Crossing the Line

CANADA AND FREE

Crossing

TRADE WITH MEXICO

the Line

edited by Jim Sinclair

NEW STAR BOOKS VANCOUVER 1992

Collection © 1992 by Jim Sinclair
Individual articles © 1992 by the respective authors

All rights reserved. No part of this work may be reproduced or used in any form or by any means – graphic, electronic, or mechanical – without the prior written permission of the publisher. Any request for photocopying or other reprographic copying must be sent in writing to the Canadian Reprography Collective, 379 Adelaide St. W., Suite M1, Toronto, Ont. M5V 1S5

First printing May 1992
1 2 3 4 5 96 95 94 93 92
Printed and bound in Canada by The Alger Press, Oshawa, Ontario

78-M

Design Kris Klaasen / Working Design
Production Audrey McClellan
Graphs Horst Maurer
Studio photography Glen Erikson Photographics

The images on the parts pages and chapter opening pages are by José Guadalupe Posada

Publication of this book is made possible by grants from the Canada Council and the Cultural Services Branch, Province of British Columbia

New Star Books Ltd.
2504 York Avenue
Vancouver, B.C.
V6K 1E3

Cataloguing in Publication Data

Main entry under title:
  Crossing the line

ISBN 0-921586-04-3

 1. Free trade – Canada. 2. Free trade – United States. 3. Free trade – Mexico.
4. North America – Economic integration. I. Sinclair, Jim, 1954-
HF1766.C76 1992   382'.71'097   C92-091237-0

Contents

vii   **FOREWORD**

x   **INTRODUCTION** by Judy Darcy

Part 1 / Free Trade and the Global Economy

2   **THE ORIGINS OF FREE TRADE MANIA** by Ken Traynor
    How to Become a 'Stealth' Advisor by Tom Hilliard / **6**
    Only the Powerful Need Apply by Jim Sinclair / **10**

14   **THE LUNACY OF FREE TRADE**
    by Marjorie Griffin Cohen

26   **MEXICO: NEO-LIBERAL DISASTER ZONE**
    by Alejandro Alvarez and Gabriel Mendoza

38   **THE U.S. AND THE GLOBAL ECONOMY** by Jim Benn
    Raiders of the Lost Art by Jim Benn / **40**
    Revolution for the Rich by Jim Sinclair / **45**

Part 2 / Front Lines

52   **CHEAP LABOUR, CHEAP LIVES** by Jim Sinclair
    Voices from the Factories / **55**
    'Never Goin' Back' by Jim Sinclair / **61**
    Jobs, Jobs, Jobs / **64**

66   **FREE TRADE AND THE ENVIRONMENT** by Zen Makuch
    No Deposit, No Return by Zen Makuch / **69**

78   **DRINK CANADA DRY?** by Wendy Holm and Donald Gutstein
    Water: The Dry Facts by Jim Sinclair / **85**

90   **FREE TRADE, FOOD, AND HUNGER** by Terry Pugh
          'How Much Lower is Low Enough?' by Wayne Easter / 93
          Marketing Boards Under Attack At Trade Talks by Terry Pugh / 94
          Food Workers, Farmers Hit Hard by Trade Deal by Jim Sinclair / 98

100   **FREE TRADE AND MEDICARE** by Chris Gainor
          American Stories by Chris Gainor / 104
          Getting Sick in the U.S.A. by Judy Haiven / 109

Part 3 / Fighting Back

118   **FIGHTING FREE TRADE, CANADIAN STYLE** by Tony Clarke
          Member Groups of the ACN / 122

128   **FIGHTING FREE TRADE, MEXICAN STYLE**
       by Fronteras Comunes/CECOPE
          Human Rights Prospects Dim Under NAFTA by Nick Keresztesi / 137

142   **FIGHTING FREE TRADE, U.S. STYLE** by Mark Ritchie
          What's Left on Wall Street by Rolf Maurer / 150

152   **WOMEN FIGHT BACK** by Denise Nadeau
          Women in the Maquiladoras by Deborah Bourque / 155

168   **SOLIDARITY, NOT COMPETITION** by Fern Valin and Jim Sinclair
          Maquiladoras Boom in Guatemala by Jim Sinclair / 172
          Solidarity via Modem by Larry Kuehn / 176

178   **THE ROAD BACK** by Maude Barlow
          Americans 'Bastards,' Says Reisman by Audrey McClellan / 181
          Alternative Proposals for Development and Trade by Tony Clarke / 184
          Creating Alternatives by Sandra Sorensen / 187

Foreword

by Jim Sinclair

The greatest fear of anyone publishing a timely book is that events will overtake it, destroying both its usefulness and credibility. In the case of *Crossing the Line*, we are writing about a North American Free Trade Agreement (NAFTA) that is being negotiated behind closed doors.

As we scrambled to meet the printer's final deadline, U.S. consumer advocate Ralph Nader leaked a copy of the proposed NAFTA to the Toronto *Star*, and later the Action Canada Network released the 408-page text across Canada. However, rather than send us into a flurry of rewrites, this leaked text confirms that the contents of this collection are more relevant than ever.

Using the Canada-U.S. Free Trade Agreement as their blueprint, the negotiators are drafting a set of rules for how every public institution and economic sector in our respective countries will operate. Like the FTA, this new agreement severely restricts the ability of governments to develop national economic and social policies aimed at meeting peoples' needs.

But the NAFTA also opens up new ground in areas excluded from the original FTA. Communications, transportation and intellectual property rights are also now open to foreign control. And although sections on the auto industry and energy resources were not included in the leaked draft, all sides agree these two issues are on the table.

The leaked text confirms our worst fears about the corporate agenda for North America. The free flow of goods, services, resources, and capital between the three nations will result in more power being held in boardrooms by executives who make fundamental decisions about our countries without reference to the ballot box or democratic process.

Fair labour standards, sustainable environmental practices, and national sovereignty are completely ignored by the architects of this deal. A few words at the beginning of the draft NAFTA make reference to full employment, but for Canadians that will ring hollow, since the trade deal with the U.S. contained the same rhetoric. Free trade, as the majority of Canadians have come to know, has little to do with trade and everything to do with the domination of the government and the economy by national and international corporations. The results of this are outlined in *Crossing the Line*.

The losers of this new deal will be the majority of Mexicans, Canadians and Americans. The priority for the majority of people in the three countries must be to solve some of the severe economic, social, and political problems facing them. These include unemployment, the destruction of the environment, widespread poverty and the lack of proper health care and basic democratic rights. The leaked text of the NAFTA reveals a set of international rules which will further entrench these problems rather than offer solutions.

With all three governments committed to signing the deal (Canada is pushing for January 1, 1993), it will take a strong and well-organized opposition to defeat this agreement and develop viable alternatives. After getting a sneak preview of the proposed North American Free Trade Agreement, the need to do this is even more urgent.

Crossing the Line is truly a collective effort. The Trade Union Group and its organizer Bill Brassington were instrumental in making the book happen. In Mexico, Nick Keresztesi of the Latin American Working Group made it possible for the excellent chapters on Mexico to appear. Joining them was Harold David, a member of the Canadian Auto Workers who has experienced first-hand the closure of his plant and the shift of production south of the border. Also crucial in this project were Rolf Maurer and Audrey McClellan of New Star Books, who spent hundreds of hours putting this book together in the form it appears today, and Kris Klaasen of Working Design, whose ideas can be seen throughout and who put up with changing deadlines.

Thanks also to the writers who took time from their busy schedules to prepare chapters for this book. Without them, none of this would have been possible.

A special note of appreciation must go to the Trade Union Group and CUSO for their continuing support of this work. This B.C. group of trade unionists recently celebrated its tenth year of solidarity work with trade unionists in Canada and Central America. It is through the work of TUG and other groups across Canada that we have come to know that it is not the workers of countries such as Mexico who

FOREWORD

are our enemies, but a political and economic system which attempts to pit us against each other. We hope this book helps to take us down another path where human solidarity takes priority over global exploitation.

I also want to thank my sisters and brothers of the United Fishermen and Allied Workers' Union, who are on the front line of the struggle to defend their communities and their country from the ravages of a "free trade" economy.

Finally, a special thanks to Susan Croll for showing me the kind of solidarity the world needs a lot more of.

Introduction

by Judy Darcy

About four years ago, I was asked to give a speech about the proposed Canada-U.S. Free Trade Agreement. I invited the audience to take a futuristic fantasy trip with me to the world of public services and social programs in 1999.

This world had high unemployment, the result of jobs that had gone south and would never return. It was rife with privatization of public services. It had a national television and radio network whose local and regional programming had been decimated and whose international news came from U.S. network feeds. Its municipal infrastructure was in decline since governments had steadfastly refused to invest in public works. And its health and education sectors were in crisis, modelled after the U.S. pay-as-you-go systems.

In short, living in Canada in 1999 was a nightmare.

I didn't know at the time that it was not going to take 11 years for this nightmare to come true – it's here right now! So spine-chilling is the reality of what's happened to Canada since the FTA was signed, that even some of its staunchest defenders, including the man who negotiated it, have started to recant.

With this nightmare all around us, one would expect that the thought of extending the free trade agreement to include Mexico would be, well, unthinkable.

It doesn't take a crystal ball to see that a North American Free Trade Agreement will have even more disastrous consequences for Canada. After all, as a result of the FTA with the U.S., Canada has permanently lost hundreds of thousands of well-paying, skilled jobs. Canadian workers will never be re-employed in many jobs lost in the current round of layoffs. The country has been forced into a deep

INTRODUCTION

recession which has placed extraordinary burdens on Canadians. And our public and social services are being threatened as never before.

Despite the recanters, there are still those who defend free trade. They talk about job creation and increased access to the American market. They claim these things will benefit *all* Canadians.

But there is only one beneficiary of free trade: the corporate elite. Free trade was designed to ensure an economic restructuring that would boost corporate profits and consolidate corporate strength in North America, primarily in American corporate hands.

This scheme only works if governments keep their noses out of the economy and ignore the social well-being of their citizens. In Canada, the federal government is locked into a mindset that encourages cuts to public and social spending. Worshipping at the altar of "global competitiveness," the Tories believe that social spending is a negative influence on competition. Thus they are only too willing to sacrifice health care, education, social services, and social security.

We only have to look at federal government cuts in transfer payments to the provinces to see that this is so. Because of these cuts, our health care and post-secondary education systems are drastically underfunded. Worse still is the fact that federal cash payments to the provinces through Established Programs Financing (EPF) – the program that provides funds for health and education – will be non-existent shortly after the turn of the century.

The government has also capped federal spending under the Canada Assistance Program for Ontario, British Columbia, and Alberta. That means those who rely on social assistance and subsidized social services in these provinces will suffer.

A popular free trade concept is that of the "level playing field." Those who subscribe to the importance of a level playing field say our social programs are unacceptable subsidies and must be cut to bring Canada closer to the competitive level of the United States.

What does it mean, practically, to move toward a level playing field? It means that private sector jobs are "crossing the line" in droves into low-wage southern states or to the maquiladoras in Mexico. And the worst features of inferior social and public services are "crossing the line" into Canada. In some cases, this means job loss for public sector workers; in others, drastic cuts to budgets and the subsequent deterioration of services.

Free trade agreements are being formulated by governments that want to curb government intervention in social and economic life. They are willingly abdicating the role of government in planning an economy that benefits the majority of citizens. Eventually, as the rules of the free trade agreements are crystallized, even progressive governments won't be able to intervene except at great cost. The rules of the free trade game enshrine corporate power. Progressive governments and ordinary Canadians pay the price. Extending free trade to include Mexico will worsen these problems. Business has one interest in Mexico – cheap labour. That's cheap labour unencumbered by environmental, tax, and other regulatory obstacles. With the maquiladoras held over the heads of Canadian workers, the pressure to accept lower wages, inferior social programs, and weaker legislative protections is enormous. There are no benefits to the vast majority of Canadians in a North American Free Trade Agreement.

Similarly, there are but a few benefits for the Mexican people. Wages in the maquiladoras are low, the social and education systems are weak, and there are serious unemployment problems. A free trade agreement won't likely have any positive impact on these areas. Mexican workers will remain exploited.

In Canada, we crossed the line when the Canada-U.S. deal was signed. Including Mexico means there will be no turning back. It will signal the death knell for progressive social programs and made-in-Canada economic policies.

The free trade agreement with the U.S. has already significantly diminished the quality of life in Canada. If we do not organize effectively to defeat the North American Free Trade Agreement, the quality of life in Canada will undergo a permanent and dangerous transformation. *Crossing the Line* provides us with the stark evidence of this threat, effective counterarguments, and, more important, a look at how we can take back our country. Now, more than ever, we must stand and fight together for the kind of society we believe in.

Judy Darcy is president of the 400,000 member Canadian Union of Public Employees, and is general vice-president of the Canadian Labour Congress.

To my son Lee and his peers.
May you inherit a decent, sovereign country
on a peaceful, healthy planet.
J.S.

PART 1
Free Trade and the Global Economy

The Origins of Free Trade Mania

The people of Canada and Mexico do not want free trade, but big business does; and big business gets what it wants

by Ken Traynor

In December 1991, the Mexican government quietly burned the ballots from the 1988 presidential elections. This act, taken to ensure that no future government could prove the fraudulent nature of the election of Carlos Salinas de Gortari, was an attempt to close the door on the past. In the run-up to the finalization of a North American Free Trade Agreement (NAFTA), it was crucial that no future Mexican government could prove just how much deceit and fraud was required to put free trade with the United States into place.

Clearly, in both Mexico and Canada, "Free Trade" is not a policy that can be rationally presented to the electorate, it can not stand alone on its own merits. It is a policy that has to be imposed through misrepresentation, fraud, and massive corporate intervention, all of it developed behind closed doors.

> **Free trade is not a policy that can be rationally presented to the electorate**

That year, 1988, was a watershed for developments on the North American continent. It was the year of a dramatic shift (although the shift was not that clear at the time) in the way the peoples of Canada and Mexico would face the 1990s and the United States, their common neighbour. As the possibility of the signing of a NAFTA gets closer, it is crucial to look into the origins of the agenda that is being imposed upon us.

GETTING THE FREE TRADE BANDWAGON ROLLING Following the dramatic conclusion of the Canada-U.S. trade negotiations (held in the late hours of October 3, 1987, in order to rush the deal to the U.S. Congress to beat the "fast-track"

THE ORIGINS OF FREE TRADE MANIA

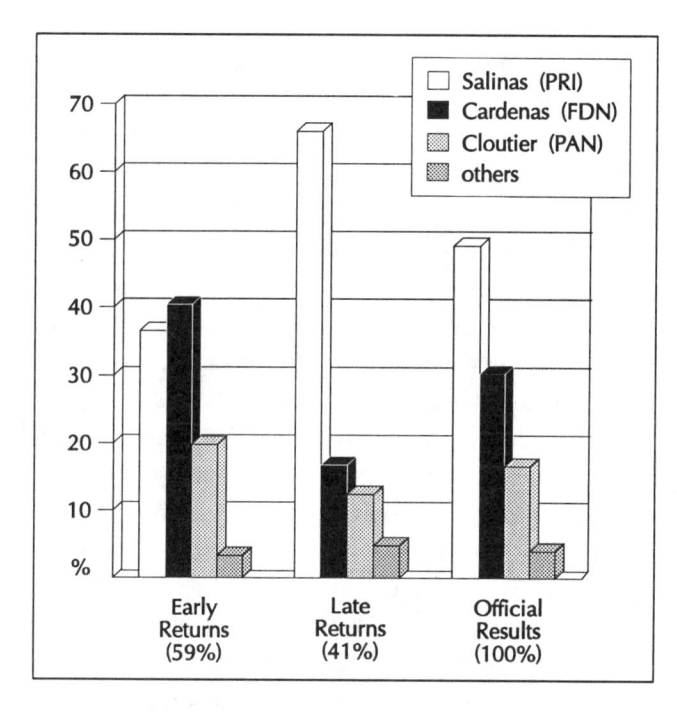

BLAME IT ON THE COMPUTERS
Mexico's 1988 election was supposed to be a cakewalk for Salinas. But when the computers showed Cárdenas with a solid lead (left), they 'broke down,' and the remaining ballots were counted by hand – a process the ruling PRI could control. Hand-counted ballots showed a whole different voting pattern.

deadline), Canadians were waking up to the threat to their future that was bound up in the detailed text of the FTA or the Deal, as it came to be known.

Throughout the early months of 1988, as discussion raged inside and outside the House of Commons, on the airwaves, around kitchen tables and lunchroom tables and even a few boardroom tables, Canadians were actively debating their future and challenging the dominant corporate view being force-fed them by the Tory government and the Business Council on National Issues (BCNI).

Throughout those same months in Mexico in early 1988, an even more profound challenge to the dominant ideology was brewing. For the first time in decades there was a serious presidential challenge from the left to the ruling Institutional Revolutionary Party, better known by its Spanish acronym, the PRI.

Carlos Salinas de Gortari, the Harvard-educated, handpicked successor to President de la Madrid, was being crowned on the pages of the *New York Times* weeks before the vote was due to be held. But despite the dominant view that the "perfect dictatorship" would reproduce itself yet again, and with the first pro-American president in Mexico's history, Mexican voters were preparing to shake the status quo to its roots.

The candidacy of Cuauhtemoc Cárdenas, son of one of Mexico's most famous and respected past presidents, had galvanized and united opposition all over Mexico in the face of the unprecedented economic hardship Mexicans had endured over the previous six years. Despite the gunning down of one of his aides days before the vote, and the overwhelming financial, media, and coercive resources available to the PRI, the unthinkable was happening.

Early returns on election night from Mexico City showed Cárdenas leading Salinas, but that was before the computers "failed." By the time the Mexican regime's "alchemists" had burned Cárdenas's ballots and inflated the PRI vote during the next week, they were able to announce that by the slimmest of margins, Salinas de Gortari had been elected president with 51 percent of the popular vote.

The near triumph of democracy in Mexico set the alarm bells ringing in Washington. In the face of regular rallies of hundreds of thousands of Mexicans protesting the electoral fraud, a complex, multifaceted program to consolidate the Salinas presidency was begun by the U.S. State Department and the Treasury. John Negroponte, U.S. Ambassador to Honduras in the 1980s and the major overseer of the buildup of U.S. support for the Nicaraguan Contras there, was quickly moved to Mexico City to manage a rescue. The rescue had a number of components.

First, a series of bridging loans worth over $2 billion was organized by the United States Treasury and provided by the U.S. Federal Reserve between August 1988 and May 1990, based on the ideas of the Secretary of State, Texan James Baker. Second came the Brady Plan in 1989, which was structured to look like debt relief but allowed Mexico to borrow further billions in the following years.

The third component of the U.S. strategy was to begin the negotiation of a North American Free Trade Agreement (NAFTA) with Mexico (it became North American after the Mulroney government pushed its way to the table) in order to promote confidence in Mexico's economic viability and to lock in the economic reforms Salinas was initiating.

In Canada, the Tory government had cynically pursued a so-called communication strategy to promote "benign neglect" among Canadians about the implications of the Free Trade Agreement. Once that policy failed and Canadians actively entered the debate, the Tories fell back on the BCNI, looking to its members to threaten Canadians into accepting an FTA. The ploy (over $56 million was spent in support of free trade by Canadian business) was successful enough that the Tories were re-elected with a majority in the 1988 election, despite the fact that 53 percent of Canadians voted against the FTA.

The realities of North America today could have been dramatically different if democracy had been respected in Mexico and if the will of Canadians had been followed in 1988. Instead of being pushed down a fast-track towards continental economic integration (the aim of George Bush's "Enterprise for the Americas" Initiative) and a hemispheric free trade bloc with all the dislocations that entails, we could have been working to build environmentally sustainable economic development in all three countries, and looking to foster development and debt

> 'The free trade agreement will not be a major creator of jobs. That was a specious claim made in the heat of an election campaign.'
>
> GORDON RITCHIE, DEPUTY CHIEF NEGOTIATOR OF THE FTA, MARCH 24, 1990

THE ORIGINS OF FREE TRADE MANIA

MEMBERSHIP DOES HAVE ITS PRIVILEGES American Express was among the first U.S. multinationals to exert behind-the-scenes pressure for the FTA.

relief, not free trade and dependence, in the rest of the hemisphere.

Where did this free trade mania come from? Whose interests are being served in this rush to integrate elite interests across the hemisphere while ignoring the needs of the vast majority? It is crucial to understand the origins of the agenda we face if we are to understand the implications of, and effectively organize opposition to, the present proposals under negotiation in the Uruguay Round of the General Agreement on Tariffs and Trade (GATT), the Canada-U.S.-Mexico Free Trade Agreement, and the Enterprise for the Americas Initiative.

ORIGINS OF THIS CORPORATE AGENDA Brian Mulroney and the BCNI would like us to believe that the push for a Free Trade Agreement was a brilliant, made-in-Canada strategy to respond to the protectionist climate of the United States corporate sector in the early 1980s. While Canadian authorities were indeed looking for a strategy to respond to the American rhetoric of that period, Linda McQuaig, in her excellent book *The Quick and the Dead*, gives us a much more detailed account of the origins of the push for free trade that so dominates our lives in the 1990s.

As early as 1974, American business interests were pushing to bring the fast-growing service industries, in which the U.S. had significant international advantages over the rest of the world, under GATT trade rules. During the Tokyo Round of GATT negotiations in 1974, a number of U.S. corporations – including Pan American Airways and the American International Group, a major U.S. insurance company – lobbied hard to get services onto the world trade agenda. They failed in 1974, but American Express, the rising U.S. financial services giant, picked up that cause again in the early eighties.

The path which brought American Express to be leading this push was an interesting one. One of the key trade officials, responsible for services in the office of the United States Trade Representative (USTR), was Gene Feketekuty. Feketekuty was a friend of Harry Freeman, who was also an executive vice-president at

American Express under Chairman James Robinson. The USTR official convinced Freeman of the importance of the issue for American Express and, in turn, Freeman got Robinson interested. Robinson was then recruited to the chairmanship of a private sector advisory committee within USTR on the services issue. Once Robinson was convinced, he became an active campaigner on the services issue and elevated it to top priority within American Express.

Jim Robinson also became the chair of the trade committee of the influential Business Roundtable in the United States, and in 1987 took over the chair of the top private sector advisory committee of the USTR. With the FTA negotiated and the Uruguay Round of the GATT underway, he could shift his focus to the world stage.

This combination of bureaucratic power and private corporate interests was an effective force, moving the services question to the centre of the U.S. trade agenda.

McQuaig outlines at length how a small group of companies allied themselves with American Express and a few trade officials, like Feketekuty, to become "an activist group that became known in trade circles as the services mafia." This "mafia," led by Harry Freeman, orchestrated a massive campaign which managed to get major changes to U.S. trade law approved in October 1984. These changes elevated "services" to equal status with "goods" as a priority for the U.S. government, and authorized bilateral negotiations for free trade agreements with Canada and Israel, agreements that could act as models for multilateral GATT

HOW TO BECOME A 'STEALTH' ADVISER

Tom Hilliard

The MTN Coalition represents a striking illustration of how an unofficial lobbying group can become a "stealth" adviser – heeded by trade officials even without official standing as an advisory committee. MTN stands for "Multilateral Trade Negotiations," the jargon term used to signify a GATT negotiating round. The MTN Coalition is a business group that lobbies Congress, the news media and the general public on behalf of the draft Uruguay Round GATT agreement.

MTN came into existence in 1989 at the urging of Carla Hills, the U.S. Trade Representative. After her appointment, Hills reportedly suggested to James Robinson, chairman of American Express, that the U.S. business community should help mobilize support for the Uruguay Gatt round.[1] Early the next year, AmEx executive Harry Freeman resigned and founded the MTN Coalition. A platoon of giant corporations and trade associations jumped on board, most of them represented on the "official" trade advisory committees: General Motors, American Farm Bureau Federation, AT&T, IBM, and Procter & Gamble, for example, all maintain representatives on ACTPN.[2] The 18 companies and 13 trade associations represented in MTN are not philanthropists for free trade. Membership magnifies their clout with trade officials by adding the role of friendly lobbyist to that of trusted adviser.

When MTN members walk out of a trade official's office, evidence suggests that they leave dirty footprints behind. The environmental and consumer-safety record of the 18 corporations represented on MTN provides a warning sign of the kind of advice and counsel they are likely to provide:

❑ As of January 1, 1990, 11 companies (or their affiliates) represented on MTN, more than a third of the Coalition, were listed as Potentially Responsible Parties for an average of more than 15 different Superfund sites per polluting company.[3]

negotiations. In fact, McQuaig quotes Feketekuty calling these agreements "dress rehearsals" for the vital multilateral GATT negotiations which were to follow.

At the centre of these vital GATT negotiations were to be three new agenda items making up the priorities for U.S. business in the eighties. The services sector promised tremendous growth for U.S. business with estimates of total services trade of $600 billion annually. Writing in the *Left Business Observer*, Doug Henwood comments on how "basic industry in the U.S. may be on the ropes but boy do we have financial services! And . . . if we could just stop Taiwanese and Kenyan pirates from making illegal copies of *Terminator 2*, then U.S. trade deficits would presumably be a thing of the past."

Investment was the second area needing to be changed. Many countries "interfered" by putting restrictions like local purchase requirements and export targets on corporate investment. They also often refused to allow foreigners the right to establish financial companies. Canada's National Energy Program was an excellent example of this tendency to require benefits from multinational corporations in return for access to markets and resources.

The third area was a demand for tighter restrictions for intellectual property (IP). "Third world countries just weren't deferential in the face of patents and copyrights on movies, drugs and chips," writes Henwood. "But IP violations are an important development strategy, as a study of U.S. history reveals. In the last century, the U.S.

❑ Six companies (or affiliates) represented on MTN, almost a fifth of the Coalition, rank among America's 50 biggest dischargers of toxic air and water pollutants.[4]

❑ Since 1980, seven companies (or their affiliates) represented on MTN, almost a fourth of the Coalition, have been assessed fines of at least $3,397,900 by the Environmental Protection Agency for illegally polluting the environment, an average of $485,414 per offender. Yet this sum represents only part of the total penalties assessed by the EPA, since it does not systematically include administrative penalties.[5]

❑ In 1986, nine companies (or their affiliates) represented on MTN, almost a third of the Coalition, spent a total of at least $380,557 in a failed attempt to defeat California's Safe Drinking Water and Toxics Enforcement Act, a statewide initiative to require warnings on potentially cancer-causing products.[6] In 1990, five of the companies (or their affiliates) represented on MTN, almost a sixth of the Coalition, spent at least $339,558 in a successful attempt to defeat another California initiative, the Environmental Protection Act, better known as Big Green. Had it passed, Big Green would have, among other provisions, set tighter standards for discharge of toxic chemicals.[7]

1. Richard Lawrence, "Industry Forms Lobby Group for Trade Round," *Journal of Commerce*, May 16, 1990.
2. "MTN Coalition Members," The MTN Coalition, undated.
3. *Site Enforcement Tracking System*, a database of the U.S. Environmental Protection Agency, January 1, 1990
4. *Manufacturing Pollution: A Survey of the Nation's Toxic Polluters*, a report from Citizen's Fund, July 1991 (September 1991 revision).
5. *EPA Enforcement Accomplishments, Field Years 1986-1990*, and *EPA Civil Enforcement Docket Database*, from the Office of Enforcement and Compliance Monitoring, U.S. Environmental Protection Agency.
6. *Californians Against Prop. 65*, California Fair Practices Commission, 1987.
7. *Capital Weekly Data*, July 15, 1991, pp. 14-16.

SOURCE: "Trade Advisory Committees: Privileged Access For Polluters," by Public Citizen's Congress Watch

was a major IP abuser, and the U.S. chemical industry didn't take off until it stole German patents during WW I." The so-called NICS (newly industrialized countries) – Thailand, Taiwan and South Korea – the new success stories so beloved by free marketeers, all were IP "abusers."

As McQuaig notes, however, "When it came right down to it, the new issues amounted to more than just an attempt to expand the scope of GATT to cover new areas of world trade. As the intellectual property issue illustrated, the focus of some of these new demands went well beyond the traditional notion of free trade and open markets. The push for the new issues was really a push for a new world order – an economic order more suited to the needs of global corporations in the eighties and nineties ... Through international trade negotiations U.S. business sought to achieve a world system that would guarantee the rights of business, that would impose laissez-faire, free market economics on a global scale, eliminating any meaningful interventionist role for government."

And the place they chose to start was Canada when the opportunity arose in the early eighties.

SETTING PRECEDENTS THROUGH THE FTA The Canadian government began to be concerned about the increasingly protectionist rhetoric coming out of the United States in the face of Canadian policies like the National Energy Program and the Canada First perspective of then Industry Minister Herb Gray. Derek Burney, now ambassador in Washington, and Robert Johnstone, now an adviser on trade with the Ontario government, undertook a review of trade policy which explicitly rejected free trade and pushed a sectoral approach focusing on informatics, steel, and petrochemicals. The basic idea was to duplicate the success of the Auto Pact.

The BCNI was also working to influence Canadian relations with the U.S. A small taskforce of chief executive officers from companies including Alcan, Canadian General Electric, and Power Corporation, began in 1982 to look at trade problems with the United States. In January 1983, this group met with William Brock, Reagan's USTR head who had spent his first two years in office touring the world, pushing everywhere for a new GATT round to discuss the "new" trade issues of services, investment, and intellectual property.

Brock was pleased to meet with the Canadians but uninterested in their proposal. The Canadians came to discuss access to the U.S. market in areas of Canadian strength, in particular goods and resource industries. The United States already had an agenda, however, and sectoral trade agreements were not on it.

During Brock's world tour he had encountered tremendous resistance, especially in Third World nations, to expanding GATT to include trade in services, investment, and intellectual property. In the face of this kind of international resistance, the

> Commenting on what he sees as the Tory government's favouritism towards American Express, the chairman of one of Canada's biggest banks said, 'What other bloody country in the world would permit that? It's bucket shop ... we look like a third-rate dummy ... as a Canadian, you're ashamed.'
> BANK OF NOVA SCOTIA CHAIRMAN CEDRIC RITCHIE

THE ORIGINS OF FREE TRADE MANIA

WHEN IRISH EYES ARE SCHEMING The 'Shamrock summit' in Quebec City in March 1985, less than six months after Mulroney took office, signalled an abrupt change in attitude toward the U.S. From now on, Mulroney promised, Canada would be wide open to U.S. corporations.
PHOTO BY RYAN REMIORZ/ CANAPRESS

bilateral option became more attractive. McQuaig interviewed Tim Bennett, a U.S. trade attaché who worked under Brock, who explained things this way: "There was a feeling of powerlessness multilaterally [but] . . . there was the belief that, gee, we've got *a lot of leverage bilaterally*." The Canadians seemed to be providing an excellent opportunity to test that leverage.

Reporting on the meeting with Brock, Alfred Powis of Power Corporation told McQuaig, "What Brock was telling us was that . . . politically the impetus had to come from Canada . . . If the United States started to talk about Free Trade, it would be torpedoed just like that. But if Canada screwed itself up to ask for it, he [Brock] would certainly go along with it."

For the BCNI the task was clear. First they had to convince their own members to support comprehensive free trade, then they had to persuade other business and government circles, and eventually the Canadian public. With the election of Brian Mulroney this task became dramatically easier and the rest is history.

Once the Mulroney government "screwed itself up to ask for it" under the constant urging of the BCNI, Harry Freeman, Jim Robinson, and American Express swung into action in the United States to take full advantage of the opportunity. They formed the Coalition of Service Industries so it would not look like a one-man show, and when the U.S. Senate almost defeated the fast-track authorization to begin negotiations, Robinson began to organize an impressive U.S. lobbying effort.

They hired four firms in what was described as a "gold plated" lobby. With the backing of the Republican White House, the challenge was to get key Democrats in the Congress on board. The former press spokesman for Jimmy Carter was hired, as was Richard Strauss, who had been Carter's Trade Representative. It was also seen as important to show broad business support for free trade. Harry Freeman organized the American Coalition for Trade Expansion with Canada and found it "amazingly easy" to get over 1,000 of the largest multinationals involved.

The biggest problem for Freeman and his coalition became how to keep the high degree of American corporate excitement about free trade quiet, so as not to arouse further suspicions in Canada. McQuaig quotes a lobbyist for AT&T as saying that Strauss "gave us the very, very sage advice: you can't appear as if this is the greatest thing in the world for Americans. Then it's going to have a negative reaction in Canada." This same lobbyist told McQuaig that American business felt Canadian business was being very sluggish in hyping the merits of free trade and that "it would

---

ONLY THE POWERFUL NEED APPLY

Jim Sinclair

In 1977, after four years of study, Canada's top business executives decided it was time for a new approach to politics.

Using as a model a similar corporate body in the U.S., this group launched the Business Council on National Issues. Its purpose was simple -- to bring the richest corporations together to speak with a single voice on key economic and political issues.

From the beginning it was a closed shop, and 15 years later the membership still stands at 150 Canadian and foreign owned corporations with assets of $725 billion, employing 1.5 million employees. No small fry allowed.

In 1977 the target was the Trudeau government and the BCNI later called for the prime minister to be more like U.S. president Ronald Reagan. Off the record, they were much more critical, according to Vancouver Sun columnist Jamie Lamb. "Privately, the council wishes Mr. Trudeau would fall down the political equivalent of an elevator shaft..."

In the 1980s, Trudeau retired and Brian Mulroney took over. The BCNI immediately set out to change government policy towards free trade. As early as 1985 they began calling for talks to begin with the U.S. As Mulroney shifted, the BCNI and its president, Thomas d'Aquino, became the strongest proponents of the deal.

He called leading opponents of the deal "intellectual terrorists," claiming that suggestions of massive job loss and the sellout of Canada were unfounded. The group also opposed an election on the issue. When the election was called, the BCNI was instrumental in a multi-million dollar campaign to sell free trade to Canadians.

Former Alcan president David Culver is honorary chairman of the BCNI. Following the 1988 election, where the BCNI played down the job losses associated with the trade deal, Culver told Canadians facing unemployment that some flowers have to die so others will grow.

The BCNI has lobbied successfully for cutting spending on social programs, cutting corporate taxes, and removing restraints on the flow of capital in and out of the country.

Despite the obvious disaster which has followed the FTA, the BCNI has turned its attention to the proposed Mexico deal. It is also championing a similar free trade deal with Japan. Aquino dismisses skeptics of a Japan trade deal by pointing to the FTA.

"In 1979 no one remotely thought that a free trade agreement was possible with the United States," he said.

No one, that is, but Canada's most powerful corporate executives.

THE ORIGINS OF FREE TRADE MANIA

be nice if the Canadian business community would get out in front on this issue."

Once the Mulroney government was committed to doing a deal or "rolling the dice" as Mulroney calls it, Canada had little negotiating leverage. The last minute walk-out by Simon Reisman and the late night negotiating sessions were just window dressing. The Americans had read things correctly; politically, Mulroney had to have a deal, any deal – so they never even considered allowing the FTA to supersede U.S. trade law as the Canadians were demanding.

For American business, the FTA was a tremendous accomplishment. They had got the breakthrough on services they wanted, made some progress on intellectual property rights with changes to Canada's law on compulsory licensing for drugs, got an unexpected windfall in the key area of energy, and put significant strictures on future Canadian government investment policy. In the words of the U.S. negotiators, from a confidential memo quoted in *Inside U.S. Trade*, "essentially, in the text, we got everything that we wanted." McQuaig quotes the head of the National Association of Manufacturers, R.K. Morris, as saying, "when we got such a great deal on energy we were crusaders for the deal."

But probably most important in the long run was the constraints that the deal put on Canadian sovereignty. R.K. Morris sees it this way: "For us it linked Canadian trade policy to Canadian investment policy. You could no longer adopt an extremely interventionist investment policy without jeopardizing the gains . . . of the trade agreement . . . Even if you have a new Liberal government, there won't be a dramatic swing back to [interventionist] economic policies, because the cost for you would be very high, it would be hard to overstate the importance of that."

Having put significant brakes on Canadian sovereignty, it was time to shift the emphasis to Mexico and beyond, to the rest of the western hemisphere, which was rapidly becoming open to the idea of economic integration. The circumstances were different but the basic agenda was the same – reform of intellectual property laws, unrestricted rights of establishment for American corporations including services companies, increased constraints on future government actions, and unfettered access to the region's oil reserves. The elimination of tariffs, the classic view of what trade agreements are about, was far down the list of objectives.

Free trade was only open to those governments in the region that first demonstrated "a commitment to economic reform" by undertaking structural

> 'We don't like being sold out, like what happened to Wayne Gretzky. What Peter Pocklington is to Edmonton, our Prime Minister is to Canada.'
>
> JOHN TURNER
> FORMER PRIME MINISTER OF CANADA

adjustments such as liberalizing foreign investment laws, tightening up intellectual property protection, and privatizing state-owned companies.

Mexico was chosen as the first Latin American candidate for a free trade agreement, partly because it had already undertaken extensive structural adjustments. It had unilaterally reduced tariffs and quantitative restrictions on trade, allowed more foreign private investment, cut back on government spending, privatized many public enterprises, and ended price controls on most items. In return for adopting these policies, Mexico became the first country to receive a small amount of debt relief under the Brady Plan, named after its author, U.S. Treasury Secretary Nicholas Brady. And it secured a place for itself as the first Latin American country to reach the free trade negotiating table.

While the International Monetary Fund (IMF) and the World Bank can enforce harsh austerity and structural adjustment policies on debtor countries for short periods, they cannot guarantee continued government support for their policies. Future governments might adopt more self-reliant and interventionist development strategies. One way to make structural reforms permanent is to enshrine them in international trade treaties which force future governments to adhere to the free trade status quo or risk retaliation.

The key role that trade agreements play in circumscribing national sovereignty was outlined very clearly by the U.S. Ambassador to Mexico, John Negroponte, in a confidential memo he sent to the U.S. State Department in April 1991, that was made public by the Mexican progressive magazine *Proceso*: "The FTA can be seen as an instrument to promote, consolidate and guarantee continued policies of economic reform in Mexico beyond the Salinas administration. I think it's reasonable to suppose that the FTA negotiations themselves will be a useful lever in prying open the Mexican economy even further. For example, I think we can reasonably expect the foreign investment law to change as a result of FTA talks. I would also foresee liberalization of the financial services regime."

Clearly this trade agreement is not about establishing a development policy for Mexico which will meet the basic needs of its already impoverished majority, just as the Canada-U.S. Free Trade Agreement was not about meeting the needs of Canadians. If we are to seriously address the overwhelming development needs in this hemisphere and respond to the environmental crisis we face, we have to reject the free trade road that is focused narrowly on liberating capital from any significant level of democratic control.

The Uruguay Round of the GATT, the NAFTA, the Enterprise for the Americas Initiative, and the Canada-U.S. FTA that preceded them are fundamentally about reorganizing production on a global scale. In Doug Henwood's words, "Free Trade is a veil for the transformation of the globe into a free-fire zone for the MNCs."

> 'I spent two and a half years in a closed room getting beaten up by a bunch of ugly Americans. I wouldn't be in a hurry to go back in.'
>
> GORDON RITCHIE, DECEMBER 3, 1990

THE ORIGINS OF FREE TRADE MANIA

WHO WRITES YOUR MATERIAL? In March 1990, Brian Mulroney visited his Mexican counterpart Carlos Salinas de Gortari to get the ball rolling on a North American free trade deal. Mulroney claimed that the Canada-U.S. deal had already created 250,000 new jobs in Canada.

PHOTO BY PAUL CHIASSON/ CANAPRESS

If we are serious about pursuing any form of alternative economic development that is more environmentally and socially sustainable, we have to reject these latest versions of the free trade onslaught and get on with the task of developing a strategy to cancel and replace the FTA.

The recent attempted military coup in Venezuela, after years of IMF-imposed austerity, provides a useful reminder of the urgency of the problems faced in this hemisphere. President Perez of Venezuela spent the week before the coup at the World Economic Forum in Davos, Switzerland, hobnobbing with the corporate and government elite from around the world. This "UN of the private and public sector where circles of overlapping power are unmatched," as the Toronto *Globe and Mail* called it, sent Perez a resolution of solidarity following the coup attempt.

In contrast, at the same time, the head of the Venezuelan textile workers, who is also the president of the hemispheric textile workers federation, was touring the United States and Canada, speaking out against the free trade mania growing everywhere in the hemisphere. His message was straightforward: we must develop continental solidarity in the face of continental integration. Whether we can organize an effective response to this call for solidarity will determine the shape of "our common future" in this hemisphere.

Ken Traynor is coordinator for the Common Frontiers Project on continental economic integration. He was formerly on staff with the Coalition Against Free Trade.

The Lunacy of Free Trade

A look at the structure of Canada's economy and international trade shows why free trade can't and won't work for Canada

by Marjorie Griffin Cohen

"The Americans are bastards,"[1] says Simon Reisman three years after he negotiated the Free Trade Agreement for Canada. He and Gordon Ritchie (former deputy trade negotiator) are trying to distance themselves from the miserable fall-out from the agreement they so ardently sold to the Canadian public. It isn't that Reisman and Ritchie are admitting they were wrong. They say the deal was fine, it is just that the Americans have been thuggish in protecting their interests and are too aggressive in pushing the new rules to the limit. They aren't being nice guys. Is that a surprise?

No surprise to anyone who knew anything about how the Americans negotiated the agreement, or who knew what they said they would do, or who knew anything about the structure of the Canadian economy. The FTA was doomed to failure and that has almost nothing to do with good or bad behaviour on either side of the border. We got what we bargained for.

> **Simon Reisman says the deal was fine; it's just that the Americans are being thuggish and aggressive**

The results of free trade have been awful. The official unemployment rate, which counts those who are still looking for work, rose from 7.5 percent in 1989 to 10.3 percent by the end of 1991. But the real unemployment rate is closer to 16 percent, if those who gave up looking for work because none was available, and those who want to work full-time but accepted part-time jobs, are counted as part of the unemployed.[2]

The most obvious unemployment problems are in manufacturing. The job losses are not simply the result of layoffs with the possibility that people will return to work when the economy begins to grow again. The vast majority of these job losses

GONE SOUTH
Free trade has hit Canada's manufacturing sector hardest. Ten years ago, 20 percent of the country's jobs were in manufacturing; today the figure is 15 percent, and in a free-fall.

PHOTO BY HEMI MITIC/CAW

are due to capital flight. Firms quickly and permanently closed down. In Ontario, 65 percent of the job losses in manufacturing between January 1989 and October 1991 were a result of permanent plant closures. This is in dramatic contrast to Ontario plant closures in the 1982 recession, which accounted for 22 percent of job losses. Now only about 15 percent of the Canadian labour force works in manufacturing, compared with 18 percent when Mulroney took power in 1984, and almost 20 percent ten years ago.

This is a very rapid decline in the significance of Canada's manufacturing sector. Change in the distribution of the labour force does not always indicate significant structural shifts. For example, as Canada became more efficient at agricultural production, we were able to produce more food with fewer people. So too, manufacturing production expanded while using a smaller proportion of the labour force over time. But the changes now are different. We aren't producing more things; since the FTA, manufacturing production has decreased by over 14 percent. Free trade has affected the very ability to produce in Canada.

Even more significant is the prospect for the future. Canada has never been particularly well managed, but in the past when things went wrong, governments could try new policies. The tragedy now is that government's ability to act appropriately when the economy deteriorates has been abdicated by almost total reliance on market forces, a turn of events that reflects not simply the political whim of the current government, but that has been codified in international trade law.

> 'Free Trade with the United States would be like sleeping with an elephant. If it rolls over, you're a dead man. And I'll tell you when it's going to roll over. It's going to roll over in a time of economic depression and they're going to crank up those plants in Georgia and North Carolina and Ohio, and they're going to be shutting them down up here.'
>
> BRIAN MULRONEY, PC LEADERSHIP CAMPAIGN, 1983

Trade law now dictates what is possible. Any new piece of legislation that, for example, might require that a certain portion of resources extracted in Canada actually be processed here, is no longer allowed. We are at the mercy of what the corporate sector perceives its interest to be in the immediate future.

The FTA rests on the belief in the power of the market to sort out all of the economic problems of any country. It rests on the idea that there is one method by which growth and development can be achieved. And it is based on a very old, almost archaic notion of how economies work. This notion is that when all players approach the market on an equal basis, no one will be able to develop a monopoly and thereby control prices. In this ideal world, everyone will be better off with free trade because each country will be able to concentrate its resources and labour on producing things it is relatively efficient at producing, and will be able to import things that it can't produce efficiently. No country will have to worry about anyone unfairly hogging the market.

The problem with this idea is that we are no longer dealing with trade between nations, but with the ability of large corporations (monopolies) to move easily between nations and to pick and choose the most advantageous conditions for themselves. These advantageous conditions depend on the historical position of countries, their geographical advantages, and their level of desperation to secure investment from large firms. When capital is free to move and labour is relatively fixed, the possibility for a happy-ever-after-ending vanishes.

Canada as a country is very different from the U.S. It is a huge land mass but has a small population. This has meant that holding the country together and moving things from one part to another has required cooperation and considerable effort and ingenuity. Much of the nation is cold most of the time, while some parts are too dry and others too wet. This makes agricultural production precarious and requires special measures to ensure that food continues to be produced in Canada.

The historical context and physical conditions of the land meant Canada developed in very different ways from the U.S. The country grew largely because we relied on exporting natural resources and because we encouraged foreign firms (mostly U.S.-based) to own and operate not only the country's resources but also a substantial proportion of the manufacturing sector.

The result is an economy that is fairly unusual for a country that is considered modern, wealthy, and developed. It is also an economy with problems that have a lot to do with the way we developed historically. Canada consistently has high rates of unemployment, and there are always a greater proportion of Canadians unemployed – even in good times – than there are in the U.S. Our regional disparities are greater than in any other western industrialized country, and we periodically experience volatile fluctuations in economic activity that are

THE LUNACY OF FREE TRADE

considerably more dramatic than those of other industrialized countries. Canada also has a relatively poor performance in the delivery of social services. Generally Canadians are proud of their social services, but that is only because we tend to compare the Canadian situation with that in the U.S. The U.S. is a particularly abysmal case, however, and if Canada is compared to almost any European country, its performance in this regard is dismal.

With free trade, the structural problems that already existed in Canada were accentuated. While the FTA was promoted by the government and business on the soundness of its economic potential and the substantial economic benefits it promised to Canadians, it was precisely in terms of the economic logic that it was bound to fail.

The major beneficiary of free trade was supposed to be the manufacturing sector. According to the economic models used by the government, manufacturing output would increase by over 10 percent.[3] The main arguments for the FTA focused on the need for a fundamental restructuring of the manufacturing sector. Canadian manufacturing was diagnosed as having poor performance in labour productivity compared with major competitors. This was related to the fragmented nature of production within firms, and to their relatively small production runs. That is, Canadian manufacturing firms tended to sell mostly within the country, and they produced a whole range of products for a relatively small market. Free trade, it was argued, would force companies to specialize in product "niches" that would find

ENGINE TROUBLE Officially, 45 percent of Canadian exports are highly processed goods, but intra-firm transfers under the auto pact account for 78 percent of these exports.

PHOTO BY
BILL MAJESKY/CAW

markets in the U.S. These companies would then be able to undertake large-scale production for specific products and would become more efficient. It was argued that with secure and increased access to the U.S. market, weak and inefficient firms would be eliminated and strong firms that carried out large-scale, specialized production would thrive.

While in theory this reasoning made sense, in the context of the real economic situation of Canada it did not.

FOREIGN OWNERSHIP Those of us who argued against free trade recognized that the high degree of foreign ownership would affect investment decisions in Canada. When the idea of free trade was first raised, about 50 percent of the manufacturing sector, 45 percent of petroleum and natural gas, 40 percent of mining and smelting, and 26 percent of all other industries were owned or controlled by foreign (mostly U.S.) firms. A substantial proportion of foreign investment in manufacturing originated in order to circumvent tariffs on imported items. If tariffs were removed, the rationale for remaining in Canada would no

CAPITAL DRAIN Increased imports of U.S. services, and a steady flow of investment payments (interest, profits) out of the country, means Canada sends more money out than we bring in.

TABLE 1

CANADA'S BALANCE OF PAYMENTS
1990 Current Account

	BILLIONS OF DOLLARS
MERCHANDISE	
Exports	146.5
Imports	135.6
Merchandise Balance	10.9
NON-MERCHANDISE	
Service Receipts	22.4
Investment Income Receipts	9.3
Service Payments	31.3
Investment Income Payments	33.2
Non-Merchandise Balance	-33.0
BALANCE ON CURRENT ACCOUNT	**-22.0**

SOURCE: Department of Finance, *Quarterly Economic Review: Annual Reference Tables*, June 1991, Table 65.

TABLE 2

RAW DEAL
Canada exports a large percentage of unprocessed goods, which means a loss of jobs and income to the domestic economy.

THE THINGS CANADA SELLS TO OTHER COUNTRIES
Exports 1990

	% OF TOTAL EXPORTS
UNPROCESSED AND SEMI-PROCESSED MATERIALS	**54.5**
Wheat	2.3
Other agricultural products	5.8
Crude petroleum & natural gas	6.4
Other crude materials	7.3
Fabricated materials	32.7
PROCESSED MATERIALS	**45.4**
Motor vehicles & parts	23.6
Other end products	21.8

SOURCE: Department of Finance, *Quarterly Economic Review: Annual Reference Tables,* June 1991, Table 68.

longer exist. Firms would be able to sell in the Canadian market without being located within the country. Because of the high degree of foreign ownership, the notion that Canadian branch-plants would be given "product mandates" for worldwide (or at least continent-wide) production was highly unlikely. With U.S. firms operating at under-capacity, it was more likely that Canadian plants would be closed.

CANADIAN TRADE Another serious problem was the nature of Canadian trade itself. Canada is much more dependent on trade than most other industrialized countries, and this dependence has grown substantially within the last thirty years. In the 1960s, exports accounted for about 20 percent of the national income. They rose to about 25 percent in the 1970s and were closer to 30 percent in the 1980s. Most of this trade (about 75 percent) is with the United States. The extroverted nature of the economy has made Canada extremely vulnerable to external forces. When things go wrong on the international market, the impact on Canada can be extreme. Canada tends to feel the impact first, experience it harder, and take longer to recover than most other industrialized nations.

The main point is that increased reliance on trade (or an export-led growth strategy) has not lessened the country's economic problems but, rather, has tended to reinforce its structural imbalances. This is because our exports are dominated by

IMPORT CRISIS
Value-added manufactured goods make up 66 percent of Canada's imports, creating a structural problem for the economy.

TABLE 3

THE THINGS CANADA BUYS FROM OTHER COUNTRIES
Imports 1990

	% OF TOTAL IMPORTS
UNPROCESSED AND SEMI-PROCESSED MATERIALS	33.3
Agricultural Products	6.1
Crude petroleum	4.1
Other crude materials	2.8
Fabricated materials	20.8
PROCESSED MATERIALS	66.7
Motor vehicles & parts	22.9
Other end products	43.8

SOURCE: Department of Finance, *Quarterly Economic Review: Annual Reference Tables, June 1991*, Table 69.

things that have relatively low labour content while our imports largely consist of things that have a high labour content.

The trade statistics periodically cited in the newspapers focus on Canada's merchandise trade balance, which refers to the physical things that are traded. It would appear from these statistics that Canada has a healthy trading pattern because in the trade of physical things, this country consistently maintains a trade surplus (Table 1). However, the cheerful picture of the merchandise trade balance masks some fundamental problems with Canada's trade.

Resource-based products account for about 55 percent of the value of all our exports. We tend to maintain a trade surplus with the United States in live animals, food, crude materials, and fabricated materials. In manufactured products we consistently have a trade deficit with the United States, although we have maintained trade surpluses in automobiles and parts. While statistics show that about 45 percent of Canada's exports consist of highly processed items, this is deceptive because a large part of this reflects intra-firm trade under the auto pact. Less than 22 percent of Canada's exports consist of non-auto manufactured items (Table 2), while our imports are highly concentrated in non-auto manufactured items (Table 3).

These characteristics of trade have important implications for the chronic problems of unemployment and regional disparities in Canada. The high reliance on

THE LUNACY OF FREE TRADE

the export of goods related to the resource-extracting sectors, which employ relatively few Canadians, means that we are exporting items with a relatively small labour content. For the most part these items leave the country with little or no processing. In contrast, a large proportion of Canada's imports consists of items with a high degree of value added. Considering that less than 6 percent of the Canadian labour force is employed in industries in which we have a trade surplus, and that the vast majority are employed in sectors where we have a trade deficit, the structural nature of unemployment becomes clear (Table 4).

SERVICES   Canada's trade in material things is only part of the whole trade picture. Services are also traded between countries. Some of the most notable are travel, transportation, and business services. Canada's economy is a service economy, yet this is not reflected in our trade figures. Services account for over 68 percent of the national income and provide about 70 percent of the jobs in Canada (Tables 4 and

JOBS...
The majority of Canadians work in the service sector, an area vulnerable to free trade. The manufacturing sector is already declining, creating serious hardships.

TABLE 4

WHERE PEOPLE WORK – BY INDUSTRY
Canada 1989

	% OF TOTAL LABOUR FORCE	% BY SEX WOMEN	MEN
PRIMARY INDUSTRIES	5.8	3.1	7.9
Agriculture	3.4	2.4	4.1
SECONDARY INDUSTRIES	23.5	12.8	31.9
Manufacturing	17.0	11.3	21.5
Construction	6.5	1.5	10.4
SERVICE SECTOR	70.2	83.5	59.7
Transportation/communications/utilities	7.5	4.5	9.9
Trade	17.4	17.6	17.2
Finance/insurance/real estate	5.6	7.8	3.9
Service	33.0	47.0	21.9
Public admin.	6.7	6.6	6.8
UNCLASSIFIED	0.5	0.7	0.4

SOURCE: Labour Canada, Women's Bureau, *Women in the Labour Force* 1990-91 Edition (Ottawa, 1990).

5). Of the new jobs created in Canada during the past decade, over 80 percent have been in the service sector. But despite this reliance on services within the country, Canada is unlike most other industrialized countries in that our export of services is poor. Canada has had a deficit in its service account for the past thirty years, and this has grown considerably in recent years. In the past, when Canada had a very large surplus in its merchandise account, the deficit in services was not considered too significant. But Canada's deficit arising from service and investment payments is now at $33 billion. Since the merchandise trade surplus has been reduced to less than $11 billion, the overall balance of payments deficit has grown to $22 billion (Table 1). The U.S., in contrast, is a service exporting country, accounting for about 25 percent of the world's trade in services. It relies on increasing its exports of services to maintain its trade position in the world.

TABLE 5

INCOME TROUBLES
Canadians are becoming more and more dependent on low-paying service jobs, as manufacturing work shifts south.

SOURCES OF THE NATION'S INCOME
Canada 1990

	% OF NATIONAL INCOME
PRIMARY INDUSTRIES TOTAL	**6.9**
Agriculture	2.2
Fish+ forest	0.8
Mining	3.9
SECONDARY INDUSTRIES TOTAL	**24.5**
Manufacturing	17.9
Construction	6.6
SERVICE INDUSTRIES TOTAL	**68.5**
Transportation	4.8
Communications	3.7
Finance, insurance, real estate	15.8
Community, business, personal service	23.0
Trade	11.5
Utilities	3.2
Government services	6.5

SOURCE: Statistics Canada, *Canadian Economic Observer: Historical Statistical Supplement 1990-92* (Ottawa 1991).

For the first time in any trade agreement in the world, services were included in the FTA in a comprehensive and extensive way. By including services trade in the agreement, Canada greatly accelerated the importing of U.S. services and substantially weakened its overall trade position. The Canadian service sector was in no position to compete internationally with the giant U.S. service firms. Even more serious was the erosion of the position of Canadian service firms within the domestic economy.

ACCESS Much of the government justification for entering the FTA was to obtain greater access to the U.S. market. This was a strange argument in many ways. Before the FTA, Canada was already the United States' greatest trading partner; most trade between the two countries (80 percent) was tariff free, and the average tariff rate on remaining exports to the U.S. was only 5 percent. Since the significant Canadian tariffs that remained (i.e., between 10 and 25 percent on imported items) were primarily on items that were particularly sensitive to import competition (textiles, clothing, footwear, and furniture), their removal would be very damaging to these domestic industries. Also, when the products of these sensitive industries were exported to the U.S., the tariff rates they faced were about half of what they were in Canada. Clearly the impact of tariff removal would be much more devastating in Canada. The removal of the remaining U.S. tariffs would not give Canadians greater access to the U.S. market, but removing Canadian tariffs could significantly improve access for U.S. firms to the Canadian market.

> **Other federal economic policies have accentuated the negative effects of free trade**

What Canada most wanted from the FTA was a means to curb the escalating harassment of Canadian importers. In the U.S. there was little recognition of the fact that vast differences in the circumstances of countries demand different ways of solving economic and social problems. Many Canadian policies and programs were perceived as either "non-tariff barriers" to U.S. business in Canada, or as unfair advantages for Canadian firms who sold in the U.S. market.

As a result, the U.S. was increasingly using its trade remedy legislation to place additional duties on Canadian imports whenever Canadian practices were deemed by them to be "unfair." The Canadian government maintained that a free trade agreement would circumvent U.S. trade law so that the irritating challenges to Canada for "unfairly" subsidizing businesses would be eliminated.

This promise never materialized. From the beginnings of the free trade negotiations, the U.S. made it absolutely clear that it would not give in to Canadian pressure to limit the power of U.S. trade legislation. The U.S. government was consistent and adamant about this issue because it had absolutely nothing to gain

CROSSING THE LINE

FORWARD INTO THE PAST
The FTA has made Canada more, not less, dependent on exports of unprocessed resource-based products. It's also made it almost impossible for future governments to pass measures requiring a minimum level of processing before goods are exported.
PHOTO BY NORM GARCIA/IWA

by changing its legislation. The sad fact for Canada is that the whole "success" of the FTA was dependent on changing the American position, but from the very beginning, the U.S. made it clear it would not give up its power on this issue.

Free trade is not a policy that stands alone. It must be seen in relation to other economic and social policies. While the current economic problems of Canada are often presented by the federal government and its business supporters as part of a vast global restructuring over which Canada has no control, the government's role in shaping the economic climate cannot be ignored. Many of the other economic policies the federal government has pursued have accentuated the negative effects of free trade.

The most notable problems have been those caused by the federal government's high interest rate policy and the overvaluation of the Canadian dollar. Reducing or eliminating the 5 percent tariffs on goods exported to the U.S. was small compensation for the 20 percent escalation in the price of Canadian products and services as a result of the revaluation of the dollar. Canadian exports became more expensive while U.S. imports became relatively cheaper. And while the absurdly high interest rates may have made lending money in Canada attractive, borrowing for business expansion and other purposes became very expensive. The result was that many capital investments in industry were delayed until interest rates came down, and the result of this was a weakening of the competitive position of Canadian industry. Labour productivity, which is directly tied to the level of capital investment, was adversely affected, and production costs increased. Since all firms operate on borrowed money, the high interest rates meant these costs were passed on to the consumer.

Free trade did not produce all of Canada's economic problems. The poor integration of the resource sector with manufacturing and service sectors has resulted in chronically high rates of unemployment and high regional disparities. In large part this was because of Canada's high reliance on the export of unprocessed resource products. What Canada needed was an economic policy which focused on processing resources within the country. Free trade was precisely the wrong policy to achieve this. It has accentuated the structural problems of the economy and has greatly weakened the ability of future governments to pursue more integrative and stimulative economic policies.

1. Vancouver *Sun,* January 19, 1992.
2. Bruce Campbell, "Canada Under Siege: Three Years into the Free Trade Era," (Ottawa: Canadian Centre for Policy Alternatives, 1992).
3. Department of Finance, *The Canadian-U.S. Free Trade Agreement: An Economic Assessment,* (Ottawa, 1988), p. 33.

Marjorie Griffin Cohen is an economist who is a professor of political science and women's studies at Simon Fraser University. She is the author of *Free Trade and the Future of Women's Work* (Garamond, 1987) and *Women's Work, Markets and Economic Development in Nineteenth Century Ontario* (University of Toronto Press, 1988). She has been actively involved in the women's movement in Canada, and since 1985 has been active in the national coalition against free trade.

Mexico: Neo-Liberal Disaster Zone

Mexico's poverty is the result of systematic state policies which have flung open the doors to national and transnational capital

by Alejandro Alvarez and Gabriel Mendoza
Translated and edited by Nicholas Keresztesi

The modern image of Mexico presented in glossy, international business magazines is of a country rich in natural resources, with 85 million potential consumers and 28 million relatively well-educated workers who earn low salaries and are largely non-unionized. The government of President Carlos Salinas de Gortari is praised for taking bold steps to open the country for business by deregulating and privatizing vast sectors of the economy. In short, Mexico is described as a paradise for capital and one of the most dynamic developing economies in the world.

While deregulation and low wages may spell paradise for a few, for the majority of Mexicans they spell purgatory. Twenty-eight million wage earners survive on some of the lowest salaries in the world; almost 23 million workers earn US$4.44 or

A SMALLER PIECE OF THE PIE
PRI policies brought about a substantial decline in the share of Mexico's net domestic income going to wages. Corporate profits and tax subsidies have gone up at the expense of workers.

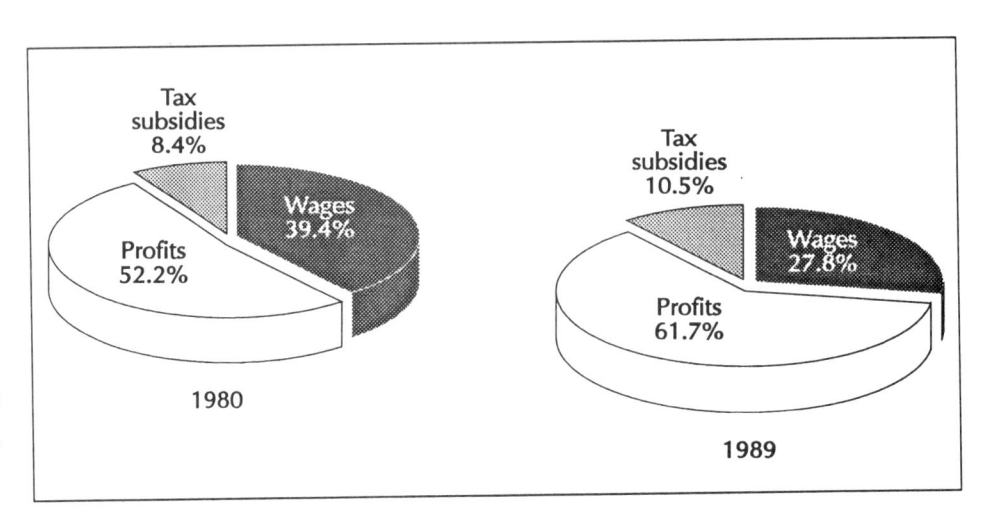

1980
- Tax subsidies 8.4%
- Wages 39.4%
- Profits 52.2%

1989
- Tax subsidies 10.5%
- Wages 27.8%
- Profits 61.7%

MEXICO: NEO-LIBERAL DISASTER ZONE

YOU SAY PEMEX, WE SAY PETROCAN
Under a Mexican law which dates back to 1938, foreigners can't own oil. A key U.S. objective in the NAFTA talks is to get rid of this restriction.

PHOTO BY
CINDY REIMAN/
IMPACT VISUALS

less for a nine-hour day; a million pensioners have a monthly income of less than US$100. Labour's share of national income has steadily declined until it currently receives only 27 percent (by comparison, in Canada, labour's share of national income is 75 percent). According to official statistics, 40 million Mexicans live in poverty. The majority live in the countryside and have no regular income, unemployment insurance, or social programs. More than half the population lacks access to health care, education, and adequate nutrition.[1]

Yet this pervasive poverty is not the terrible destiny forged by our own ineptness. It is the result of systematic state policies which have flung open the doors of the economy to national and transnational capital.

ECONOMIC CRISIS AND GROWING DEPENDENCY   Mexico, like Canada, has a long history of dependence on the U.S. economy. The U.S. is Mexico's most important trading partner, accounting for two-thirds of all Mexican imports and exports. U.S. influence has grown since the oil crisis of the mid-1970s. The quadrupling of international oil prices led Mexico into an unprecedented spree of foreign borrowing to finance petroleum extraction for export. In a few short years, Mexico became an important petroleum exporter and, through PEMEX, the state petroleum monopoly, oil earnings became the largest source of state revenue – but it was at the cost of Mexico's becoming one of the world's biggest foreign debtors.

MEXICO'S GROWING DEBT BURDEN
The light bars represent what the Mexican government spends on programs (in pesos, adjusted for inflation). The dark bars are what's spent on foreign debt servicing. This figure has fallen slightly in recent years, but is still many times what it was just a decade ago.

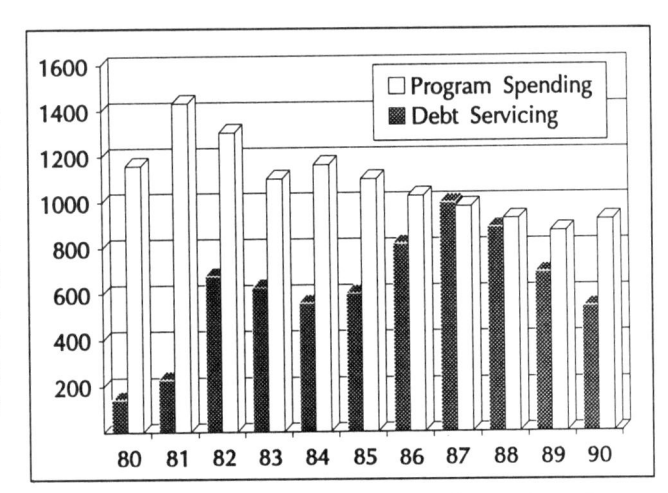

As Mexico's foreign debt grew, so did U.S. leverage on Mexican domestic policy. Almost one-third of Mexico's foreign debt is held by U.S. banks, and much more is held by U.S.-influenced international financial institutions. Leverage is reinforced by U.S. ownership of the most important part of the manufacturing industry, and by the fact that more than half of petroleum exports go to the U.S.

By the early 1980s, rising interest rates on the foreign debt, and falling oil prices, virtually bankrupted the state treasury (at that time, 75 percent of foreign earnings came from oil exports). To qualify for an International Monetary Fund (IMF) bailout, Mexico adopted a program of "structural adjustments" to reduce state spending and increase export earnings. Agricultural subsidies were reduced, and spending on health, education, housing, and other social services was cut drastically. Agricultural output began to drop and inflation skyrocketed to 160 percent in 1987. Mexico fell into virtual stagnation throughout the 1980s, with a .8 percent annual growth rate, and real wages lost 50 percent of their purchasing power.[2]

GOVERNMENT AND PRIVATE SECTOR ASSAULT WAGES The unprecedented decline of wages is a product of a number of factors, including population growth that outstripped economic expansion. During the 1980s, the workforce grew by one million people a year. Even the large migration of workers to northern Mexican cities and the U.S. southwest could not compensate for the lack of job creation caused by IMF-induced stagnation.

Fiscal austerity made problems worse. To cut its deficit, the state, Mexico's biggest employer, cut jobs and put a lid on public employee salaries. Cuts in social spending aggravated already dismal working and living conditions. Reduced access to education and training will increase the ranks of the unskilled workforce for generations to come. The private sector, also reeling under heavy foreign debt, took advantage of the depressed job market to freeze wages.

MEXICO: NEO-LIBERAL DISASTER ZONE

Government strategy to promote maquiladoras – assembly facilities for many of the Fortune 500 U.S. transnational corporations – as a way of increasing foreign exchange earnings for debt servicing, further integrated Mexican and U.S. economies and kept wages low.[3] The Mexican government offers attractive terms to lure maquiladoras to its northern border area. These terms include: low wages, the absence of effective unions, lax environmental controls, low health and safety standards, special tariff and taxation rules, and proximity to the U.S. market.

During the early 1980s, government policies to keep the peso undervalued in relation to the U.S. dollar helped promote exports and made Mexican wages even more "competitive" internationally. A Mexican worker earning the minimum salary in 1980 brought home the equivalent of US$7.02 per day. In 1986, the average daily salary in the maquiladora dropped to US$4.24. By 1990, the minimum daily wage had fallen to US$3.13.[4] Foreign companies took advantage of the profit-making opportunity, and maquiladora investment grew rapidly. In 1980 there were 620 factories employing 120,000; by 1990, 467,000 Mexicans were employed in 2007 factories, primarily producing electronics, auto parts, and textiles. Despite their location on Mexican soil, maquiladoras buy only 2 percent of total inputs from Mexican sources, so their capacity to stimulate Mexican industry is nil.[5]

AUTO INDUSTRY PUSHES FOR INTEGRATION Government policies to promote exports have also benefitted U.S. car companies and the Mexican petrochemical and petroleum industries, all of which have been strong promoters of North American integration.

In 1980, the automobile industry in Mexico was divided into three segments, all foreign controlled: the older assembly plants and parts suppliers in central Mexico

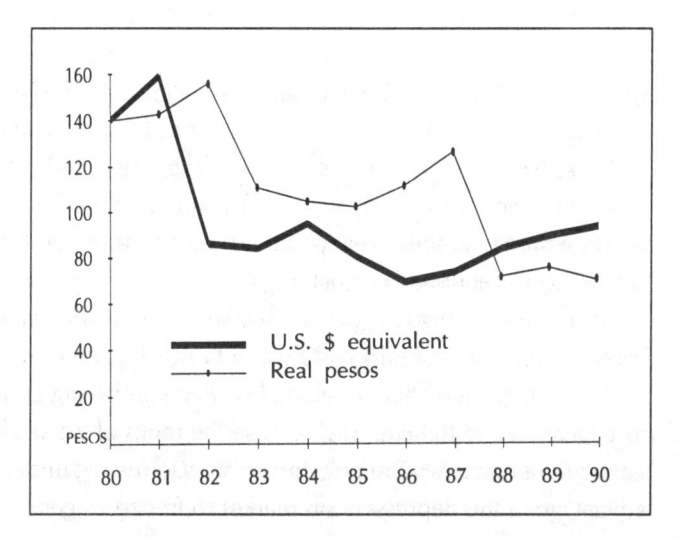

GOVERNMENT HELPING INDUSTRY Mexico's official minimum wage under the de la Madrid and Salinas governments has not kept up with inflation. The lighter line shows the minimum wage expressed as 1980 pesos, the dark ribbon shows its U.S.-dollar equivalent.

mainly served the internal market; the newer, export-oriented assembly plants were set up in the north; parts manufacturers operated maquiladoras on the border. High-tech plants in northern Mexico proved enormously profitable. For example, the stamping and assembly plant in Hermosillo "cost Ford $500 million to launch in 1986 and employs 1,600 workers for an annual labour bill of about $7 million. In the United States, labour costs (including wages and benefits) run about $30 an hour or $100 million a year for a plant this size."[6]

PRO-GOVERNMENT UNIONS FAIL TO DEFEND WORKERS' INTERESTS

Workers' ability to reverse the devastating decline of wages and living and working conditions has been eroded by Mexico's powerful trade union structures, which have tended to support government policies. Only 22 percent of the active workforce is unionized, and the biggest unions have been allied to the state since 1936 through their affiliation with the governing Institutional Revolutionary Party (PRI), which has ruled continuously for 62 years. The largest labour central, the CTM (Confederation of Workers of Mexico), has fought against independent rank-and-file union movements that struggle for greater democracy within the labour movement.

Through the 1980s, much of the growing resistance to government policy was led by the small but militant movement of "independent trade unionism." Hundreds of thousands of workers throughout the country and from diverse sectors – industry, services, commerce, public sector, education, agriculture, and even the unemployed – have been active in opposing government policy. But the fight has so far been isolated and unable to break the domination of capital. During the period that real salaries lost 50 percent of their purchasing power, strikes were used in only 2.7 percent of all contract negotiations, and only one union was certified through all of the 1980s.

Today, government-linked unions continue to back policies that hurt their membership. The leader of the petroleum workers' union quietly accepted PEMEX plans to lay off almost 35,000 workers this year. Many more thousands of workers are threatened with layoffs in the railway, steel, and textile industries, as well as in the public sector. These layoffs go unchallenged by the unions, as they are seen to be necessary to make the industries more competitive.

While unions have been unimaginative in their dealings with capital, management has been more adept at manipulating labour in Mexico's rapidly evolving economic climate. For example, business adopted a strategy of artificially prolonging strikes in 1980, resulting in a 130-day strike at Industrial Automotriz de Cuernavaca, and a 106-day strike at General Motors. Similar strategies were used at the airline Mexicana de Aviacion, and at two soft drink plants: Mexicana de Envases and Coca-Cola. The 1980s also saw systematic layoffs and partial restructuring in the

> 'In Mexico alone, 3 million children work on the streets. They work as clowns, they wash cars or windshields, and they sell chocolate and household items to passersby. Others work in markets or as prostitutes. Close to 10 million children under the age of 15 work as prostitutes in the region [Latin America]. Many of these children are the sole wage earners in their families.'
> LATINAMERICA PRESS, MAY 30, 1991

MEXICO: NEO-LIBERAL DISASTER ZONE

automobile and machine tool industries, and deteriorating working conditions and pay scales for workers in education and health services. 'The Renault auto-plant 'lockout' was a major blow to labour in 1985, as was the 1986 closing of state steel company Fundidora de Monterrey. Workers' demands for wage increases and the renegotiation of collective contracts were met in 1986 and early 1987 with massive layoffs and reduced shifts. Some companies even shut down rather than deal with employee demands. Ford Motor Company closed its Cuautitlan plant in September 1987 and reopened it several weeks later, and the airline Aeromexico illegally declared bankruptcy in April 1988 and immediately resumed operations under the name 'Sindicatura de Aeromexico'."[7]

During the past decade, government policy and demands of capital for austerity, deregulation, and restructuring have led Mexico to greater economic integration with the U.S. These policies delivered benefits to multinational corporations and to a few big Mexican financial and industrial groups, while delivering growing unemployment, lower wages, and a strong anti-labour climate to working people.

MASSIVE MEXICAN MIGRATION CHEAP THREAT

Salinas de Gortari has used Mexican migration as a way to divert Canadian opposition to NAFTA. On two trips to Canada, he insisted that only a NAFTA could ensure that Mexico would export high quality, inexpensive products rather than Mexican workers. The fear of massive migration is conjured up to disguise the role he seeks for Mexico: a haven for Canadian companies paying wages of hunger. Labour market integration between Mexico and the U.S., already well advanced, reveals the role Mexico is playing in the restructuring of the North American economy.

The U.S. has used immigration policy throughout the 1980s to create a special zone along both sides of the U.S.-Mexico border in the U.S. states of California, Arizona, New Mexico, Colorado, and Texas, and in the Mexican states of Baja California, Sonora, Chihuahua, Nuevo Leon, Coahuila, and Tamaulipas. This zone has a large but highly segmented labour force with a low rate of unionization and great salary differentials. The most difficult jobs and the lowest wages go to the

PUPPET ON A STRING This cartoon from the progressive Mexican weekly PROCESO plays on the view of Salinas as George Bush's pet. Salinas is saying, 'The deal's practically tied up.'

migrants who work in the U.S., and to those who work in the maquiladoras in Mexico. Legislation designed to control this labour force (like the U.S. Immigration and Reform Act) offered amnesty to undocumented workers who had entered the U.S. illegally but were able to prove a certain number of years of residency. In reality, these measures have facilitated police persecution, frightening and disorganizing hundreds of thousands of migrant workers. The resulting labour instability serves to suppress wages and labour rights of both U.S. and migrant workers in the vital economic zone. For domestic political reasons, the U.S. prefers to exercise control over Mexican immigration through unilateral mechanisms rather than by putting it on the NAFTA negotiating table.

FREE TRADE MEANS MORE JOB LOSS IN MEXICO Over the past decade, the Mexican government has pursued neo-liberal, anti-democratic, and unpopular policies under banners like "stabilization" and "modernization," but always with the claim that the austerity measures were "bitter but inevitable." In the past two years, Salinas de Gortari has accelerated Mexico's sell-out to international capital with a new, positive twist: now he claims that free trade will create jobs and allow Mexico to form part of the biggest market in the world.

For Mexicans, punished by almost 50 percent underemployment or unemployment, the NAFTA promise of sustained economic growth and abundant jobs sounds sweet. It is a lure cast to win support for a NAFTA which will make the structural changes suffered by Mexicans, Canadians, and Americans irreversible.

Mexico's experience of economic liberalization and modernization during the 1980s has already shown that the claim that economic integration will bring many well-paying jobs is a hoax. The job market has not even recovered from the severe economic restructuring launched in 1982, when Mexico's unilateral lowering of tariffs devastated industries that had been protected since the 1930s. Technologically backward industries were hardest hit: 50 percent of the textile factories and 28 percent of the leather industry disappeared; domestic production of household appliances and capital goods virtually shut down.

> **Half the textile factories and 28 percent of the leather industry disappeared during restructuring in 1982**

With the dramatic drop in salaries in the past ten years, the domestic market shrivelled and businesses shut down, throwing hundreds of thousands of workers onto the street. The automotive workforce alone fell by 50 percent between 1980 and 1984. Layoffs in the steel industry between 1985 and 1990 affected 25,000 workers. More than 35,000 primary school teachers lost their jobs. "Modernization" in the health sector left 60,000 doctors and 20,000 nurses unemployed.

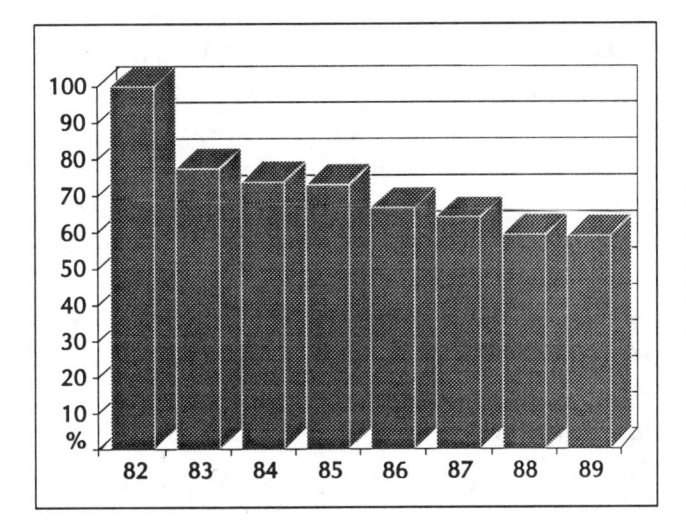

PAYING THE PRICE FOR NEO-LIBERALISM Average real wages have fallen 50 percent in Mexico since 1982. At the same time, the cost of living is rising, approaching U.S. levels.

Integration into a North American regional economy will tend to cause further unemployment in Mexico, just as it has done in Canada and the U.S. Even in the case of a gradual lowering of tariff barriers, around 30 percent of manufacturing jobs will be lost. That is, almost 1 million of the less productive jobs in older small and medium-sized enterprises will be wiped out by high-tech, modern industries producing massive volume, but with a reduced workforce. The sectors in biggest trouble are food and beverages, clothing, chemicals, petrochemicals, and precision instruments. U.S.-based multinationals are already investing heavily in these sectors, buying out Mexican companies and pressuring for ever greater deregulation.

In agriculture, reduced state and private investment, combined with a credit squeeze aggravated by rising interest rates and reduced subsidies, has led to rising unemployment, reduced rural incomes, deteriorating infrastructure, and diminishing land under cultivation. Opening the economy to food and agricultural imports has displaced domestic production of traditional crops like soya and other beans, sorghum, corn, wheat, and oil grains. Reforms to landholding laws pave the way for financial and industrial capital to establish agricultural maquiladoras, drawing production away from food that will meet domestic needs in order to supply the North American market with beef, fruits, and vegetables.

Overall productivity of the Mexican economy grew, on average, 3.7 percent a year between 1963 and 1977. During the period 1977 to 1987, when production for export was expanding, the rate of productivity growth fell to 1.8 percent per year.[8] This illustrates that manufacturing exports grew, not as the result of rising efficiency or modernization, but rather due to the undervalued peso, which subsidized labour and energy costs. These advantages tended to disappear as the peso value was fixed at its real level in comparison to the U.S. dollar.

> 'El Paso [Texas] is a great place to live, but we wouldn't be here if it weren't for the maquiladora industry in Juarez [Mexico]. The lower labor rate for manufacturing and assembling is the honey that attracts all of us bees. Juarez is a city of over one million. It has developed from a city catering to farming and ranching, to a large industrial city . . . Sure, you can see temporary cardboard houses which look bad, but those people are up here because there are jobs available.'
>
> DON NIBBE, TWIN PLANT NEWS (PRO-MAQUILADORA MAGAZINE), OCTOBER 1990

Most working Mexicans labour in small and medium-sized enterprises. Experts estimate that 900,000 Mexicans work in 135,000 industrial establishments with less than 100 employees each, where the average annual value produced per worker is US$7,800. Workers in comparable industries in the U.S. produce on average US$53,000 worth of value.[9] Large U.S. companies which benefit from economies of scale achieve an even higher productivity rate, estimated to be 11 times that of the Mexican average. Despite dramatic productivity differences, per unit cost of production in Mexico and the U.S. is roughly the same when Mexico's low wages are factored in.

FREE TRADE IS NOT OUR AGENDA   Former U.S. President Ronald Reagan stated that free trade would write a new economic constitution for North America. Salinas de Gortari's regime is, in part, a product of Reagan's political and economic visions. His policies are from the same school. He is aggressively deregulating and privatizing the state sector, starting with banking and telecommunications, and he is now exploring ways to privatize social security, health care, and pension funds. Proposals to decentralize the education system directly threaten teachers' unions, and open the way for privatization. Reforms of church and state relations brought in by Salinas allow the powerful Catholic Church to erode public education, something denied it since the Mexican Revolution (1910-1917). Constitutional limits on foreign investment are being systematically erased, and constitutionally protected communal landholdings are being privatized. These are all preconditions for Mexico's entry into NAFTA.

The government which is administering the shock treatment to the Mexican economy keeps itself in power through electoral fraud. Small, controlled openings in the political system are being made available to opposition parties, but obtaining a fully respected democratic process is the highest priority for Mexico's diverse social movement.

IF NOT FREE TRADE, THEN WHAT?   Mexico's entrance into a NAFTA is one more damaging step in a decade-old process of handing our human and natural resources over to transnational capital. Neo-liberal policies have changed people's lives, producing growing unemployment, poverty, reduced access to health care and education, growing hunger and malnutrition, more children dying of diarrhea, and the return of cholera. These are the daily consequences of neo-liberal economic policies for 50 million Mexicans.

But NAFTA not only integrates the Canadian, Mexican, and American economies, it also integrates our peoples. And a people's alternative to NAFTA must be

MEXICO: NEO-LIBERAL DISASTER ZONE

HOW THE OTHER 95 PERCENT LIVE Mexico does have considerable wealth, particularly in oil and gas reserves, but the vast majority of its 85 million people live in unsanitary shanty communities like this one in Mexico City.
PHOTO BY NICK KERESZTESI

coordinated among us. We must develop a common response, one based on mutual respect for our differences and strengthened by our common interests. We must coordinate our struggles around common demands. We must insist that NAFTA raise living and working conditions to the highest levels enjoyed by North American workers, not be used to lower them to the poor conditions prevalent in Mexico. Similarly, economic integration must lead to improvements in environmental protection and enforcement, not make it easier for polluting industries to relocate to escape controls, or to dump toxic wastes. We must also support each other in our particular demands. For Mexicans, our highest priority is for the democratization of the political system. Without democracy, the Mexican people cannot participate in the development of alternative economic strategies. Canadians and Americans must support us in this demand by insisting that a NAFTA not be signed until free and fair elections have been held in Mexico. An agreement signed by an illegitimate government must itself be seen as illegitimate.

No one is opposed to increased trade among our countries, but we oppose the NAFTA because it is founded on cut-throat competition, not on constructive cooperation. It allows the free flow of investments, profits, and products, but restricts the dissemination of ideas, technology, and know-how, so vital for the development of backward economies. It seeks to weaken unions and other efforts working people make to improve their lives, instead of promoting democratic participation in society. By treating as equals economies that are fundamentally unequal, it forbids the kinds of policies necessary to develop weak and underdeveloped economic sectors and regions of the country. It is unacceptable

CROSSING THE LINE

SEPARATE REALITIES Since Mexico's government began deregulating the nationalized banking system in the late 1970s, between $35 and $50 billion in capital has fled the country. The gulf between the jet-set world of international finance represented by this bank, and the man who keeps its sidewalk clean, is growing every day.

PHOTO BY NICK KERESZTESI

that NAFTA thrives on poverty and advances only those parts of the economy that are profitable to transnational capital.

Mexico needs an alternative economic strategy, one that stimulates sustainable development of poor and underdeveloped regions of our country, and strengthens weaker sectors of the economy. We seek policies that improve education, health care, food security, and that create meaningful and well-paying jobs. More than free trade, we require fair trade that permits the sensible use of trade regulation to protect vital sectors of the national economy. We want a strategy for economic growth that develops, not plunders, our national resources, and that uses an active public sector to ensure the provision of accessible and quality social services.

These principles must form the basis of any international trade agreement that seeks development, not simply economic growth. They are ambitious and go against current neo-liberal trends. They set out goals for international trade and economic relations in which working people throughout North America can find common cause. We are challenged today to develop closer relations and join together to fight for our common interests.

1. The predatory features of recent development have been examined in greater detail in Alejandro Alvarez and Gabriel Mendoza, "Mexico 1988, un capitalismo depredador in crisis," in *Cuadernos Politicos*, enero/abril 1988, Editorial ERA, Mexico.
2. These aspects are documented in greater detail in Alejandro Alvarez and Gabriel Mendoza, *Mexico 1988-1991: Un ajuste economico exitoso?*, Facultad de Economia, UNAM, Mexico, 1991.
3. A fuller view of the maquiladora industry is in Alejandro Alvarez, "Mexico: Maquila Country?" a speech presented at the conference "Solidarity, Not Competition: Canada-U.S.-Mexico Free Trade," Toronto, May 3-5 1991, published by *Common Frontiers*.
4. See note 2 above.
5. See note 3 for more detail on this topic.
6. See the article by Kim Moody and Mary McGinn, "From the Yukon to the Yucatan: Free Trade Goes Continental and So Must Labour Solidarity," in *Dollars and Sense*, No. 171, Boston, November 1991, pp. 10-12.
7. See Alejandro Alvarez, "Economic crisis and the labour movement in Mexico," in Kevin Middlebrook, ed., *Unions, Workers and the State in Mexico*, Centre for U.S.-Mexican Studies, U.C. San Diego, 1991, p. 45.
8. Overall productivity growth rate fell even though it increased in the automotive sector as modern plants employing high technology achieved internationally competitive levels of productivity.
9. This theme of productivity is developed by Edur Velasco, "El Desafio Sindical al NAFTA: empleos, salarios y productividad," in *El Cotidano*, No. 41, May-June 1991, Universidad Autonoma Metropolitana-Azcapotzalco, Mexico, pp. 21-28.

Alejandro Alvarez is a labour economist and teaches in the Faculty of Economics at the National Autonomous University of Mexico (UNAM). He is a member of the Academic Council of the Mexican Action Network on Free Trade.

Gabriel Mendoza teaches economics at the Faculty of Economics of the UNAM and coordinates the faculty's *Current Economy Workshop*. He also advises the Partido de la Revolucion Democratica (PRD) members of the federal Chamber of Deputies.

The U.S. and the Global Economy

Global competition, for the U.S., has meant lower wages and disappearing jobs, but there are alternatives

by Jim Benn

There's no doubt about it – it's a changing world for U.S. business and for the relationship between business and the U.S. people. The North American Free Trade Agreement and the rest of the administration's free trade agenda – GATT and a hemispheric common market – are shaping up to be trademarks of that world. Still, free trade is only a part of a more general policy of liberating capital from all social restrictions, a policy that includes privatization and deregulation. It is a policy that demands that only corporate investment should have the authority to define domestic and global society. With the implementation of this policy we can see how business, assuming growth as a birthright, has simply tolerated social standards in the past. Now faced with global competition and redefined market identities in Europe and the Pacific Rim, U.S. capital has dropped social accountability as if it were a luxury it can no longer afford.

Business has dropped social accountability as if it were a luxury it can no longer afford

MISMANAGEMENT, TECHNOLOGY, COMPETITION AND GREED For over a century, capitalism frolicked in America. With seemingly unlimited potential for land development, and an unrelenting tide of immigrant labour, U.S. productive forces couldn't help but expand. Nowhere else has an expanding domestic market played such a prominent role in capital's growth. It didn't bump its nose until the 1930s, and then World War II came along and wiped out the prospects of serious world competition for another twenty years. In 1945 the U.S. steel industry controlled 80 percent of the world's steel production. Steel management didn't free themselves of

THE U.S. AND THE GLOBAL ECONOMY

GOING, GOING... Skilled manufacturing jobs in the U.S. are disappearing. According to the U.S. Bureau of Labor Statistics, the country lost 9.7 million jobs due to plant closings and lay-offs between 1983 and 1988.

PHOTO BY CATHERINE SMITH/ IMPACT VISUALS

that sense of dominance until the early 1960s. By then times had changed.

When the steel leadership learned that European and Asian steel production was getting back on its feet in the late 1950s, they didn't do much about it. They had been on top of the heap and had more capacity than any newcomer would logically dream of. These industrialists had become fat and contented, complacent about marketplace issues and unimaginative when it came to innovation. Conservative to the core, they scoffed at the idea of assessing the impact of new technologies in furnace designs and rolling facilities as absurd. After all, they were the U.S. steel industry, they controlled all the production that mattered.

By the early 1960s, all Japanese and most European steel companies were on-line with state-of-the-art technologies, including Basic Oxygen Furnaces that cut the time for cooking a heat of steel from 8 hours to 20 minutes. By the 1970s, giant state-of-the-art facilities had begun appearing throughout the Third World. By the end of the 1970s, rising costs in the construction of basic steel mills gave them ever-climbing, multi-billion dollar price tags. For the U.S. steel industry, now facing losses from competition in a big way, a reassessment finally occurred.

Generally the conclusion was that they had missed the boat. Yes, they should have paid attention and kept up with innovations. They hadn't, and now to catch up would require risking everything they had in costly investments. They did have an option. They could sell much of their traditional core business and pool their money into new, more profitable sectors.

For the money managers who began to take control of basic industry, confronting foreign competition was more of a God-send than a disaster. It supplied the motivation to liberate capital from low-profit industry and give it the freedom to exploit high-profit opportunities wherever they might be found. In 1980, David Roderick, the first CEO of the U.S. Steel Corporation who hadn't grown up within the steel industry, put the new direction succinctly: "You've got to understand that we're not in business to make steel, we're in business to make money." Roderick came from the banking industry and represented a new trend in the management of America's big corporations, away from industrialists and toward money managers. Industrial strategy faded into the shadows of returns on investment, commitment to shareholders' quarterly reports, and maximization of profits.

U.S. Steel restructured, dropping steel production to less than 25 percent of its holdings. Management then used a promise to invest in new steel technologies to

---

RAIDERS OF THE LOST ART

Jim Benn

The Owens-Corning Fiberglass raid is one example from a list of thousands that speaks to the role of speculative capital freed from the responsibility of being productive. In 1987, OCF had never had an unprofitable year. It had over 30 percent of the U.S. fiberglass market, the bulk of it in housing insulation. As insurance against cyclical downturns in housing starts, they had diversified into plumbing supplies, aerospace, and a variety of other interests. OCF was a dominant manufacturer of what many considered a material for the future, fiberglass having already replaced much of steel's uses in automobiles. Then the Wickes Corporation in Texas took a look at the value of OCF stock and, being good samaritans, decided that they could help OCF shareholders do better. They began buying OCF shares in a raid on the company.

OCF management panicked. The raider's justification was that too many resources were being used too unproductively and that meant bad management. Wickes would streamline operations, improve investment return, and increase stock value. That would mean trimming fat, which meant non-core investments and non-profit-making employees. A leaner OCF would mean thousands of jobs lost and a less strategic commitment to corporate growth. It would also mean new leadership. OCF management reacted with the only decision their egos could handle—if the company was going to be mismanaged, then by-God they'd be the ones to do it. They fought back.

Management began borrowing money, which allowed them to buy back OCF stock. This caused the value of the stock to skyrocket; it became too expensive for Wickes. The Texans ended their raid and sold back their OCF shares, claiming a moral victory and walking away with $75 million profit. OCF management, still in control, could measure their victory with the corporation's newest acquisition, a $1.5 billion debt.

From this point on, OCF's defense began to look remarkably like the raider's original intention. Their reorganization plan started with the closing of their Research and Development labs and the dumping of over 400 technicians. Goodbye to innovation. They then cut the Toledo headquarters staff in half, dumping 450 office workers (so much for the service sector). Then they got down to business. They sold off all of their non-core diversified holdings and began chopping away at production facilities across the country. Within a few months, a number of departments and plants had been closed and over 5,000 production workers had lost their jobs.

THE U.S. AND THE GLOBAL ECONOMY

NIGHTMARE IN DETROIT
The Japanese are usually blamed for this scenario. In fact, U.S. corporations are closing their own factories to escape unions and decent wages. General Motors is now the largest employer in Mexico, and the auto industry is the fastest growing sector of the maquiladoras.

PHOTO BY JIM WEST/ IMPACT VISUALS

rob steelworkers of over $1.5 billion in contract concessions, which helped to buy Marathon Oil. By the mid-1980s, the business was primarily an energy company and they had changed their name to USX. The X was their New York Stock Exchange identification – they had changed their name to money.

INVESTMENT VS. PRODUCTION Technology's impact on American industry had a one-two punch. One, it was competitors' effective application of new technologies that broke U.S. dominance in manufacturing. Two, it was new communications technologies that allowed U.S. corporations to rapidly diversify and abandon their U.S. base for high-exploitation opportunities world-wide. Split-second movement of capital resources introduced speculation into industry on a scale undreamed of. Whole industries transformed themselves from giant manufacturing complexes to complex global networks of computer connected "outsourced" contracts. Capital cowboys on Wall Street and beyond played with junk bonds, buyouts, and corporate raiding to redesign the face of profit-making in industry by eliminating production as a requirement for money making.

At the centre of this economic chaos was a frenzy of blackmail leveraging by corporations anxious to exploit local and state governments' desperate need for

CROSSING THE LINE

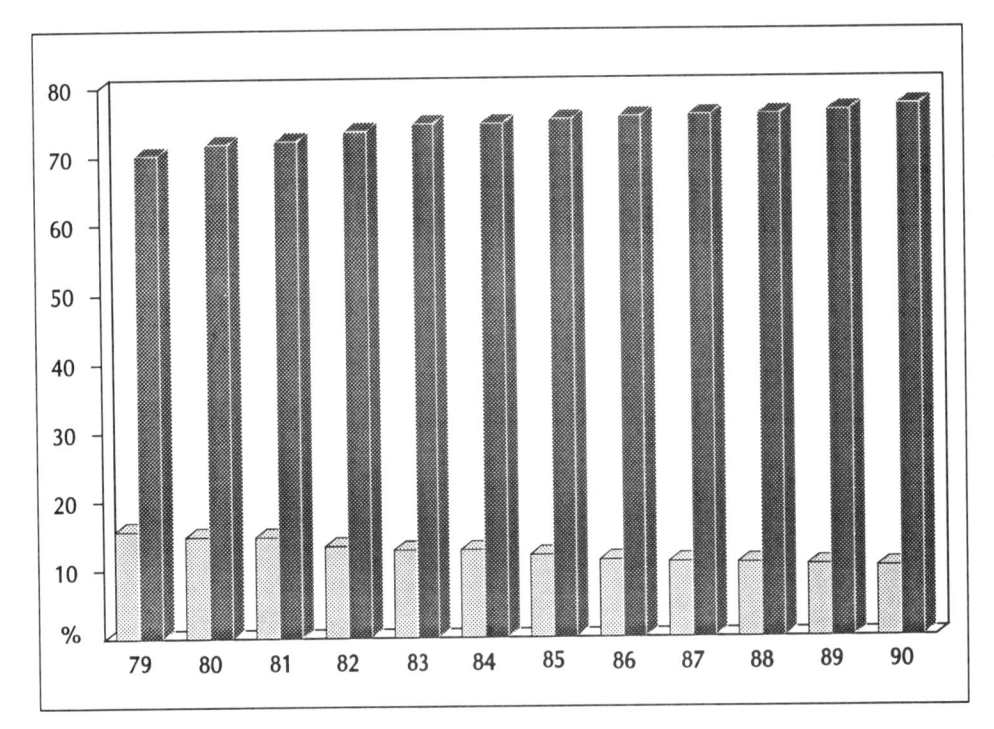

FIRST, THE GOOD NEWS... Lighter bars show skilled manufacturing jobs as percentage of workforce; darker bars are unskilled service sector jobs. Disappearing manufacturing jobs are, by and large, being replaced by service sector jobs.
SOURCE: BUSINESS WEEK

investment. Plants moved across county lines to take advantage of tax break packages, run away from union contracts, and dramatically cut wages. As manufacturing jobs disappeared from the landscape of the early 1980s, collapsed economic bases created the perfect conditions for whipsawing – potential investors pitted one community against another for the biggest tax break. General Motors unleashed a bidding war for its Saturn plant. American Motors pitted Kenosha against Toledo to determine which of the two plants might stay operating. In economic development offices across the country, any kind of investment proposal was worth selling a city's integrity for.

Of course industrial restructuring was global and part of a worldwide recession in the early 1980s, but for industrial communities – those neighbourhoods where blue-collar families live – the recession never ended. In 1982 the U.S. official unemployment rate averaged 9.7 percent. In communities that had large populations employed in basic industry, official unemployment made it to 25 and 30 percent. Unofficially, the numbers were much higher. As benefits ran out, or as workers developed a more transient character or fell back onto "underground" economies or a handful of minimum wage part-time jobs, the statistics began to lighten up. But the conditions didn't. It has never stopped being 1982 for most "industrial" communities in the U.S.

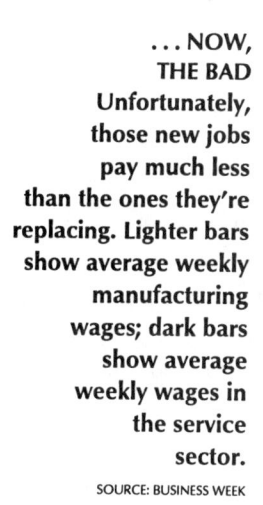

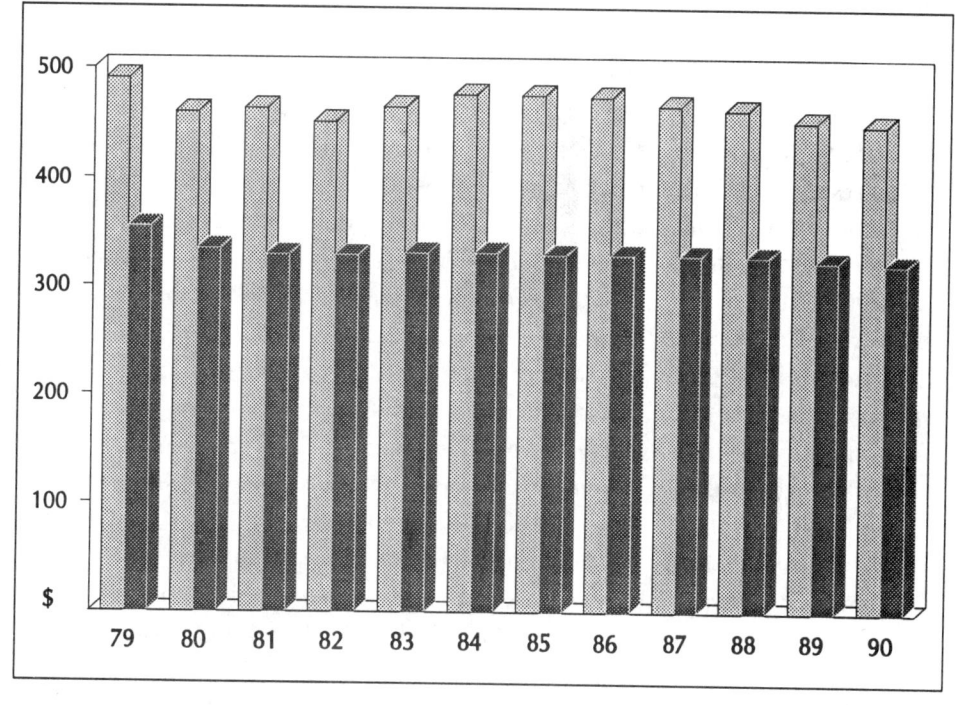

THE U.S. AND THE GLOBAL ECONOMY

...NOW, THE BAD
Unfortunately, those new jobs pay much less than the ones they're replacing. Lighter bars show average weekly manufacturing wages; dark bars show average weekly wages in the service sector.

SOURCE: BUSINESS WEEK

SOCIAL IMPACT – THE RICH GET RICHER AND THE POOR GROW... It's hard to say what unemployment means today. The whole concept has changed over the last fifteen years. Today, few can survive on the wages from a single job, yet having a single job is considered being employed, even if it's not survivable. Most of Pittsburgh's steelworkers, who lost their jobs in the early-1980s collapse of the region's basic steel industry, wouldn't consider themselves employed. In fact many of them aren't, under anyone's definition (among that population unemployment still runs at about 40 percent). Only 20 percent have found jobs that offer close to the wages they lost. An additional 40 percent found work, but at 40 to 60 percent of their previous income. For those who have found minimum wage occupations that require welfare supplements or assistance from pensioned family members, employment has always meant earning a living – and they are not earning a living.

> **It has never stopped being 1982 for most 'industrial' communities in the U.S.**

One of the most graphic examples of the new relationship of employment to poverty is seen in the city of Cleveland, Ohio. In 1979 the crisis of deindustrialization had brought official unemployment there to over 11 percent. As in most other U.S. industrial cities, many development advocates argued for a

> 'Canada will supply natural resources; Mexico cheap labor; and the U.S. will enjoy the fruits of both. But only the more fortunate citizens of the U.S. will enjoy these fruits. Behind all the hype for the globalized post-industrial economy lies this reality: high-wage production jobs disappear; an affluent minority of managers, designers, lawyers, marketing specialists, propagandists, and financiers plan and administer the global economy; and an increasingly immiserated mass of janitors, nannies, manicurists, and clerks serve them.'
>
> DOUG HENWOOD, LIES OF OUR TIMES, SEPTEMBER 1990

strategic shift away from manufacturing. They didn't have much of a choice. Investors did not want to spend their money on manufacturing, and developers make it a point to give investors what they want.

Development in Cleveland, and across the country, was hobbled by the taskmaster of "business climate." Business climate is an ideological measure of the comfort level for investors doing business in a community. Make them uncomfortable and you have a bad business climate, which discourages new investment. Business climate is a concept that limits governments to grovelling before anyone with investment dollars in his pockets. Setting rules, disciplining violations of agreements, demanding social responsibility of any kind, are all factors that lead to a bad business climate.

For Cleveland, as for most cities, grovelling generally took the form of government subsidies, mostly aimed at real estate development which would build office and convention complexes tied to a new service sector. Tax breaks became the first step towards any investment that could vaguely be tied to jobs. The bulk of these breaks were real estate tax abatements.

The headlines tell the tale. A recent Chicago *Tribune* article reports on Cleveland as the "Comeback City." It focuses on the flats, an old industrial area that has been transformed into a riverfront entertainment complex. Others have pointed to the new office towers and other skyline and lakefront transformations. Without a doubt, pandering, with abatements and other tax breaks to a small group of local investors, has dramatically redefined the role of the service sector in the economy of the city. It has brought BMWs to a small but developing cultural scene of nightclubs and restaurants, and to an ever-growing array of downtown shopping malls. It has created new jobs for the more traditional working class population too, replacing manufacturing opportunities that have been forever lost. By 1989 the unemployment rate had dropped to 6 percent.

Unfortunately, that number was overshadowed by an even more startling statistic. The poverty rate had increased over those same years by 35 percent. Today, 47 percent of the population of Cleveland is at the poverty level or below ($12,000 a year for a family of four). The public school system has collapsed and a dramatic loss in promising entry-level jobs in manufacturing – jobs that teach skills and build future potential – have left young people with the choice between scarce openings at fast-food chains, and the streets. And the psychology of the streets has begun to mirror the cynical psychology of abandoned workers. If there is any promise in a futureless urban decay, where a black male isn't likely to live past 40 in any case, then selling crack doesn't seem like such a desperate option.

It seems fair to suggest that the future of Cleveland is the future for the United States. Across the country, the impact of federal policy has transformed a nation with tremendous productive resources into the home of the poor and the land of the desperate. That policy is an ideologically guided promotion of unleashed capitalism. It runs on the belief that what's good for business – big business – is good for the country, and any mucking around with business' freedom to act only further jeopardizes the economy. In every aspect of economic life, domestic and international, we have seen government policy committed, unwaveringly, to the liberation of capital. It is Reagan's "trickle down," and it plays itself out with tax breaks, deregulation, privatization, and "free" trade. Its product has been an incredible polarization of society between rich and poor. It has fostered the mismanagement and gutting of basic industry. It has fed the collapse of regional economies and produced a landslide of bankruptcies that has threatened the national pension fund insurance program. It has promoted a speculative

REVOLUTION FOR THE RICH

Jim Sinclair

"The most important story about the U.S. economy in the eighties is the economic warfare that the wealthy and powerful have been waging against the vast majority of Americans."

With those words, David Gordon of the New School for Social Research, describes a decade of U.S. history which has seen a dramatic shift in wealth from working Americans to the rich.

A combination of a massive cut in personal income taxes for wealthy Americans–the rate plummeted from 70 percent to 28 percent–and monetary policies that encouraged speculation, offshore investment, and deregulation, was responsible.

In 1988 approximately 1.3 million individual Americans were millionaires by assets, up from 574,000 in 1980, 180,000 in 1972, 90,000 in 1964 and just 27,000 in 1953.

In 1982 there were 13 billionaires, but by 1988 the number had jumped to 51 billionaires.

Between 1980 and 1989, the number of people reporting incomes of more than a half a million dollars rocketed from 16,881 to 183,240–an increase of 985 percent.

The 1 percent at the top of the economic pile control 26.9 percent of all wealth. The top 10 percent of U.S. households control 44 percent of the country's wealth.

On the other hand, the bottom 10 percent share only 4.6 percent of the wealth, a drop from 5.6 percent in 1969. Americans earning $15,000 to $26,000 saw their share drop to 10.7 percent from 12.4 percent in 1969. Perhaps more startling is the fact that if you don't count government assistance, the bottom 20 percent receive only 1 percent of the wealth.

Almost 50 percent of all Americans who filed income tax returns in 1989 earned less than $20,000.

During the same period, pay for executives has climbed dramatically. In 1987, corporations paid their officers $200 billion in compensation, while they paid only $83.9 billion in federal income taxes. Compare this to 1953, when corporations paid their officers $8.8 billion compensation, but paid federal income tax of $19.9 billion.

Today a handful of corporate executives take home more than double the amount the government collects. Compensation to corporate officers accounts for 78 percent of corporate profits in 1987.

In the same year, Texas Agriculture Commissioner Jim Hightower commented, "Indeed, Reagan's administration took so much money from the pockets of middle and lower-income Americans and shoved it up to the wealthiest 10 percent in our society that a top-heavy structure now threatens to come crashing down on us."

SOURCES: Kevin Phillips, *The Politics Of Rich And Poor* (Harper Collins, 1991); "America: What Went Wrong," in the *Philadelphia Inquirer*

environment that has led to crisis in the financial industry, threatening the savings and loan's and banking industry's deposit insurance programs. It has nurtured a disdain for discipline among the federal regulating agencies, affecting occupational safety and health, labour relations, civil rights, and the environment.

Most of these programs grew from the spirit of New Deal reforms that argued that government regulation was key to avoiding economic chaos. These reforms recognized that business, left to its own devices, would lose all socially responsible perspective in the quest for profits. The shapers of the New Deal were trying to end the Great Depression of the 1930s while building a body of safeguards against future depressions. Of course that was the 1930s and the world has since seen a lot of changes, not least the collapse of communism as a global contender with capitalism. A recent Chicago *Tribune* political cartoon showed two fallen and broken statues. On the right was Lenin, on the left was Franklin Roosevelt.

A WHIPSAWING BUSINESS CLIMATE GOES GLOBAL

North and South Carolina have aggressively advertised their non-union, non-taxing business climate as bait for northern businesses. To keep or attract a business, a northern state had to match what North Carolina was willing to offer. By the end of the 1980s southeastern Ohio was becoming a more attractive business climate by achieving wage parity with the Pacific Rim.

And what about North Carolina? When technology brought whipsawing, based on the worst possible social conditions as the best possible business climate, to the Third World, then nowhere was a sure bet for investment. The fact that Mexico's maquiladora industries have grown to over 2,000 sites, employing nearly 500,000 workers, had an impact on all of America's industrial communities: north, south, east and west. At $4.00 a day wages, the maquiladora workers are the lowest paid manufacturing workers in the world. The maquiladora industrial sites are some of the most unregulated in the world. When it comes to whipsawing, even North Carolina may have met its match.

And that's where the "free" trade concept comes in. Within the United States, industrial communities have already established quite a shameless history of cutting each other's throats for the smallest business investment. In doing so, they have not made their hometowns any more attractive to a corporation that's willing to move overseas for an advantage. What they have demonstrated is a willingness to bring that overseas advantage home. In a country that has been indoctrinated on "what's good for GM is good for America," the idea of confronting abusive capital with discipline requires quite a leap of consciousness.

WHO ARE WE TO BLOW AGAINST THE WIND?

The biggest threat to the

'In the five years from 1983 to 1988 – the longest peacetime economic expansion in U.S. history – 9.7 million workers lost their jobs through plant closings or layoffs. As of January 1988, 30 percent remained unemployed among those counted officially as displaced workers – the 4.7 million who had held their jobs for three years or more. Nearly half of those with new jobs took pay cuts, with deep cuts of 20 percent or more reported for 30 percent of the re-employed.'

BUREAU OF LABOR STATISTICS

THE U.S. AND THE GLOBAL ECONOMY

American people and their communities is the myth that all of these economic forces are beyond their control. The relationship between production, the distribution of wealth, and the protection of social standards are not the products of some absolute economic law. These are, for the most part, ideologically guided political decisions reflecting one point of view on how to deal with the changing times. It is a wrong point of view, but it does have a hold on political power, which gives it the ability to build arguments around self-fulfilling prophecies.

The only option to the pain of deregulation, abandonment of social standards, and more deregulation, is organizing collective muscle behind another point of view. On the face of it, that seems like a simple enough concept. Yet many of the United States' social justice institutions have built into their traditions strong independent identities that don't easily lead to long-term cooperation. Perhaps it was the country's history of economic growth that gave social justice institutions faith in the future, and the luxury of independence from each other's political agendas. If the current crisis offers us anything, it is its environment of desperation – an environment that pleads for a new commitment to a common agenda.

FRIES WITH THAT SHAKE?
As high-paying skilled jobs are exported to the Third World, U.S. workers are forced to turn to 'McJobs' – service sector work which is poorly paid, demands few skills, and tends to be non-union.

PHOTO BY
CINDY REIMAN/
IMPACT VISUALS

That argument is being shaped in industrial communities across the United States. There, coalitions are being created that oppose the abandonment of traditional economic anchors, while demanding participation in economic decision making. They're shaping an alternative for dealing with the changing times that points to planning and democratization for a more just economy. In Duluth, Minnesota, the Diamond Tool Company was forced to return machinery, already relocated to a new site in South Carolina, because of its failure to comply with obligations attached to the use of Industrial Revenue Bonds. In Pittsburgh, failed efforts to stop steel mill shutdowns gave birth to a community-led "Steel Valley Authority" that has the full eminent domain powers (the right to seize private property in the public interest) of the State of Pennsylvania. Across the country, breakthroughs involving regional planning, Planned Manufacturing Districts, compliance with contracts for government subsidies, plant closing legislation, community/employee ownership,

Early Warning Signal Networks, training tied to economic development strategies, and a host of other ideas have come from the grassroots and begun to influence debate about how economics can be just. Many of these coalitions have joined together to form a national organizing network called the Federation for Industrial Retention and Renewal (FIRR).

> **Building opposition to 'free' trade must necessarily mean building economic empowerment**

FIRR, as a community-based organizing initiative, has a long way to go in shaping the details of a national vision for changing times. However, it does suggest a starting point, captured in a five-point industrial policy outline that calls for:

1) Locally administered regional planning bodies to guide the future of regional economic resources; 2) A federally supported Industrial Capital Fund to assist in the implementation of regional plans; 3) Dislocated and other worker training programs tied to economic development strategies and funded by employers; 4) Plant closings legislation that promotes viable alternatives to shutdown; and 5) A "fair" trade policy that is committed to the mutual development of trading communities.

Central to any community-based strategy is the involvement of the national leadership of two of the most important social justice institutions – organized religion and organized labour – while there is still time to have an impact. It is unlikely any national community-based initiative that doesn't include the organizational resources of these two sectors could long survive as a model. It's also unlikely that labour or religion will be able to deal with their own problems without some dramatic new direction. If organized labour is ever to see the good side of its current 16 percent representation of the workforce, it will have to change its role within the broader working class community. Labour's losses and government's promotion of unions as a "special interest," hungry for dues dollars, are a real barrier to winning the confidence of the unorganized. Demonstrating a commitment to working people in and out of the bargaining unit should help restore organized labour's image as a reliable fighter for workers' rights. And if mainline religious denominations want to stop declining membership, they too might consider becoming more materially relevant to communities in crisis. They can do so by practicing what they preach, demonstrating more commitment to a theology of socially responsible stewardship. Local economic justice coalitions offer both groups ways to fight the collapse of our communities while restoring their place in them.

'FAIR' TRADE AND INDUSTRIAL POLICY FIRR has brought its community-based affiliates into two coalitions dealing with trade issues. The first is the Coalition for Justice in the Maquiladoras (CJM), made up of 88 members including a number of

THE U.S. AND THE GLOBAL ECONOMY

> 'The demand for an industrial policy is born from an understanding that the people of the United States have no real voice in shaping their economic destinies. Business decisions that determine the resources and futures of all Americans are made without reference to the desires or concerns of those people. These decisions are, in fact, often made without any reference to the needs of the nation or any community within the nation.'
>
> TRI-STATE CONFERENCE ON STEEL

national religious and labour organizations. CJM focuses on strategies that will compel U.S.-based corporations that invest in the maquiladora zones of Mexico to comply with basic environmental, community, occupational safety and health, and labour "Standards of Conduct," as outlined by current U.S., Mexican, and UN law. The second is the Fair Trade Campaign (FTC), a less structured effort which also includes labour and religion. The FTC is organizing opposition to the array of "free" trade initiatives being spawned by the Bush administration, with a special focus on GATT and NAFTA.

FIRR's role in both these groups is to support their agendas by connecting them to its community-based economic development coalitions. The intent is to establish a link between the destruction of social standards globally by the maquiladora program, NAFTA and GATT, and the already free-falling quality of life in American communities. Focusing on the administration's attack on social standards, FIRR demands "fair" trade – trade that generates mutual development within the communities of the trading partners. It has been the experience of FIRR affiliates that as long as one community, anywhere, can be super-exploited, the condition exists, through whipsawing, for all communities to be super-exploited. For FIRR, building opposition to "free" trade must necessarily mean building economic empowerment in working class communities. Fighting capital flight will mean strengthening social standards that support the rights of labour and the community.

Every crisis is an organizing opportunity. It would be a shame to look too narrowly at this one's potential. NAFTA is a reflection of a broader problem that has to be addressed – the failure of democracy to penetrate economic decision-making. Beating NAFTA in Washington, DC, will be nice, but if it doesn't build the base for challenging the other related problems, we'll have missed our chance. Whipsawing across and within borders will go on.

Jim Benn has worked as a tenant organizer, a steelworker, a union activist, and was co-founder of Cleveland's Regional Industry Center, a labour, university, and neighbourhood cooperative venture in regional industrial planning. He is currently the executive director of the Federation for Industrial Retention and Renewal.

PART 2
Front Lines

Cheap Labour, Cheap Lives

The maquiladoras prove the truth of an old Mexican saying: 'Poor Mexico: So far from God, so close to the United States'

by Jim Sinclair

We climbed up the cement embankment in Tijuana and peered out over the Mexico-U.S. border. It was dusk, and a nightly ritual which pitted the hungry of Mexico against the border patrols of the United States was about to begin.

On the U.S. side, patrol cars moved into position under spotlights we normally associated with baseball stadiums. But nothing we were about to witness had much to do with our reality.

We were on the Mexican side, looking across a quarter-mile-wide concrete valley that was split in half by a small drainage ditch polluted with chemicals and sewage. Suddenly we heard a yell and a group of more than 20 people started running across the water and up through a hole in the fence at the U.S. border. Within minutes the border patrol was there and half the people retreated to the shadows, to try again later.

As we continued our watch, a helicopter spotted a group of Mexicans in a darkened area further along. A giant spotlight shone down and the lights of a speeding patrol car soon zeroed in on the group. There is little time for sympathy, as other potential border-crossers, seeing the preoccupation of the border patrol, use the opportunity to try their luck. Once a month someone dies making this run, shot by either the border patrol or muggers who line the border waiting for victims.

For us, six Canadians who were there to discuss free trade, it was hard to imagine a country so desperate that more than one million people a year would risk their lives trying to leave. For our host, Jose Luis Canchola, the scene was not so

> **More than one million people risk their lives trying to leave Mexico each year**

DOUBLE STANDARDS Maquiladora managers travel freely between their factories and their comfortable U.S. homes, but Mexican workers seeking U.S. jobs face a much tougher commute.

PHOTO BY DAVID MAUNG/ IMPACT VISUALS

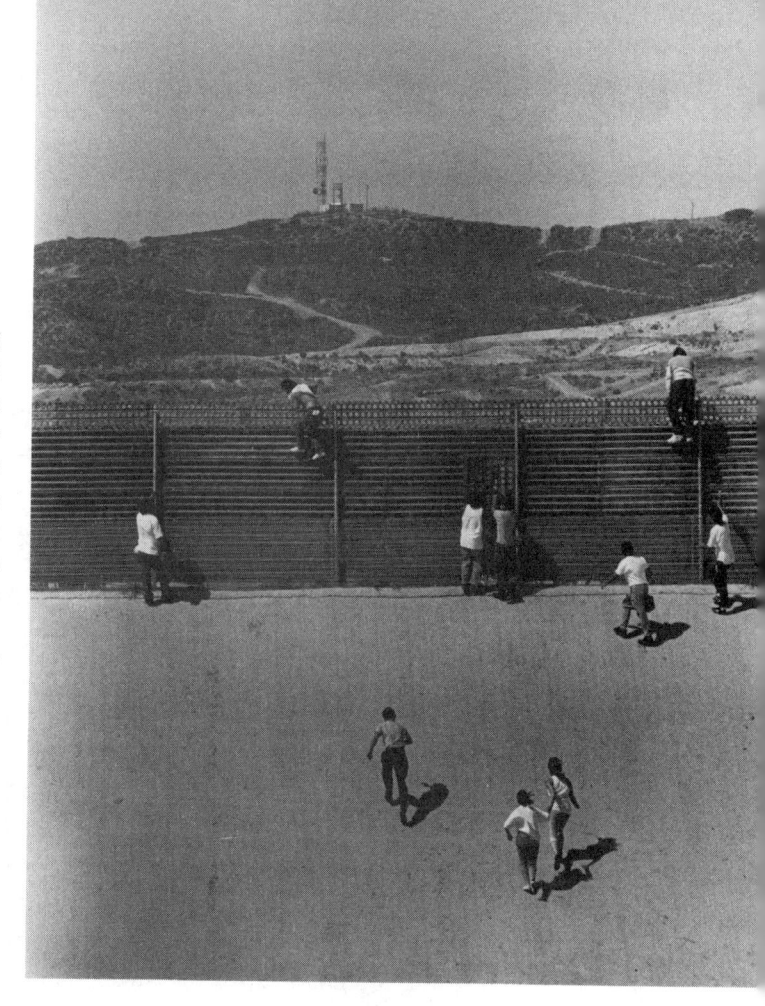

shocking. Canchola's father went across the same border years earlier. Canchola followed and ended up working illegally in Alaskan fish plants. Unlike his father, who never returned, Canchola came back home and has been fighting to improve conditions in his homeland for more than 20 years. He is now the human rights director for the state of Baja.

When asked why the number of Mexicans who take such risks is increasing, Canchola points a finger at the policies of the Mexican government. He claims that the 60 percent drop in wages since 1982, the privatization of more than 600 crown corporations, the huge national debt, and the opening of Mexico to foreign investment, are at the root of the growing crisis for millions of Mexicans.

JOBS AND POVERTY The backdrop for this daily game of "chicken" with the U.S. border patrol is the city of Tijuana, where industrial growth has exploded unlike anywhere else in the world. Those making this journey to the United States pass through miles of brand new factories that would be the envy of any Canadian city. Each factory displays huge banners crying out for employees.

These factories are part of the maquiladoras, the cornerstone of the "New Mexico" and a model for the development of the entire country as envisioned by the government of President Carlos Salinas de Gortari. For millions of other Mexicans, like Canchola, the maquiladoras have become a symbol of why the proposed free trade deal will destroy their country.

More than half of Mexico's population of 86 million people lives in poverty. More than 17 million live in dire poverty and 15 million are unemployed. That the maquiladora factories suffer labour shortages in a country with these statistics says much about an economic strategy which fails to meet the basic needs of Mexicans.

> **The maquiladoras have become a symbol of why the free trade deal will destroy their country**

Many trace the birth of the maquiladoras to a decision in 1964 by the U.S. government to clamp down on Mexicans working in California. The move resulted in hundreds of thousands of unemployed Mexicans living along the border.

In response to this, the Mexican government set up these "free trade" zones along the border. Dubbed the Border Industrialization Program, the plan was aimed at attracting U.S. capital to northern Mexico. To do this, Mexico lifted tariffs and removed virtually all taxes normally charged to traditional Mexican industries.

Corporations are allowed to bring in parts without duty, assemble them using cheap labour, and export them without penalty. Taxes are paid on the value added, not on the actual value of the goods. Because labour, the only value added, is cheap, taxes are very low.

Firms are also subject to income taxes on corporate profits, but companies duck this by ensuring they make little profit. According to a Price Waterhouse report: "Since they are designed to be cost centres and not profit centres, net profits tend to be a small percentage of costs incurred by the maquiladoras (usually 1% to 4%). All the equipment, raw materials and finished goods are the property of the parent (imported duty free under bond) and sale of the manufactured goods gives rise to income in the parent. The parent is not considered to have a permanent establishment in Mexico."[1]

But even these breaks were not enough. Tough controls that restricted foreign ownership of Mexican land and businesses were removed. Restrictions on foreign personnel working in Mexico were also waived. In order to sell this incredible holiday from government restrictions to existing Mexican business, the government agreed that products from these plants could not be sold in Mexico. They also held out the hope that parts for production in maquiladoras would come from Mexican plants in the future. Mexican businesses are still waiting for this to happen.

U.S. ECONOMIC INVASION In one sense, the 1964 program started a process which simply redrafted the southern border of the United States to include northern Mexico. Profits and finished goods flow without restriction to the United States. As the U.S. magazine *Business Week* pointed out recently, "For all the dynamism, maquiladoras are little more than foreign enclaves on Mexican soil."[2]

The maquiladoras did not take off in earnest until 1982 when the government, faced with a massive foreign debt and a major flow of capital out of the country (US $25 billion was taken out by wealthy Mexicans between 1978 and 1982), dramatically devalued the peso. The immediate effect was to lower the basic wage rates in the maquiladoras to US$0.75 per hour from $1.50.

U.S.-based corporations turned their eyes south and began a shift which would leave hundreds of thousands of American and, more recently, Canadian and Japanese workers unemployed. Today there are more than 2,000 factories employing 450,000 workers, making the maquiladora program the only significant area of growth in Mexico. A new plant opens nearly every day; by 1994 employment is expected to increase by an additional 150,000 workers.[3] The maquiladoras have gone from producing 4 percent of Mexico's exports to nearly 50 percent.

The main investors have been U.S.-based corporations, who control 90 percent of the maquiladoras. General Motors leads the pack, employing 25,500 workers in 30 plants. Recent announcements that the U.S. auto giant will close plants in

---

VOICES FROM THE FACTORIES

"At Dimit [Farah] there are a lot of problems. There's no ventilation, no exhaust fans – even though there's a lot of dust in the factory, the dust came from the fabric we were sewing. At the end of the day you would walk out there covered with dust all over your body. It caused a lot of illness. Headaches, sore throats, eye infections – all caused by dust."

Luisa, a garment worker

"Most of the workers live in conditions that have no dignity. They live in houses made out of adobe, scraps of wood or even cardboard. They have to pay a lot just for water. They don't have electricity for lighting or other necessities. Without proper drainage, conditions are very unsanitary. You cannot drink the water, it is full of germs. People get sick from it. It's quite a contradiction. These companies arrive and say to the workers, 'Come and grow with us.' But you can spend 10 years working in the maquiladoras and you'll still be living in these same conditions."

Roberto, a garment worker

"There are an infinity of problems. Chemicals are spilled on the floor. Trays of solvents are left uncovered – methylene chloride [a known carcinogen], thinner, acetone, alcohol, flux. All these things are in the environment. In one job you measure the width of capacitors. On each tiny piece you take five or six measurements, making the same motions of your wrist all day long. Eventually the workers get a growth on their wrists and then they have to have an operation."

Gloria, an electronics worker

SOURCE: *The Global Factory* (Philadelphia: American Friends Service Committee, 1990)

Canada and the United States, did not extend to Mexico's maquiladoras, where plans are on the drawing board for 27 new plants by 1995.[4] Following closely behind GM is Zenith Electronics, with 11 plants and 21,500 workers. Chrysler, General Electric, United Technologies, and a French company called Thomson fill out the list of the largest companies. Others include Sony, Ford, Honeywell, Johnson and Johnson, and Phillips.[5] All of the 100 largest U.S. corporations have at least one plant in the border area. A key area of growth is the automotive parts industry, which has grown from 53 plants and 6.3 percent of the workforce in 1980 to 121 plants and 21 percent of the workforce by 1987.[6]

Japanese corporations have also tuned in to the advantages of the maquiladora zones; between 1987 and 1990 they built an average of 100 plants annually. New investment is also starting to flow from the "Gang of Four" – Taiwan, Hong Kong, Singapore and Korea – who see a chance for tariff-free access to the U.S. market.

Low wage rates remain a key attraction. Labour costs, including benefits and government payments for health and education, are estimated at 98 cents an hour. This is in sharp contrast to U.S. and Canadian manufacturing labour costs of US$14.31 per hour and US$14.72 per hour respectively. Hourly costs in other so-called "cheap labour" countries, such as South Korea at US$2.94 per hour and Taiwan at US$3.71 per hour, make Mexico one of the cheapest wage zones in the world (U.S. Department of Labor Statistics).

But it is not just in the cities and towns of Canada and the United States that the factory doors are closing as a result of runaway plants. Within Mexico itself, the maquiladoras are beginning to undercut jobs and development. Contrary to earlier promises, the government has moved to soften restrictions on the sale of maquiladora goods within Mexico, and this is putting economic pressure on domestic producers. Domestic sales could absorb 50 percent of the products made at a maquiladora. Free trade will accelerate this integration. U.S. Department of Labor statistics show the labour costs of manufacturing in Mexico are $2.32 an hour compared to 98 cents an hour in the maquiladoras. At the same time as an estimated 90,000 auto jobs have been created in the maquiladoras, there has been a loss of 100,000 jobs in the domestic Mexican auto and auto parts industry.[7] The maquiladoras undermine national industries and institutions by hiring trained professionals away from Mexican companies and universities.

> **Labour costs, including benefits, are estimated at 98 cents an hour**

AN EXPLOITED PEOPLE If the obvious losers are the workers of the national industries in the rest of Mexico, Canada, and the United States, the obvious winners are not the 450,000 maquiladora workers or their families.

CHEAP LABOUR, CHEAP LIVES

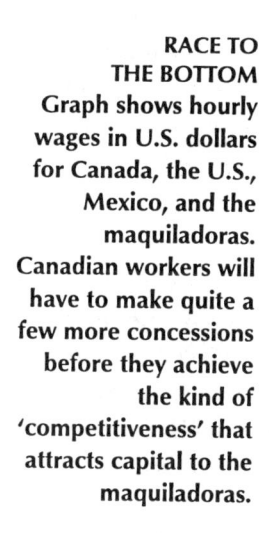

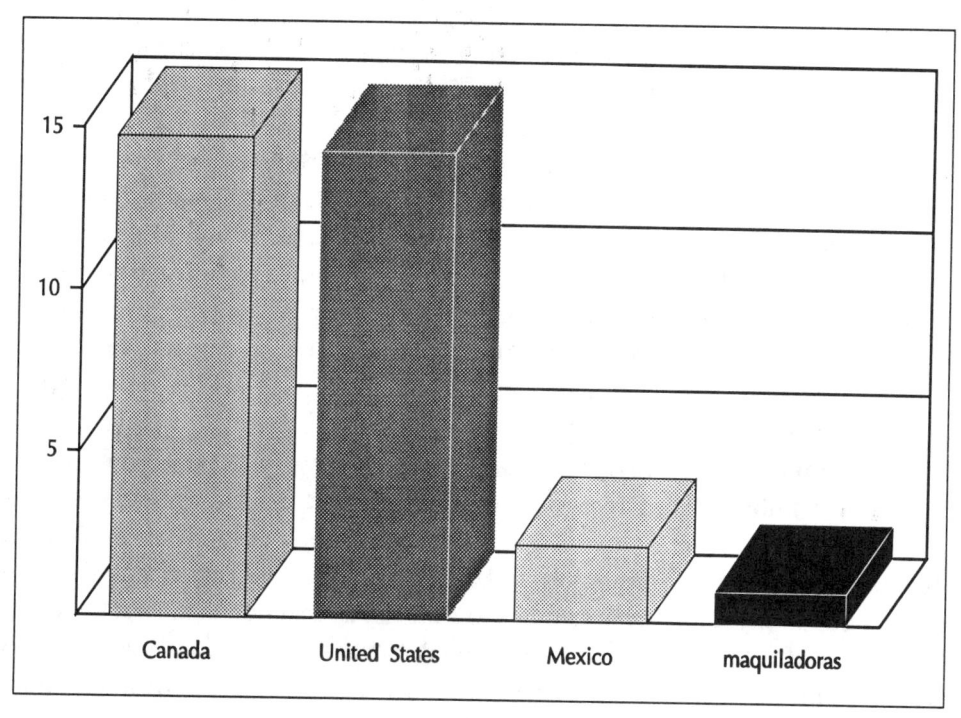

RACE TO THE BOTTOM Graph shows hourly wages in U.S. dollars for Canada, the U.S., Mexico, and the maquiladoras. Canadian workers will have to make quite a few more concessions before they achieve the kind of 'competitiveness' that attracts capital to the maquiladoras.

Nowhere is this clearer than in Tijuana. Visually, it is a city of extreme contrasts. More than 500 modern factories, on four-lane paved streets, with plush green lawns, give the impression of prosperity and modernization. Out in front of each factory, a smattering of BMWs, Mercedes, and other high-priced cars belonging to the owners and managers completes the image of wealth. But the cars have U.S. plates and, like the profits the factories produce, they line up nightly to return home to the U.S.

Inside the factories and in the communities that surround them, the impression of prosperity gives way quickly to conditions that led a reporter for the conservative *Wall Street Journal* to describe Mexican maquiladora workers as "joining the ranks of the most crudely exploited humans on the planet. The result has been conditions along the Mexican side of the border that rival any of the well-publicized disasters of the worst Stalinist regimes."[8]

At the Martinez Mexican Manufacturing Company in Tijuana, owner Alfonso Martinez is clearly proud of his accomplishments. His company has no product of its own – its main business is selling cheap labour. From an office in California, Martinez bids for contracts to assemble U.S. companies' products.

At his Tijuana plant, more than 50 teenage women work from 7 a.m. to 5 p.m., six days a week, for an average of $4.00 a day. (Women, mostly young, account for 68 percent of the maquila workforce.) The plant itself is simply a large room with wooden benches and folding tables covered in brown paper. Today women are putting together tiny computer components under fluorescent lighting. Martinez employs a piecework system of bonuses for increased production, similar to the system in most plants.

This is one of the few plants without a help wanted sign outside, and Martinez says that's because he pays a little better and always celebrates the birthdays of "his girls." At break time the workers gather outside the plant. They are young, some under 16, and most have worked at other plants. Workers do not want to stay at these jobs, and they leave at an amazing rate, even though there are few alternatives. Annual turnover rates in the maquiladoras can run as high as 180 percent in certain areas.

RISKING WORKERS' HEALTH   This turnover is confirmed by Victor Osanu, the purchasing manager for Ceyboom, a large computer firm which recently moved from a 2000-square-foot plant into a brand new 94,000-square-foot building at an industrial park in Tijuana. Unlike the Martinez company, Ceyboom is far more typical of the growth that has occurred in the last ten years. Osanu explains that Ceyboom's 300 workers have a turnover rate of 20 percent a month.

In the plant itself, rows of women, some wearing masks, huddle over miniature computer parts that they assemble with the help of magnifying glasses. The smell of epoxy greets us as we enter the production area, and chemicals and solvents are used in several stages of production. Osanu says the plant meets all safety standards and workers are in no danger, but the Canadians find his assurances of safe working conditions hard to believe.

"These women are not only poorly paid and have no protection but their health is probably being seriously endangered," said Québec labour leader Monique Simard. "If there is a turnover of 20 percent per month like he [Osanu] told us, then it is probably for health reasons."

Scientific studies of the health and safety of maquiladora workers are virtually non-existent, but one U.S. survey of 267 maquiladora workers (81 percent female) in the Reynosa-Matamoros region on the Atlantic coast found workers had widespread complaints about their health.[9]

Nearly half of those surveyed by a study team from the University of Lowell, Mass., reported that on every shift they were exposed to gas or vapours, chemicals, and dust. "Nausea or vomiting, stomach pain, urinary problems and breathing problems were significantly related to the frequency of exposure to airborne contaminants," the study reported. The authors conclude that the widespread exposures were an "indication of the likelihood that there will be substantial chronic health effects in the future."

Health and safety inspection is almost non-existent at the plants. In Matamoros,

> 'There is great potential for success in the maquiladora along the border, tourism and drugs along the Pacific Coast and export-driven growth in traditional northern industrial cities like Monterrey. But these regions and sectors barely include a fifth of the population; the other 80 percent will be left out in the cold. Not only would this larger segment of the population not participate in a regional boom, it would lose ground.'
>
> JORGE CASTENEDA, ECONOMIST, NATIONAL AUTONOMOUS UNIVERSITY IN MEXICO CITY

CHEAP LABOUR, CHEAP LIVES

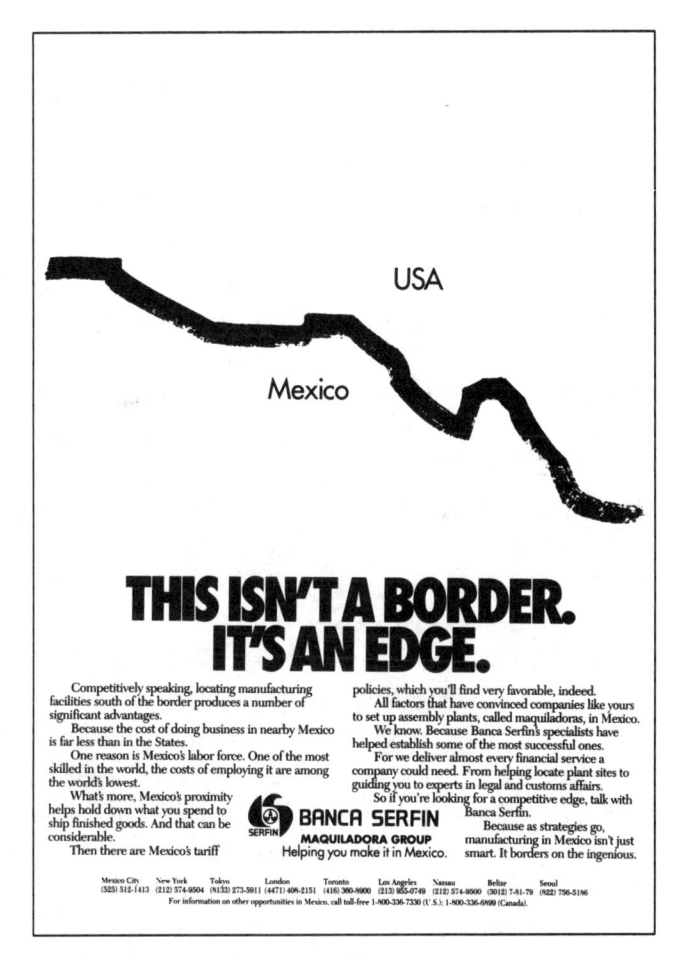

THIS ISN'T A BORDER. IT'S AN EDGE.

COME ON DOWN! This ad from a Mexican bank appears in TWIN PLANT NEWS, an American magazine that is little more than an elaborate ad for the maquiladora concept. Almost half a million jobs have disappeared into maquiladoras.

where there are more than 100 plants, there is not a single ministry of labour inspector in the city. The nearest one is 200 miles away. This is symptomatic of the lack of enforcement of even minimal standards.[10]

For some workers, the future predicted by the U.S. study team has already arrived. Dr. Isabel de la O. Alonso has identified 20 retarded children whose mothers worked with toxic chemicals at a battery plant. The mothers all breathed battery acid fumes containing PCBs without any kind of protective masks. One plant manager refuted health and safety concerns at his plant by pointing to the high turnover rate "We don't worry too much about these matters; these girls don't stay on the job long enough to get sick."[11]

CONTAMINATED COMMUNITIES Unsafe and dangerous conditions do not stop at the factory gate. When employees leave work, often on company buses that can cost them 10 to 20 percent of their incomes, they are dropped off in chemically contaminated communities where poverty is widespread.

Unable to afford proper housing, they live in squatter slums lacking such basic services as electricity, water, or sewage facilities. Their houses are often made of scraps of wood and cardboard left over from the construction of nearby plants.

The staple diet is beans and rice, and many families cannot afford to buy meat or milk on a regular basis. While wages may only be a fraction of what their U.S. counterparts receive, Mexicans heading for the grocery store find prices for food and household goods that are only slightly below U.S. prices. A survey of supermarket sale ads in Tijuana papers revealed that a small jar of Hellman's mayonnaise cost one hour's pay; it was two hours' pay for a small bottle of dish soap, shampoo, toilet paper, baby powder, or Reynolds foil wrap. It cost three hours' work to pay for a kilo of bologna, a box of laundry soap, mouth wash, or hair spray. It takes half a day's pay to buy sanitary napkins, a kilo of cheese or meat, furniture polish, or hand cream.

> **Families store water in drums that maquiladora industries used to bring in toxic chemicals**

Drinking water and wash water, in most cases, is brought in by truck. Families store water in metal drums that maquiladora industries used to bring in toxic chemicals – but water problems run much deeper than just the contaminated drums. The discharge from the factories can be seen flowing, untreated, directly into the rivers and streams of Tijuana. A survey found that 86 percent of the factories produce toxic wastes which run through communities such as Fracionamiento Murua, where Carmen Parra, a mother of three, says her people suffer rashes, hair loss, persistent sore throats, and other ailments. They hold the plants responsible and there is ample evidence to back them up.

"This is a contaminated zone," said Juan Manual Sanchez Leon, a physician who lives down the street from Parra's home. "People complain about it, but no one listens."[12]

Independent tests of the water, initiated by the Los Angeles *Times*, showed that mercury levels were five times the acceptable U.S. levels. Mercury is a highly toxic metal linked to brain damage and birth defects. Studies conducted in 1990 on the Tijuana River found levels of lead – another highly toxic metal that can attack the brain and nervous system – on the U.S. side that were 100 times the U.S. standard for human health purposes.[13]

Other Tijuana communities report an increase in diseases among farm animals using the water. Salvador Sanchez told the Los Angeles *Times* that his pigs were undersized now, and that the number of miscarriages and of pigs born with deformities and terminal liver damage is growing. "It's the stuff they're dumping in from the American factories. This water has acid in it. It has chemicals. Sometimes it's yellow, sometimes it's green. Unfortunately I can't keep my pigs out of it."

The long-term implications for the people of the border region are impossible to tell. Michael Kaltofen, U.S. laboratory director at the National Toxic Campaign Fund in Boston, paints a bleak picture. "There's no way we can predict what risk people are running for increased cancer, liver and kidney diseases and for other problems, all we know is that the outcome will be bad."

The Lowell University study concluded that the "parallels with the Union Carbide [Bhopal, India] disaster are ominous: the reported numerous small chemical leaks previous to the massive leak of a toxic chemical; mismanagement of safety procedures; untrained work-force; poorly maintained equipment and large numbers of poor living in neighborhoods immediately adjacent to the plants. All of these Bhopal features were present in the accounts of the accidents described by community leaders and press accounts of chemical release accidents from maquiladora plants... The warning signs of a potential acute environmental catastrophe should not be ignored."

This ongoing disaster is downplayed by government agencies on both sides of the border. Regulations do exist but environmental enforcement in Mexico is almost non-existent. Originally, toxic waste was to be shipped back across the border with the finished products, but this has not happened. Mexico's environmental agency, SEDUE, does not have the resources to deal with the problem. In Tijuana, only seven maquiladoras actually have an operating permit approved from SEDUE. In 1990, only 37 companies reported shipping wastes back to California or Arizona. John Hall, chairman of the Texas Water Commission, confirms that "tons and tons of

---

'NEVER GOIN' BACK'
Jim Sinclair

Like tens of thousands of rural Mexicans, Martin and Antioco Aldaco came to Tijuana four years ago to search for work. They were carpenters who found work quickly in the maquiladoras, but they didn't stay. Now they have a wood-working shop in a small community. The streets are dirt, there is no electricity, and water is brought in by truck. A small Honda generator provides electricity for the tools.

Many people in the community work in the maquiladoras, but both brothers shake their heads when asked if more maquila factories are the answer.

"The big companies exploit you," said Antioco. "It is like slavery to work in the factories. The worst part is you are only a part of the machines."

In a nearby community, Rosa Maria Palicio, sitting on a frayed red velveteen couch that is the only furniture in her cardboard house, echoes these sentiments in an interview with the *Wall Street Journal*. "Women only work at them because there is no other work." She left her maquila job – cleaning gun chambers – to survive as she could: making tortillas, working as a maid, cooking for a church. She swears, like thousands of other Mexicans who have tasted life in the maquiladoras, that she will never work there again.

Studies show that workers who stay last between five and ten years in the industry before they burn out and are replaced by younger workers.

toxic materials are being improperly disposed of along the borders."

Compounding this problem has been the population explosion in border cities like Tijuana, which has overwhelmed local sewage, housing, and sanitary facilities. This prompted the American Medical Association to declare the border area "a virtual cesspool and breeding ground for infectious disease."[14]

Getting tough with polluters would require strong government action, a move which seems unlikely since the maquiladoras are the centrepiece of so-called "economic recovery." Any crackdown would destroy a key incentive for foreign companies to locate here.

KEEPING UNIONS OUT The Mexican government will not take any action which might raise the cost of operations for companies. In response to the crisis in infrastructure, the government recently proposed a tax of two percent on the total gross wages paid by maquiladoras, to help build roads and housing. This proposal was quickly withdrawn after strong opposition from the corporations. The threat is that companies will simply pack up and move if they don't like what the government or workers are doing.

Workers trying to organize find themselves having to fight not only the companies, but also the government and, in some cases, organized labour. Most plants are non-union, and any suggestion that a union may come to organize usually results in the immediate firing of the workers involved. High turnover rates make it difficult to organize. Also hampering organization is the mainstream labour movement, which is closely aligned with the government.

> **The AMA called the border area 'a virtual cesspool and breeding ground for infectious disease'**

"We had some labour problems, so along with a dozen other plants we went to Mexico City to make a special arrangement with the Confederation of Mexican Workers (CTM)," says Don King, general manager of West Bend Industries in Reynosa, Mexico. "It was time-consuming and expensive, but we arranged to have a special union leader that our companies can deal with. Unions here are much different than in the States. If you have any disruptions in the plant, they are helpful with that too. And they were very understanding when we negotiated our first contract."[15]

Where unions have asserted themselves, the government has stepped in. At the Louisiana Pacific sawmill operation south of Tijuana, local longshore workers thought they should be the ones unloading logs and raw lumber from the U.S. for reprocessing. After a brief skirmish with the local union, the company halted construction on the plant and went to the government to demand action against the

CHEAP LABOUR, CHEAP LIVES

CUTTING DEALS
Forestry companies, led by U.S. giant Louisiana Pacific, are beginning to exploit the maquila concept. Raw logs that used to be finished in U.S. mills are instead heading straight to maquiladora operations like this one near Tijuana.

union. The government decreed the unloading would be non-union for 20 years.[16]

Louisiana Pacific has recently announced a $100 million expansion, including a 12-factory industrial complex.[17] The introduction of wood processing is a new development for the maquiladoras, which have historically been based on electronics and assembly work. The growing threat to traditional secondary wood processing should not be lost on a country like Canada where the largest single export is forest products.

As the maquiladora zones and their production spread to the interior of Mexico, the result will be an economy more and more controlled by foreign capital and geared for the export market. The next major sector being developed is the agriculture and food processing industry. This is already affecting the ability of Mexicans to meet their own food needs, as increasingly large sections of land are used for export crops. The government plans to privatize millions of acres of community land to encourage foreign exports of food, and the number of frozen vegetable plants has climbed to thirty from six in the last five years.

Once again, the pattern of development is being repeated. Mexico will sell cheap labour and allow the destruction of its environment and local communities. In return, foreign corporations will invest heavily, knowing they will receive a high return on investments. Exports will help pay for the foreign debt owed to major foreign banks. While this is called free trade in 1992, a century ago, when foreign capital dominated every aspect of Mexican life, it was called colonialism.

THE RESELLING OF MEXICO   In the late 1800s, President Profirio Diaz swung open the doors to uncontrolled foreign investment, as Salinas is doing now. All the major industries, including oil, agriculture, mining, and manufacturing, were owned by foreign interests. Mexicans were forced off their land and ended up working on large haciendas or in the mines, in terrible conditions.

"The foreign investors not only reaped the benefits of exploiting Mexico's natural and human resources, but also received preferential treatment in many cases from the Mexican government in their dealings with it," notes financial lawyer Jose Cruz, a member of one of Mexico's largest law firms, which actively assists foreign investors. "One historian, Henry Parkes, summed up the situation with the comment: Mexico had become the mother of aliens and the step-mother of her own children."[18]

Mexicans, according to Cruz, did not receive the benefits of this type of development at the turn of the century, and "most hacienda workers for all intents and purposes were used as slave labour." Eventually the complete foreign dominance of the economy, and the lack of democracy, led to the Mexican revolution in 1910. Reforms brought in by the revolutionary government included

---

JOBS, JOBS, JOBS

An August 1990 article in *CLC Today* says thousands of Canadian jobs have been lost to Mexico. Below is a partial list of companies with Mexican plants.

COMPANY	LOCATION	JOBS LOST
General Electric	Montreal, Que.	200
Ford Motor Co.	Windsor, Ont.	900
Motorola Corp.	Brampton, Ont.	186
Square-D	Edmundston, NB	156
Square-D	Port Colbourne, Ont.	107
General Motors	Oshawa, Ont.	800
General Motors	St.-Therese, Que.	1700
General Motors	Scarborough, Ont.	2700
Black & Decker	Trenton, Ont.	100
Black & Decker	Montreal, Que.	150
Sheller-Globe	Windsor, Ont.	350
Norton Abrasives	Cap-de-la-Madelaine, Que.	116
Whirlpool Corp.	Cambridge, Ont.	870
Echlin Canada	Niagara Falls, Ont.	58
Echlin Canada	Rexdale, Ont.	125
Northern Telecom	Aylmer, Que.	680
Northern Telecom	St. Laurent, Que.	250
Northern Telecom	Belleville, Ont.	240
Northern Telecom	Brockville, Ont.	145
Northern Telecom	Bramalea, Ont.	120

major restrictions on foreign ownership and a bill of rights for Mexican workers.

Today, maquiladora workers have replaced the hacienda workers as the new slaves, and foreign investment is once again given carte blanche in Mexico. The return from the gross national product that goes to capital has risen dramatically to 65 percent from 41 percent since government reforms in 1982.[19] This rise closely parallels the growth of maquiladoras. Not surprisingly, labour's share of the GNP dropped in the same period to 27.7 percent from 41.7 percent.

Foreign capital, mostly from the U.S., is again dominating the country, and the results can be seen in places like Tijuana, where Canchola predicts the proposed free trade agreement would simply extend exploitation to the rest of Mexico, and accelerate the economic domination of Mexico by the United States.

"Free trade means open borders where they can bring in anything they want to, even toxins. They can bring part of their production without taxes, use cheap labour and then take it back. With free trade this process can take place across the entire country. I think free trade is simply a nice fancy word which means to sell our country, our resources, our cheap labour – and lose our sovereignty," Canchola said.

There can be little doubt that the seeds of the next Mexican revolution are being sown today in the foreign factories and slums of Mexico's border towns, where foreign capital, once again, has free rein over the people of Mexico.

> 'The Canada-U.S. border is an imaginary border. And free trade with Mexico is coming. We've just done a study that determined that we can manufacture in Mexico and ship to Vancouver, including duty and freight, cheaper than we can manufacture in Vancouver.'
>
> JIM PATTISON, CHAIRMAN OF THE JIM PATTISON GROUP, DECEMBER 3, 1990

1. Donald L. Furney, Thomas K. Falconer and Ruben E. Calles (Guadalajara, Mexico), "Taxation of Revenue Earned in Mexico," Price Waterhouse, 1 November 1991, p. 4.
2. Stephen Baker, "Mexico: A New Economic Area," *Business Week*, 12 November 1990, pp. 105-106.
3. Irwin (Sandy) Somerville, "Manufacturing in Mexico: Prospects for the 1990s," paper for the Asia Pacific Institute, 1 November 1991, pp. 1-8.
4. Somerville, p. 8.
5. Rafael Moure-Eraso, Meg Wilcox, Laura Punnett, Leslie Copeland, Charles Levenstein, "Back to the Future: Sweatshop Conditions on the Mexico-U.S. Border," University of Lowell-Work Environment Program, 11 April 1991.
6. Alejandro Alvarez, "Mexico, A Maquila Country?" *Briarpatch*, September 1991, p. 33.
7. Kim Moody, "Free Trade, Promise or Menace?" *Against the Current*, Vol. 33, July-August 1991, p. 22.
8. Listening Post, *Financial Post*, 25 April 1991.
9. Rafael Moure-Eraso, et al.
10. Rafael Moure-Eraso, et al.
11. Annette Fuentes and Barbara Ehrenreich, *Women in the Global Factory*, (Boston MA: South End Press, 1984), p. 31.
12. Patrick J. McDonnell, "Foreign-Owned Companies add to Mexico's Pollution," Los Angeles *Times*, 18 November 1991, pp. 14-15.
13. *Ibid.*
14. Rafael Moure-Eraso, et al.
15. Vicki J. Northcott, "Women in the Maquiladoras," *Briarpatch*, September 1991, p. 29
16. *AFL-CIO News*, 21 September 1991.
17. Somerville.
18. Jose I. Cruz, "Foreign Investment in Mexico, Yesterday, Today and Tomorrow," 1 November 1991.
19. Labour and Employment Committee of the National Lawyers Guild, "The Connection Between Mexican Labour Struggles and the Free Trade Agreement," (no date).

Jim Sinclair is an organizer for the United Fishermen and Allied Workers' Union in Vancouver, and an executive member of the B.C. Trade Union Group.

Free Trade and the Environment

Canada's experience with the FTA and GATT should make it clear that trade and environment issues are inextricably linked

by Zen Makuch

Negotiations for the proposed North American Free Trade Agreement (NAFTA) have proceeded at a breakneck pace. The Bush administration has been in such a hurry to sign this deal that it has been placed on "fast track," a procedure calling for the enormous expansion of presidential authority while severely limiting any congressional role.

Similar backroom, last-minute wheeling and dealing produced the Canada-U.S. Free Trade Agreement (FTA). Thus far, at a minimum, this deal has cost Canadians 300,000 jobs, and has already produced visible, irreversible, negative environmental impacts while undermining Canadian sovereignty over resource conservation and management initiatives, and environmental regulation. One may well ask why this assault on our environment has taken place.

The simple explanation is that each of the governments involved in the trade negotiations have denied that there is any connection between trade agreements and environmental issues. In 1987, when questioned in the House of Commons about the potential environmental impacts of the FTA, John Crosbie, the Minister of International Trade, offered the conclusion that "the Free Trade Agreement is a commercial accord between the world's two largest trading partners. It is not an environmental agreement." So the environment was not a subject for negotiations nor are environmental matters included in the text of the FTA. The Bush administration has responded in a similar fashion, stating, "We are negotiating a free trade agreement not a common market."

> **The FTA has already produced visible, irreversible, negative environmental impacts**

HIGH COST OF FREE TRADE This resident of the Sacramento River in California was having a pretty good day until he ran into a toxic chemical spill. Corporate pressure for a 'level playing field' under free trade means environmental laws will be watered down, not strengthened.

PHOTO BY MARK LUDAK/ IMPACT VISUALS

Fundamental components to sustainable and equitable economic development, such as human rights, labour rights, and environmental regulations, are not only being kept off the negotiating table as such, but are often put on the chopping block as "non-tariff barriers to trade" that negotiators are trying to eliminate in order to facilitate "liberalized trade" and the unaccountable pursuit of profits. The three administrations negotiating the NAFTA have agreed that the environment in all of its aspects will *not* be dealt with in any provision of the agreement.

Canadian experience with the FTA and the General Agreement on Tariffs and Trade (GATT) should make it clear that trade and environmental issues are inextricably linked. A new free trade deal which does not address environmental issues will create even more obstacles to environmental protection. We can only hope that the recent protectionist mood of the American Congress will prevent

President George Bush from signing a deal in an election year. This will offer us the opportunity to convince our governments of the necessity of making the crucial connections between trade and environment which provide an essential precondition to the conclusion of any future trade agreement.

> 'Canada will continue to set and adopt environmental protection standards in keeping with our own national goals. It is absolutely false that Canada will have to adopt American environmental standards.'
>
> THE CANADIAN ALLIANCE FOR TRADE AND JOB OPPORTUNITIES, NOVEMBER 3, 1988

ENVIRONMENTAL REGULATION In its report entitled *Our Common Future*, the Brundtland Commission recognized the intimate link between trading activities and environmental protection when it stated that the activities of GATT and other inter-governmental organizations "should reflect concern with the impacts of trading patterns on the environment and the need for more effective instruments to integrate environment and development concerns into international trading arrangements." In a similar vein, members of the Canadian environmental community anticipated that an FTA without environmental guarantees would result in challenges to existing and future environmental protection efforts. Any evaluation of our environmental laws which characterizes them as "non-tariff barriers to trade" undermines the democratic processes and, indeed, the national sovereignty which created such regulations. In effect, the agreement severely impedes the ability of citizens to see high environmental aspirations realized in our environmental protection regimes.

As soon as the ink on the FTA dried, the assault on our environmental regulation regimes and our natural resource conservation began. In the area of environmental regulation, consider the Canadian challenge to the United States' Environmental Protection Agency announcement that it was introducing regulations to phase out the production, import, and use of asbestos over seven years pursuant to the Toxic Substances Control Act. Asbestos is a known carcinogen, the ban of which was expected to save 1,900 American lives in the next ten years.[1] The Canadian government challenge was presented to the U.S. Fifth Circuit Court of Appeals in a brief which characterized the EPA asbestos regulation as creating an unnecessary obstacle to trade. This American environmental initiative was soundly defeated at the instance of the Court along the lines of the FTA analysis.[2] The Canadian challenge arose not only from a desire to protect the Quebec asbestos industry but also as a means of curtailing a similar ban in Europe.

In view of the above, it is an interesting irony that the Canadian government should challenge the validity of a U.S. environmental regulation when, in a similar context, it has sought to protect its own regulatory power over the environment from U.S. encroachment. The U.S. Non-Ferrous Metal Producers Committee has criticized the Canadian government for providing support to help industry prevent acid rain and reforest denuded land. This Committee has challenged pollution control programs that include loans and investment credits aimed at reducing emissions from, and improving workplace safety in, a number of lead, zinc, and copper smelters. If the U.S. challenge succeeds, the federal government may choose to eliminate these environmental programs rather than face any countervailing trade action.

Free trade challenges to environmental legislation are not unique to North America. A recent decision of the Court of Justice of the European Community illustrates the incompatibility of liberalized trade and environmental protection, and it establishes yet another unfortunate precedent by overturning a Danish regulation that required all beer and soft drinks to be sold in returnable containers (see sidebar).

On August 21, 1991, a GATT dispute resolution panel produced a report overruling the 1990 U.S. ban on selected tuna imports under the Marine Mammals Protection Act. This ruling supports the proposition that imported products (in this case Mexican tuna) should be given the same treatment as domestic products (i.e. American tuna). The ban, effective early in 1991, was against tuna products imported from Mexico and other nations that caused dolphins to be unnecessarily trapped and killed in tuna fishing nets. Mexican commercial fishermen set purse seine nets around schools of dolphins because of a tendency for tuna to congregate below the marine mammals. If adopted by GATT member nations, the report will have a wide, potentially disastrous impact on international conservation efforts.

According to the panel's report, the U.S. ban violates GATT regulations and is

---

NO DEPOSIT, NO RETURN

Zen Makuch

In 1988, the European Court heard a challenge to an anti-pollution initiative.

At issue was a Danish waste reduction regulation that required all beer and soft drinks to be sold in returnable containers. As noted by the European Court, the Danish regulations were "highly effective" and made no distinction between beverages manufactured or bottled domestically and those imported to the country. Nevertheless, other member states of the European Community objected, as did retail associations who complained about the cost of establishing collection systems and argued for the right to market non-refillable containers.

In considering the case, the European Court noted mandatory obligations established by the EEC Treaty to preserve, protect, and improve the quality of the environment. It found the Danish regulations to be a bona fide and successful effort to accomplish environmental objectives. But even after taking these findings into account, the Court found that Denmark had failed to satisfy the onus of having to prove that its measures were "not disproportionate to achieve a legitimate aim."

Acknowledging the fact that no restraint of trade had actually arisen, the Court reasoned that re-use regulations could be more expensive for importers than for domestic producers. The Court concluded: "There has to be a balancing of interests between the free movement of goods and environmental protection, even if in achieving the balance the higher standard of protection sought has to be reduced."

It then proceeded to strike down the waste reduction regulation.

SOURCE: "Re: Disposable Beer Cans, E.C. Commission V. Denmark," European Court Of Justice, 1988, as reported in [1989] 1 *CMLR* 619.

illegal because it uses domestic measures to protect dolphins living outside the territorial jurisdiction of the United States. The panel decision is a setback for conservation because it disregards national legislation designed to provide environmental protection for common resources. In many cases, these national legislative initiatives are the only effective means for achieving conservation goals. The GATT decision rules out the only domestic legislation available to the U.S. to protect the dolphins. It is a further problem that the panel was encouraged by many countries to interpret GATT rules to prevent member countries from discriminating between "like products" on the basis of the method of production. This would mean, for example, that GATT members could not apply trade restrictions which distinguish between sustainably and unsustainably harvested tropical timber, or between tuna caught in purse seine nets and those caught in "dolphin-safe" nets.

The panel decision further underscores the reality that, since its implementation in 1948, the GATT has never adequately addressed concerns about environmental protection and resource conservation. This is not a problem which is unique to GATT, given the fact that both the FTA and the NAFTA negotiations refuse to acknowledge the intimate links between trade and environmental protection. The consistency with which these rulings undermine valid environmental regulation initiatives underlines the need to persuade NAFTA negotiators to re-evaluate their decision to ignore any consideration of environmental measures in the agreement.

These cases stand as a strong disincentive for governments that plan to bring forward any new environmental regulation. A number of Canadian environmental initiatives have already been put aside by government policy-makers on the basis that they would be challenged as a non-tariff barrier to trade. One wonders how many other environmental regulations have not seen the light of day due to this fear.

What is more discouraging is the trend among commercial sectors, at home and abroad, towards relocating in countries where environmental regulations are less stringent, in order to improve profit margins. By locating in countries where the cost of environmental regulation is the lowest, these companies are more free to despoil domestic environmental conditions while exerting an overall pressure towards lower environmental standards around the world, as individual countries take steps to become more attractive to foreign investors. This failure to regulate commercial activities affecting the environment should be treated as representing a subsidy, which would in turn be vulnerable to countervailing trade measures.

> **The GATT decision rules out the only domestic legislation available to protect the dolphins**

Given the alarming tendency to dismantle environmental regulatory regimes, some have suggested that it would be logical to harmonize standards among

ANOTHER VICTIM OF GATT A recent GATT ruling overturned a U.S. ban on tuna caught with driftnets as a non-tariff trade barrier. The U.S. law was intended to stop the slaughter of dolphins by drift-net fleets.
PHOTO BY GRACE/GREENPEACE

member countries to any multilateral trade agreement. In view of the deregulatory nature of liberalized trade principles, it is not surprising that standard-setting bodies such as Codex Alimentarius, a GATT institution, have tended towards a level of standardization at the lowest common denominator of environmental regulation. The clearest example of this phenomenon here at home occurred in the area of pesticides, where Canada's more stringent regulations, which base the approval of a pesticide on its proven "safety," are being sacrificed for harmonization with U.S. regulations which are based on a "risk/benefit analysis." The tangible difference in the two approaches is noticeable in that the U.S. has registered over seven times as many pesticide products, and has 20 percent more active pesticide ingredients registered for use, than Canada has.[3]

These standardization proposals, which impose only a very low floor and not a

SOMETHING IN THE AIR
Pesticides and herbicides banned in Canada are widely used in Mexico and the U.S. The Americans allow seven times as many crop spraying substances as Canadian laws do, and DDT is still widely used in Mexico.
PHOTO BY KAY TREAKLE/ GREENPEACE

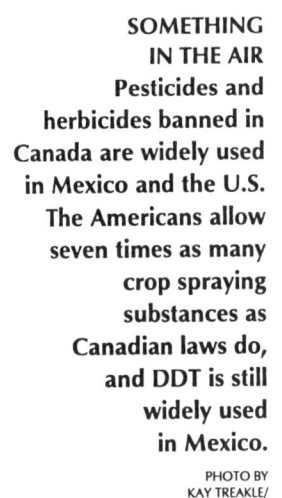

ceiling for environmental regulations, would preclude the introduction of any innovative environmental initiative in these areas. This will significantly undermine the traditional tendency among progressive nations towards setting the highest environmental standards, thereby encouraging other nations to raise their standards to similar levels.

It is a further disturbing fact that, like the GATT and the FTA, the NAFTA is being negotiated under a veil of secrecy which prevents any substantive analysis of the standard-setting tendencies taking place during the negotiations. It will be difficult if not impossible to resolve these discouraging tendencies if we are to be provided with a NAFTA in final form. For this reason, the negotiations, if not the draft text itself, must be more widely accessible to the general public in a manner consistent with our democratic principles.

FREE TRADE AND THE ENVIRONMENT

THE MEXICAN EXPERIENCE While Canada and the United States have had three and a half years' experience with a liberalized trade regime, Mexico has had its own trade experiment in place in the maquiladora "free trade" zones established along the U.S. border area since 1965. These zones were formed for the purpose of attracting jobs to the border regions, resulting in the relocation of approximately 1,500 industries enticed by the cheap labour, lax environmental regulations, and minimal taxes.[4]

Not surprisingly, this experiment has resulted in devastating environmental problems in the border zones: acute and widespread air pollution, raw sewage and hazardous waste problems, and an inadequate supply of housing and drinking water.

The condition of the environment in the Mexican "free trade" zones should be part of our wider concern for the environment in North America in view of the fact that the NAFTA would greatly add to the amount of industrial activity in Mexico and, more specifically, in the maquiladoras. This will only deepen Mexico's already serious environmental crisis, and exacerbate the unsustainable patterns resulting from Mexico's existing model of development. This will contribute further to the environmental problems that already exist in every sector of industrial activity.

There is much to support the claim that multinationals build the least environmentally and occupationally safe part of their operations in developing countries as a means of escaping government regulations. It is clear that Mexico allows multinationals to follow more lenient occupational and environmental standards than those to which they must adhere in their own nations. The result is a toxic time-bomb that Mexico and its neighbours must address for generations to come. In the short term this means the intensive and unsustainable exploitation of natural resources, the further debilitation of the ecosystems, higher levels of toxic air emissions and effluents into water, and the further degradation of soil conditions. At present the Mexican government is not in a position to address these environmental difficulties, because government cost-cutting to meet the massive costs of debt financing has resulted in an inadequate amount of public spending on the environment.

Furthermore, any attempt to address the environmental crisis stands in complete contradiction to the liberalization contemplated by NAFTA, whose fundamental principles rest on the ability of multinational corporations and other large enterprises to exploit Mexico's low-wage labour force and lax enforcement of environmental regulations. Mexico is aware that these advantages, in addition to those brought on by favourable tax policies and other non-tariff barriers, are the key to attracting foreign investment. Therefore, the logic of NAFTA betrays the basic truth that Mexico cannot afford to be tough on environmental protection issues.

> 'It is a fact that if unnecessary or excessive costs are introduced unilaterally by any country, (or province), innovation and development will simply cease or be transferred to jurisdictions with a more favourable business climate. Should this happen in Canada, it would be quickly reduced to a warehouse for chemicals.'
> CANADIAN CHEMICAL PRODUCER'S ASSOCIATION

> 'We don't know what's happening, but you can see the [tree] is sick. The fruit just drops off, and the leaves never get green. The same thing happens with the peaches. And my children, they are sick all the time.'
>
> MARIA ELENA MARTINEZ-MATA, WHO LIVES NEAR A CHEMICAL PLANT IN MATAMOROS, MEXICO

On February 23, 1992, the United States and Mexico agreed on details of an environmental clean-up program to reduce pollution and improve water quality along their common border.[5] The United States has dedicated $241 million to border environmental problems, including $75 million for drinking water and waste water needs in border areas on the U.S. side that have substandard housing and poor water quality. It will also spend $80 million for waste water treatment in the border regions near San Diego and Imperial Valley, California, and Nogales and Laredo, Texas. For its part, Mexico is committing $147 million for various border projects, including waste water treatment, solid waste management, transportation infrastructure, and dedicated land areas for low-income housing. This strategic move on behalf of the United States and Mexico stems from an eagerness to secure support from the U.S. Congress for NAFTA.

This $147 million commitment will barely scratch the surface in terms of the massive environmental cleanup which must take place over several decades. As well, such an expenditure will only be neutralized by future industrial activity.

Unfortunately, there have been few attempts to quantify in any objective fashion the cost, benefit, and the lost opportunities involved in the experience of the maquiladoras. What is certain is that the environmental and human health risks, and any representative voice for those who have been victimized by "free" trade, have been silenced. Among the environmental health risks in the maquiladoras are the following: workers are known to be exposed on a frequent basis to excessive amounts of lead, methylene chloride, thinner, acetone, alcohol and flux. According to Noam Chomsky there have been several instances in which young children have been working beside open vats of toxic waste, with no protective face covering.[6] Safety labels are almost exclusively written in English. Not surprisingly, an alarming number of mentally retarded infants have been born to mothers who worked in maquila plants. In "The Maquiladoras and Toxics: The Hidden Costs of Production South of the Border," Leslie Kochan writes of 24 such children, called "Los niños de la Mallory," who were born to women who worked long hours with PCBs at a company called Mallory Capacitors. Their only protection was rubber gloves.

Aside from the myriad of reproductive health and fetal development risks, there are the further issues of the indiscriminate dumping of waste in landfill sites; the threat of toxic poisoning through transportation or industrial accidents; the lack of adequate waste treatment facilities both in Mexico and the United States; the skyrocketing cost of cleaning up bacterial and industrial contamination; the pitiful hazardous waste disposal practices which affect populations on both sides of the border through groundwater contamination; and the decimation of fish and wildlife which are facing extinction.

In a recent study, the American Medical Association called the U.S.-Mexican

FREE TRADE AND THE ENVIRONMENT

DON'T GO NEAR THE WATER
Toxic waste from factories in Mexico have poisoned the New River, which runs north into California. Rather than press Mexico for tougher environmental laws, the U.S. is spending $241 million on an after-the-fact cleanup.
PHOTO BY JOHN W. EMMONS/ IMPACT VISUALS

border "a virtual cesspool and breeding ground for infectious disease."[7] It also observed that "the major factors affecting environmental health in the area are water and air pollution." The rivers used to irrigate nearly two billion acres of farmland in the border area are governed by agreements which address neither sewage problems nor pollution control. Given these discouraging features, if the maquiladoras were permitted to expand and to continue at their present rate, no amount of money spent for environmental purposes would undo the permanent damage done to the environment or the health of citizens living in the area.

CONCLUSION Although it will not admit this, the Mulroney government is extremely concerned that the FTA has thrown Canada's economic destiny to the wind. Having wrongly anticipated an exclusive deal with the United States with measurable benefits, our experience with the FTA has been a dismal one, not only from the environmental and social perspective, but also in economic terms. Approximately two thirds of Canadians are against a trilateral deal, and yet this government is hell-bent on delivering one.

This raises the question of who it is that would be served by such a deal. The answer is: very few people indeed. Canada's large banks are hoping that the NAFTA will provide them with the chance to move many of their activities to the United States. Then there are the multinationals and other Canadian businesses who see a grand opportunity for relocating in Mexico in order to take advantage of the "environment for enterprise" described above. Such a move would hardly encourage our commercial institutions to better serve Canadians. On the Mexican side, there should be no illusion that the Mexican poor will benefit from such an agreement, given that it is consistent with an economic development policy which Mexico has pursued for some years at their expense. What can be done?

Canadian environmentalists, unionists, and social activists have a duty to relate their unfortunate experiences with the FTA to fellow citizens and our continental counterparts. Our understanding of the social and environmental impact of free trade is born out of direct experience and a well-reasoned analysis of its inevitable outcomes. It is clear that, while our governments state that trade agreements are commercial accords – not environmental and social accords – they are indeed aware of the linkages between intercontinental trade

THE ENVIRONMENT

Brainless births spark toxin watch on border

Baltimore Sun

BROWNSVILLE, Texas — In less than 36 hours last spring, three children were born without brains at Valley Regional Medical Center here.

CHILDREN PAY PRICE
Better use of their brains by some grown-ups might have prevented this tragedy. Such stories are becoming increasingly common, as toxic waste dumping by maquiladora plants continues unchecked.

and the larger environmental and social milieu. They have clearly decided to subordinate social and environmental concerns to the liberalized trade agenda.

It is essential that any further trade negotiations be broadened to assess their social and environmental impacts, and to provide the mechanisms to counteract potential losses in these areas. We must deal decisively with a political agenda that favours trade at the expense of broader environmental and social considerations. These costs have been demonstrated in decisions under the FTA, the GATT, and in the maquiladora experiment. The following are the minimum environmental requirements for a workable NAFTA:[8]

1. Maintain control over export flows where a valid natural resource conservation purpose can be demonstrated.

2. Employ import controls to maintain and promote effective environmental protection legislation, such as regulations on the movement of hazardous waste.

3. Treat an externalized environmental or resource cost from a commercial activity as an inadmissible subsidy.

4. Create an environmental fund in which monies received by way of import controls applied to Mexico go towards improving its environmental programs.

5. Require domestically owned businesses operating abroad to use domestic environmental, health, and safety standards, and to file environmental and workplace compliance certificates where applicable foreign standards are less strict.

6. The trade dispute resolution body must possess the professional expertise and the institutional ability to address environmental concerns in an informed, transparent process which guarantees full public participation supported by intervener funding.

7. There must be a series of environmental assessments of NAFTA which examine potential impacts and alternatives for remedying such impacts. Such assessments must take place during any negotiation, implementation, dispute resolution, and

enforcement of the agreement.

8. Enhance environmental standards through a transparent, accessible negotiation process which allows for the subsequent enactment of higher national standards without penalty.

9. Set up a trade and environment panel with the jurisdiction to identify, monitor, and resolve environment and trade issues pertaining to the agreement itself (such a committee should in no way resemble the composition, mandate, or secretive processes of Codex Alimentarius or the Multilateral Trade Organization being proposed at the GATT Uruguay Round). This trade and environment panel would give direction to national governments to promote environmentally sound practices and to call for amendments to the trade agreement where necessary in order to accomplish this goal. Representation for non-governmental organizations on this panel would be required.

If trade deregulation and effective environmental regulation continue to be seen as incompatible by our governments then, as environmentalists, we must campaign against any further assault on our environmental protection regimes and our natural resource conservation options at the hands of a liberalized trade agenda. Failing any resolution of these matters, we must take the government position that the free trade agreement is a commercial accord rather than an environmental agreement, and turn it on its head. If trade agreements are not environmental agreements then environmental regulations and natural resource conservation measures should be exempt from trade rules. This fundamental principle, if properly observed, would ensure that any potential adverse environmental impacts of the NAFTA, the FTA, or the GATT would be neutralized.

1. This section is informed by the work of my colleagues Michelle Swenarchuk and Steven Shrybman. In particular, see: Michelle Swenarchuk, *Environmental Impacts of the Canada-U.S. Free Trade Deal*, Toronto: CELA, 1988; Steven Shrybman, *Selling Canada's Environment Short*, Toronto: CELA, 1988; Steven Shrybman, *Selling the Environment Short: An Environmental Assessment of the First Two Years of Free Trade Between Canada and the United States*, Toronto: CELA, 1990.
2. *Corrosion Proof Fittings et al. v. The Environmental Protection Agency and William K. Reilly, Administrator*, U.S. Court of Appeals for the Fifth Circuit, No. 89-4596, October 1991.
3. Shrybman, 1990 at p. 16.
4. "Integrated Border Plan for the Mexico-U.S. Border Area (First Stage, 1992-1994)," Washington: U.S. Environmental Protection Agency, 1991.
5. "U.S., Mexico to clean up border area," Ottawa *Citizen*, February 23, 1992.
6. Noam Chomsky, "The Victors: II," in *Z Magazine*, January 1991, p. 11.
7. Mary B. Benant, "Border Called Cesspool," in Tucson *Citizen*, June 23, 1990, p. 1.
8. Zen Makuch, Janine Ferretti, Ken Traynor, "International Trade and the Environment," an Issue Paper from CELA, Pollution Probe, Common Frontiers, 1991.

Zen Makuch is a staff lawyer with the Canadian Environmental Law Association, specializing in toxic chemicals, hazardous waste, administrative law, and international environmental law. This paper is written from the author's personal point of view and does not necessarily reflect CELA's position on the issues raised.

Drink Canada Dry?

Sooner or later the U.S. is going to go after our water, said Simon Reisman in 1985. Now it looks like it may be sooner rather than later

by Wendy Holm and Donald Gutstein

Water is the most essential element of life. Wars have been fought over it, empires have flourished and crumbled because of it. The American dream of transforming the vast stretches of semi-arid and desert territory west of the 100th meridian into lush, fertile farms and prosperous cities was accomplished only with the aid of massive water projects. For Canadians, abundant water sources – lakes, rivers, streams, and glaciers – may be what defines Canada's uniqueness.

But all that is changing. Today's abundance is becoming tomorrow's scarcity as global warming dries up rivers and lakes, and acid rain, pesticide runoff, and industrial wastes pollute those that remain. The Americans, because they have squandered their resource on such a massive scale, are fast approaching a major crisis in their water supplies. Accustomed to unlimited water even in the desert, so far they seem more interested in finding new sources than in cutting back in the quantities they use. Canadians fear that Americans will soon come after their water, and they do not trust their federal or provincial politicians to protect Canadian interests.

All continental water-sharing schemes show Canada's water flowing south through the U.S. and into Mexico

Further, it is not at all clear that the growing U.S. interest in Canada's water is limited to fulfilling the needs of American cities and industry. With the advent of the North American Free Trade talks, the concern escalates considerably, since water is currently the greatest limitation to growth of the maquiladora zones which will most certainly be dramatically developed and extended under a continental trade arrangement. All continental water-sharing schemes on the drawing boards –

including the Grand Canal – show Canada's water flowing south through the U.S. and into Mexico via the Rio Grande or Colorado River.

Brian Mulroney and his Tories lost credibility during the 1988 federal election when agricultural economist Wendy Holm and thirteen of Canada's most distinguished writers on economic, political, and environmental issues presented compelling evidence, in the book *Water and Free Trade*, that water was indeed included in the Canada-U.S. Free Trade Agreement. While the Tories have continued to vociferously deny this, many Canadians remain gravely concerned. In a national Gallup poll conducted during the summer of 1988, Canadians overwhelmingly identified water as Canada's most essential natural resource, well ahead of farm land, forests, minerals, oil, and gas.

CALIFORNIA SCHEMING While shortages in the U.S. are becoming increasingly severe in many areas, much of the demand recently in the public spotlight centers around Los Angeles. Five years of drought have left this sprawling megalopolis of 15 million parched, its lawns brown, its toilets unflushed, its swimming pools unfilled. Drought busters – employees of the L.A. Department of Power and Water – write citations for water runoff.

NICASIO RESERVOIR
MARIN COUNTY, CA
Water shortages have hit California's agro-industry hard. A steady supply of cheap, Canadian water would be just the thing to hit the spot.
PHOTO BY
MARVIN COLLINS/
IMPACT VISUALS

In February 1991, California Governor Pete Wilson cut off all state water to farmers in the lush Central Valley, the most productive agricultural region in the world, and cut urban users by 50 percent. There is a drought, and there will undoubtedly be more droughts in the future, but is there really a water shortage? The four biggest users of water in California are grass for livestock, alfalfa for livestock, subsidized cotton, and subsidized rice, all low-value uses which contribute little to the state economy. In fact, agriculture uses 85 percent of the water, while half of the rest is used to keep lawns and golf courses green.

The prodigious squandering of water is a result of decades of operation of the Iron Triangle: the government bureaucrats in the Department of Interior, Bureau of Reclamation, and Army Corps of Engineers; the agricultural and urban users; and their congressional representatives, who have all conspired to ensure that plentiful,

> 'In parched Santa Barbara county, rich residents are paying $200 to have water trucked in for their thirsty lawns. Those who can't afford the sprinkling service are paying $50 to have green dye sprayed on their brown grass. Water rustling is rampant, forcing residents to buy locks for their outdoor taps. A Santa Barbara man with a leaking toilet got a water bill for $2,775. So far, it's farmers who are taking the brunt of the cutbacks – principally because they account for 85 percent of water consumption.'
>
> VANCOUVER PROVINCE, FEBRUARY 2, 1991

heavily subsidized water was available for politically powerful farmers and developers who wanted to build new subdivisions. Wilson himself is a former mayor of San Diego, the fastest growing area in the U.S., which relied almost exclusively on imported water for its growth. He is unlikely to make major changes to the system.

THE ARID U.S. WEST   California may get the headlines, but the rest of the arid west and southwest, with an average annual rainfall of less than 20 inches, is just as heavily dependent on water projects for its survival. El Paso County, Colorado, has adopted, and the courts have upheld, a land-use regulation that requires a 300-year water supply for new subdivisions.

The damming and diversion of the once-mighty Colorado River is so extensive that hardly a drop now travels the entire length of its natural channel to the Gulf of California in Mexico. And every drop has been fought over in the courts by the seven states through which the Colorado flows.

Meanwhile across the Great Divide from the headwaters of the Colorado, Denver developers want to raise a huge dam on the South Platte River at Two Forks to supply that growth-crazed city with 32 billion gallons of water a year. If that venture is defeated, Vancouver's Belzberg family is standing by, 350 kilometres to the south, to pump water to Denver from the aquifer which underlies the Raca Ranch, which was first developed by Canadian environmentalist-businessperson Maurice Strong. To the east, the great Ogalala Aquifer which underlies the high plains of west Texas, the Oklahoma panhandle, Kansas, and Nebraska, is being rapidly sucked dry, and those states are getting panicky.

MEXICO   The implications of the North American Free Trade Agreement (NAFTA) exacerbate the need for Canadians to retain control over Canada's water resource. Mexico's maquiladora plants have been limited in size because of their limited access to water. In fact, insufficient water access has been their prime limit to growth. Now that the Americans have rights to Canada's water, they could place this resource squarely on the table in their dealings with the Mexicans. All continental water-sharing schemes on the drawing boards – including the Grand Canal – show Canada's water flowing south through the U.S. and into Mexico via the Rio Grande or Colorado River. Interestingly, Mexico's new ambassador to Canada, Jorge de la Vega Dominguez, left his cabinet post as minister of agriculture and hydraulic resources to come to Canada.

ECONOMIC RESPONSES IN CANADA   Instead of reapportioning existing supplies and practicing demand management, Los Angeles and California are looking further afield for new sources, like a 1000-mile pipeline from the Columbia

THIRSTY LITTLE TUBERS Each kilogram of potatos requires 1,000 kilograms of water while it's growing. Is it sensible to concentrate food production in what is basically desert?

PHOTO BY NICK KERESZTESI

River (where some consider the 90 billion gallons a day flowing into the Pacific to be "wasteful and sinful") to Lake Shasta and from there into the State Water Project. Supplying water is becoming an economic proposition and has attracted the big engineering firms and corporations. There are few inexpensive, accessible sources of water left in the U.S. Neo-conservative interests are pushing to privatize water rights; they see water markets as one means, albeit misguided, to ease the shortage. As well, corporate eyes are turning to Canada.

For Americans, Canada is a land of vast untapped flows of fresh, clean water. That is only partially true. Canada has an estimated 70 to 90 percent of the continent's surface supply of fresh water, although 60 percent of that drains north into the Arctic Ocean and is virtually inaccessible. Even so, with 10 percent of the population and industry of the U.S., Canada has twice as much available water,

CROSSING THE LINE

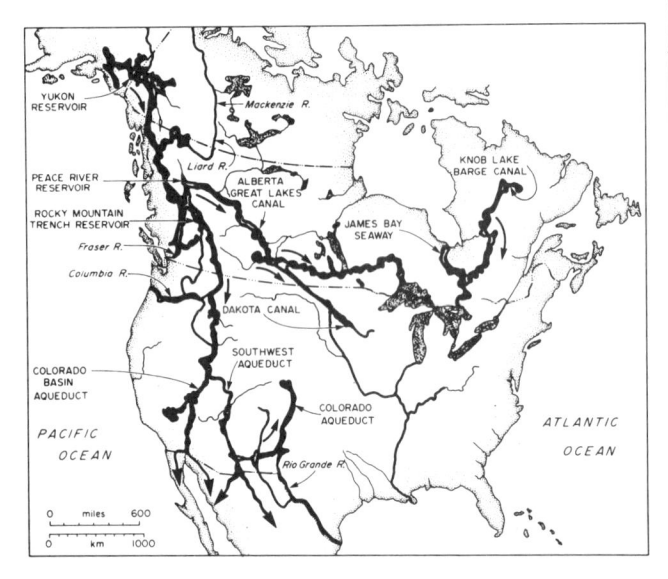

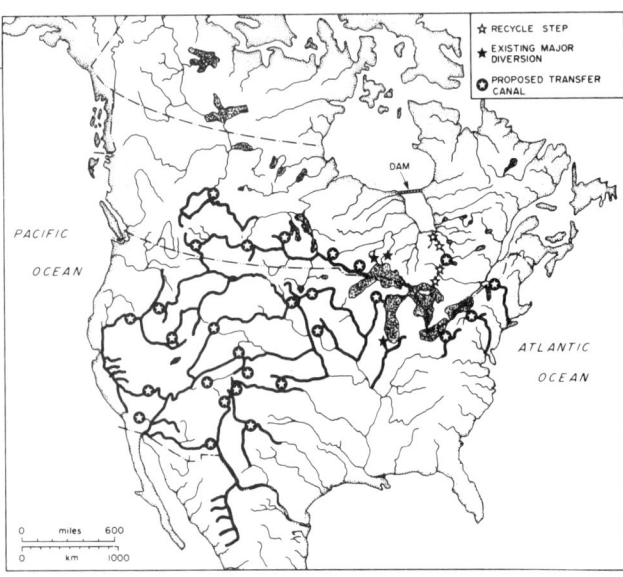

DOWN THE DRAIN? These maps show two schemes to divert water from the northern part of the continent south, toward the sunny southern U.S. and, to a lesser extent, Mexico. The NAWAPA scheme is shown on the left; the GRAND canal plan is on the right.

MAPS FROM DEPARTMENT OF FISHERIES AND OCEANS

although many large bodies of water near populated areas are fast becoming polluted and unusable. Certain regions of the west also suffer from chronic drought.

Nonetheless, Americans have expressed interest in Canadian water at least since the North American Water and Power Alliance (NAWAPA) proposal to divert massive flows of water from northern Canada and Alaska south into the U.S. in the early 1960s.

Tom Kierans' $100-billion Great Recycling and Northern Development (Grand) Canal proposal is the darling of the engineering industry. It would dam James Bay and turn it into an immense fresh water lake, divert the water into the Great Lakes, and send it from there into the mid-western states or, alternately, to Lake Diefenbaker in Saskatchewan and from there to the parched American south and southwest and perhaps even further afield to Mexico.

While these projects may still seem unrealistic today with their price tags in the hundreds-of-billions-of-dollars range, large-scale water diversions are not new: with more than 600 *large* dams and 60 large-scale domestic interbasin diversions, Canada already diverts more water (mainly to create hydro-electric power) than any other country on earth.

Nor are the early schemes dead. In 1988, NAWAPA supporters gathered in Washington D.C., to rekindle support for the project. And Tom Kierans has said that the U.S. Army Corps of Engineers was still encouraging him to continue work on his project. Simon Reisman, former deputy minister of finance under John Turner and a person made famous by his central role in the free trade talks, was a key lobbyist for the Grand Canal scheme. Companies like Bechtel Canada – John Turner was a director in the early 1980s – continue to lobby the federal government to reconsider its declared ban on large-scale water exports.

CANADA'S POLITICAL RESPONSE In 1985, Simon Reisman, soon to become Canada's free trade negotiator, said that water sales were the carrot that could entice the Americans to the table to negotiate a free trade agreement. Reisman tried to convince his friend John Turner to become an outspoken advocate of water exports. Turner wouldn't but Reisman found an ally in Mulroney.

Politicians have a difficult time with water exports. While Canadians see water as their most essential natural resource and the vast majority of Canadians oppose large-scale water exports, the alleged benefits of large-scale exports – big resource revenues plus a chance to cozy up to the American giant – compel private sector participants to lobby hard for an "open-tap" policy.

Former B.C. premier Bill Bennett said it all in 1981: "Not today, but come and see me in 15 years." Meanwhile he quietly started the process of granting water export licences. This issue lay dormant until 1990.

So governments have had to tread stealthily. That's why there was such Watergate-type intrigue surrounding the place of water exports in the Canada-U.S. Free Trade Agreement. When the Agreement was signed in October 1987, water was excluded; when the Free Trade Agreement was released to the public in December 1987, the exclusion had been removed. This surprised people like Pat Carney and Vancouver lawyer Chris Thomas, who were both intimately involved in the negotiations. There is no question that water is in the FTA; it can be found under tariff heading 22.01, the national treatment provisions (article 105), the quantitative restrictions clause (article 409), and Chapter Seven (Agriculture). The FTA gave the Americans substantial new rights relating to Canadian water and reduced Canada's freedom to meet its own water needs.

> **Reisman said that water sales were the carrot that could entice Americans to negotiate a free trade agreement**

The Mulroney government has consistently denied that water is included in the FTA, but it refused to amend the agreement or explicitly exclude water the way it did beer. The government put forward Bill C-156 to prohibit large-scale water exports, but allowed the bill to die on the Order Paper. It was never reintroduced.

Now the provinces are moving to reduce and perhaps eliminate the federal role in environmental regulation and controls on resource exports including water. The Rafferty-Alameda episode in Saskatchewan made it clear that the federal government is not serious in its efforts to develop and enforce a national water policy which prohibits large-scale water exports. Quebec likes being courted for its water because it ties in so nicely with its hydro-electric export sales strategy. Premier Bourassa is an ardent advocate of large-scale water exports.

CONVEYING THE WATER TO MARKET   Water can be moved to the U.S. by supertankers, pipelines, or by interbasin diversions like Rafferty-Alameda. Transport by tanker is not included in the federal government's ban on water exports. In March 1985, the B.C. government established a fee schedule to license the "commercial bulk export of water by marine transport vessels." In 1990, three B.C.-based companies were bidders to supply the water-starved community of Santa Barbara, California, with as much as 12.4-billion litres of water a year. Santa Barbara council opted for an expensive desalination plant (which would remove salt from sea water) but said it was "keeping the door open" to future supertanker imports. Western Canada Water Enterprises is the most aggressive player in this new game.

In B.C., a group of mining promoters has been secretly developing a water pipeline proposal since 1988. This group has close links to the former B.C. Social Credit government and is backed by Canadian and Japanese interests.

The Rafferty Dam on the Souris River and the Alameda Dam on Moose Mountain Creek in southeastern Saskatchewan make little economic sense. They are in semi-arid country without enough water to fill and maintain their supply levels. The dams will provide irrigation but will flood more farmland than they irrigate. They are also supposed to play a role in flood control, but the only built-up area requiring flood protection is Minot, North Dakota, where the Souris makes a 180-degree turn and flows back into Manitoba. The U.S. paid Saskatchewan $50 million for the dams.

Rafferty-Alameda make sense only as part of a larger scheme, the Grand Canal project. In fact, Simon Reisman was advising Saskatchewan Premier Grant Devine in 1990 on agricultural trade while Devine was ramrodding Rafferty-Alameda past the federal Ministry of Environment. Rafferty-Alameda are the linch-pins in the entire system. "They are being put in the right place except those that are putting them there don't really know that they're part of a much bigger puzzle, a much bigger picture," Grand Canal promoter Tom Kierans said recently. An interesting part of this puzzle is that the growing demand for water to fuel expanded industrial development in Mexico under the proposed North American Free Trade Agreement will be coincidentally met directly by the projected flow of Canadian water south under the Grand Canal scheme.

IMPLICATIONS FOR CANADA   Air and water are commodities for which there are no replacements. Canada will suffer a serious diminution in its power and authority as a sovereign nation if the FTA shifts jurisdiction over water policy

> 'I think one of the reasons the U.S. wants to negotiate a free-trade agreement with Canada is because Canada has the water resources that this country is eventually going to need. The marriage of these two nations is to take a resource-rich country like Canada and merge it with a capital-rich country like America. And that, I think, is something that we are looking at down the line.'
>
> FRED GRANDY, IOWA CONGRESSMAN, QUOTED IN VANCOUVER PROVINCE, JULY 31, 1988

decisions to the Americans by placing their hands on the tap.

Canadians may lose their ability to grow their own food if they lose their ability to irrigate the land, a cornerstone of sustainable agricultural development. Drought, desertification, global warming, and a reduction in agricultural production are forecast for American exporting regions such as California, and Canadian producers could win new markets if they had assured water supplies. At issue for the Canadians is not only the irrigation of existing farm land, but the ability to alter cropping patterns, bring new land into production, and increase the volume, diversity, and location of domestically produced food stuffs to reflect changing market trends.

Water exports pose serious risks to the environment. Supertanker sales and large-scale diversions could result in the exportation of micro-organisms to other environments, changes to the salinity and micro-climate of ocean outfall sites, and the loss of biological diversity, wildlife habitat, and large tracts of prime land because

---

WATER: THE DRY FACTS
Jim Sinclair

While most Canadians take water for granted, many Americans and Mexicans cannot.

❏ Of the three countries, Canada has the lowest population and by far the largest supply of water. Its renewable supply is listed as 696 cubic miles – 20 percent of the world's total fresh water supply. The United States has 595 cubic miles, but is consuming it at a rate ten times faster than Canada. Mexicans have only 86 cubic miles, and consume it at about the same rate as Canada. Canada's water use doubled from 1972 to 1981, although the population only increased 5 percent.

❏ Agriculture is the main consumer of water in North America. In Mexico, farming accounts for 86 percent of water usage; in the U.S., 42 percent; in Canada, 8 percent. In the U.S., this translates into 600 gallons per person per day. Water is especially critical to states like California, where one quarter of all U.S. food – half of its produce – is grown. There, 85 percent goes to agriculture. Water shortages forced a 75-percent reduction to farmers in January 1991. It takes 40 gallons of water to produce a single egg, 1000 kilograms of the stuff to grow a kilo of potatoes.

❏ Domestic use accounts for 11 percent of total consumption in Canada, 12 percent in the U.S., and 6 percent in Mexico. The average Canadian family of four consumes 243 gallons of water per day, with toilet flushing taking 100 gallons. A five-minute shower uses 100 litres of water. Canadians use only 5 percent of their domestic water for cooking and drinking, while bathing counts for 35 percent, laundry and dishes 20 percent, and toilets 40 percent. Running water or safe drinking water is just a dream for millions of Mexicans. More than 50 percent of rural Mexicans have no access to safe drinking water, and only 15 percent of the rural population has some form of sanitation. This is particularly true in the maquiladora zones, where sewage and toxic waste have polluted every single river. In developing countries as a whole, 80 percent of illnesses are related to the lack of clean water.

❏ Industry accounts for 46 percent of water use in the United States. In Canada, the figure is 80 percent. Thermal power generation accounts for 60 percent of this, while manufacturing uses 18 percent. Mexicans use only 8 percent of their water for industry. It takes 100,000 gallons to build a car, 280 gallons to produce your Sunday newspaper, and 86,900 litres to make 310 kilos of steel.

SOURCES: Environment Canada publications; World Resources Institute, *1992 Environmental Almanac* (Boston: Houghton Mifflin Co., 1992)

of flooding. Increasingly such concerns are being met by promises of full-blown environmental impact assessments, but these offer little security in the face of the terms of the Free Trade Agreement.

Canada's economic and industrial development policies are also at stake. If Canada's water resources, either as coastal outflows or river diversions, are committed to meeting the needs of American consumers, Canadians will not be able to harness the flows for new domestic industries.

NATIVE IMPACTS   Water is central to North American aboriginal societies, whether they are located in the parched southwest, in the temperate rain forests of northern California, Oregon, Washington, and British Columbia, or on the tundra of northern Quebec. Water is integral to many native religions; its importance is reflected in native myths throughout the hemisphere.

In the U.S., Indian water rights have become one of the country's hottest water resources issues. The landmark Supreme Court *Winters v. United States* (1908) decision ruled that water rights existed on Indian reservations in order to allow the reservations to achieve economic independence. Today, after dozens of cases have been heard in the courts and Congress has approved some major Indian water claims settlements, the magnitude of potential Indian reserved water rights claims is perceived by the water lobby to be "staggering." One expert suggests that the annual diversion of water required to meet such claims could easily exceed 3-1/2 times the annual flow of the Colorado River (40-million-plus acre-feet). The water lobby is now working to deny to the Indians as much of that water as possible.

Canada's aboriginal peoples remain decades behind their American counterparts. They are intimately acquainted with large-scale water projects because they usually end up paying most of the costs while receiving few of the benefits. In the name of progress, traditional hunting and gathering grounds have been flooded, wildlife decimated, and pristine streams polluted.

> In the U.S., Indian water rights are one of the country's hottest water resources issues

The massive James Bay hydro-electric development project in northern Quebec – which is linked to the Grand Canal project – will see hundreds of dams and dykes reshape an area the size of France. Proponents call it the "project of the century." However, in *eeyou astchee* (literally, "people's homeland") there is widespread fear about the effects of the project on Cree culture and lifestyle, and on migratory birds, whales, and aquatic ecosystems.

When La Grande, the first phase of James Bay, was launched 16 years ago, the Cree were an unorganized and ineffective opposition to all-powerful Hydro-Quebec.

INVESTMENT TIP: BUY WATER Western Canada Water, listed on the Toronto Stock Exchange, is a would-be major water exporter. Its stock is probably undervalued if the NAFTA goes through.

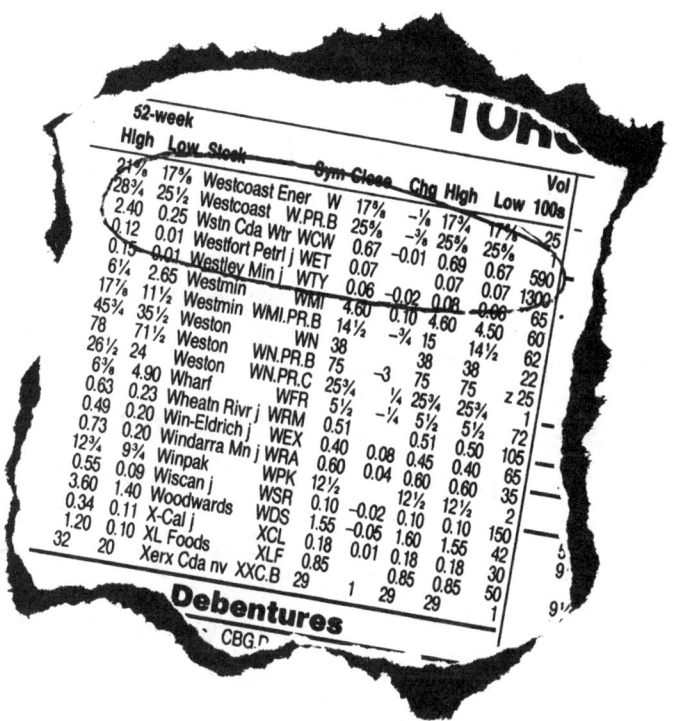

When they lost their legal battle to halt the project, they saw no option but to enter into a land-claims settlement.

Today, faced with James Bay Two and Three, the Cree are no longer powerless. Their national government holds authority over health, education, municipal government, and hunting and fishing rights over 75,000 square kilometres of land. The Grand Council of the Cree enjoys the support of an increasing number of Canadian and American environmental and native groups in their fight to halt the projects. It will be a long and bloody fight.

British Columbia's native community is also fighting the right of the state to enter into water-export agreements without acknowledging the constitutional and aboriginal rights of the native community over the resource. One factor leading the Santa Barbara council to opt for desalination over B.C. supertanker exports was strongly worded correspondence from lawyers representing several B.C. native groups, warning the council about unsettled land and water rights claims.

B.C.'s powerful First Nations Council has called for a moratorium on water-export proposals and water-licence applications pending a full airing of legal, trade, and environmental implications. The Coast Salish nation, representing 50 bands, has resolved to "take whatever actions are required to ensure that such a massive giveaway does not occur within our traditional territories without our consent..."

POLICY IMPLICATIONS   During the 1988 election campaign, business paid for full-page newspaper ads which claimed that water exports were not part of the FTA: "The people who say that water was put on the free-trade table mistook 'bottled' water for bulk water exports and they are wrong. Top officials on both sides of the border have made this crystal clear."

Business is now pointing to Canada's abundant water resources and saying Canadians are not being good neighbours if they do not share their bounty with the Americans.

Opponents argue that Canada must conserve its water to meet the needs of its people now and in the future. Besides, we don't really understand all the environmental implications.

> An unthinking water export policy repeats the Canadian pattern of 'hewers of wood and drawers of water'

The opponents are in the majority. In a Gallup poll conducted during the summer of 1988, more than two-thirds of Canadians disapproved of including water exports in the Free Trade Agreement and 71 percent said they would be less likely to support a political party which approved large-scale exports of fresh water to the U.S.

Canada's agricultural professionals first took up the issue. Delegates to the Agricultural Institute of Canada's 1989 annual meeting in Montreal unanimously called on the federal government to enter into a Memorandum of Understanding (MOU) with the U.S. to limit the terms of the deal to include bottled water only and to place a moratorium on all bulk-water sales to the U.S. until the MOU was signed. The resolution has since been endorsed by environmental, labour, agricultural, and aboriginal groups.

The Save Georgia Strait Alliance wants public hearings on water exports, citing environmental risks related to the transmission of undesirable organisms in ballast water, changes to the salinity of B.C.'s coastal inlets, the destruction of salmon habitat, and damage to the oceanic micro-layer.

For these groups, the issue is not prohibiting all water exports. Limited sharing – small in scale, strictly monitored, and within drainage basins – may contribute significant revenues for social programs in Canada. But because of the behind-closed-doors approach being taken by business interests and the politicians, a full public airing will not likely occur.

There are serious flaws in the way water use and water exports are regulated. Water is mainly a provincial responsibility with significant federal involvements (fishery, inter-provincial and trans-border flows, major environmental impacts). Disputes between the governments in Quebec, Saskatchewan, and Alberta

> 'Only by accepting that water is a tradeable commodity, like coal and oil and timber, will sensible decisions be possible. Many countries once abhorred the idea that water is just another raw material. No longer: at an international conference in Dublin earlier this year, a large number of governments signed a statement saying, in effect, that water was an economic good and should be treated as such.'
>
> THE ECONOMIST, MARCH 28, 1992

(Oldman Dam) have diverted attention from the central issue. The provinces still see their mandate to develop their resources whatever the social and environmental consequences, while most citizens feel, rightly, that they are being shut out of the decision-making process. For example, a 1991 review of B.C.'s water export policy did not include even one public meeting.

If the planet is to survive, all countries must utilize their remaining resources according to the principles enunciated by the Brundtland Commission in *Our Common Future*. As American agricultural production shrinks because of global warming, declining water supplies, and increasing salinization, Canadian farm land will become more valuable, but only if the water is available to irrigate it.

Water is a key ingredient not only in agricultural production but also in Canada's industrial strategy. Many more jobs could be created in Canada by focusing on the world-wide demand for products and processes which monitor, control, clean up, and reclaim the environment. One promising area is technology to solve water-scarcity problems. University grants, tax credits, and stiff penalties for non-compliance could redirect Canadian markets from low value-added products like water to higher value-added technology. Such initiatives will also help the Americans use their water resources more efficiently, since they will not be able to gain easy access to Canada's water.

An unthinking water export policy merely repeats the traditional Canadian pattern of "hewers of wood and drawers of water." Once again Canada will export a low-value commodity – water – which is used to add value elsewhere, either to grow food or to produce manufactured goods which are then imported back into Canada.

Donald Gutstein, B.Arch., M.Arch., is a research and public policy expert currently teaching documentary research methods and introductory journalism in the Department of Communication at Simon Fraser University, and investigative techniques in the Journalism Program at Vancouver Community College. Author of two books (*Vancouver Limited*, Lorimer 1975, and *The New Landlords*, Porcepic Books 1990), Gutstein is a founder and past director of the Centre for Investigative Journalism.

Wendy R. Holm, M.Sc, P.Ag, is a Vancouver-based resource economist with a strong background in competition and trade policy. President of W.R. Holm and Associates, and editor and contributing author to *Water and Free Trade* (Lorimer 1988), Holm is currently B.C. Director, Agricultural Institute of Canada, Director, Vancouver City Savings Credit Union, and Past-President, B.C. Institute of Agrologists.

This chapter presents the framework of material to be covered in considerably more depth by the authors in their new book, *Liquid Assets – America's Thirst for Canada's Water* (Douglas and McIntyre Ltd.), scheduled for release in the spring of 1993.

Free Trade, Food, and Hunger

Canada and Mexico have 'given away the farm' to multinational food producers; now Canadians and Mexicans are going hungry

by Terry Pugh

The food system in Canada is big business, worth $21 billion a year. While only about 4 percent of the Canadian population live on farms, the commodities they produce account for 10 percent of the total Canadian economy.

A lot of what farmers grow is exported either in raw or processed form. In fact, about 8 percent of Canada's total exports are agricultural commodities, and most of those exports are in the form of a single crop: wheat. Canada's traditional image as the "breadbasket of the world" is more myth than reality, however, despite the fact that this country is the world's second largest wheat exporter behind the United States. Canadian farmers actually grow less wheat than China, the Commonwealth of Independent States (formerly the Soviet Union), the United States, India, and France. It's just that we export 80 percent of our production, making us extremely dependent on overseas markets and therefore highly vulnerable to the vagaries of global grain prices. The sharp fall in grain values (50 percent) in the last three years has been a major factor in the dispossession of thousands of Canadian farm families from their land.

Virtually all the grain that flows through the global market is handled by five highly secretive companies

The real breadbasket is the United States, the third largest grain producer in the world. More importantly, it is the biggest exporter. It is a country which sells 50 percent of its grain production in foreign markets – and therefore policies made by the U.S. government are the most important factor in determining global grain prices and market flows. When the U.S. Congress elects to lower the floor price for

FREE TRADE, FOOD, AND HUNGER

TOUGH TIMES ON THE FARM
Canada's farmers have been hit hard by free trade. The destruction of marketing boards by GATT and the NAFTA could finish off the family farm.
PHOTO BY ELAINE BRIERE

grain and to provide export subsidies to transnational companies in order to boost exports (as it did in 1985), the rest of the world's exporting nations must follow suit if they want to retain their markets. The European Economic Community (EEC) consumes 80 percent of its grain domestically, exporting only 20 percent. The EEC has matched the U.S. in providing the corporate sector with export subsidies (which are not the same thing as domestic support measures to farm families), therefore driving down global grain prices even further.

Like all big businesses, the global grain trade and the food system in general operate on the basis of a "market system" – a system dominated by a relative handful of very large multinational corporations. In fact, virtually all the grain that flows through the global market is handled by five highly secretive and tightly controlled companies: Cargill, Continental, Louis-Dreyfuss, Bunge & Borne, and Mitsui. Somewhat smaller transnational companies such as Archer Daniels Midland (ADM) and Feruzzi hold significant market control over specific smaller-volume crops. Cargill's Canadian subsidiary recorded over $6.1 billion in sales alone in fiscal 1990, according to the *Globe and Mail*'s "Report on Business Top 1000 Companies" (July 1991), about one-quarter of the sales volume achieved by the Canadian Wheat Board (CWB). However, there is a major difference between the operations of the CWB and Cargill Canada Ltd. The CWB functions as a semi-autonomous arm of the federal government solely to market western Canadian farmers' wheat, durum, and barley. It seeks out the best price it can get on the world market, and returns its earnings to the farmers that finance its operations. It reports annually to Parliament and accounts for all the public money which occasionally goes toward it. The only secretive aspect of its operation is the day-to-day marketing negotiations with customers. In contrast, privately owned companies like Cargill are totally unaccountable to farmers, the public, and even governments. Cargill's corporate information-gathering network dwarfs the resources available to most governments, and the data is used solely to accumulate profits for the company.

Private transnational grain companies have tremendous economic leverage in the global food system, not only because they are diversified into other commodities, but also because grain prices are pivotal in determining prices for other basic commodities such as red meats, poultry, and dairy products. Cheaper grain leads to cheap meat because grain is the basic input in livestock production. It is this push for cheap grain at the farm gate which underlies the corporate strategy for global free trade in agricultural commodities. Transnational grain companies make their money on the volume, not the price, of grain which passes through their facilities.

It's important to point out that cheap grain prices at the farm gate don't necessarily translate into cheap bread prices at the consumer level. Prior to the Canada-U.S. Free Trade Agreement, Canada had a "two-price wheat system" in place which differentiated between wheat bound for export and wheat consumed domestically. Millers paid roughly $7 per bushel for Canadian wheat, which was then processed into bread, while the world price was roughly half that. The federal government eliminated that pricing structure as a concession to the U.S. under the FTA, rationalizing the move by suggesting that because millers' costs would be halved, bread prices would fall accordingly. This, of course, didn't happen. Bread prices continued to rise, allowing processors to be more "competitive," as well as taking advantage of cheaper inputs to generate higher profits.

The drive for "efficiency" in agriculture centres around the objective of trying to produce greater yields for less cost. Under a theory known as "comparative advantage," only those producers who can generate commodities for the lowest possible cost are considered efficient. Driving down the price of this basic raw material then allows processors to reduce their costs in order to be competitive in the global market.

This free trade strategy benefits the corporate industrial sector at the expense of farmers and workers in the food industry. Both groups receive less for their labour as companies cut costs.

The emphasis on exports of both raw commodities and processed goods is also aimed at generating foreign exchange in order to pay for imports of other commodities, including foodstuffs, which are produced elsewhere. This rise in trade for the sake of trade itself limits national or regional policies of self-sufficiency in

> 'What does change under free trade is that U.S. food companies can for the first time ship goods into Canada from south of the border – as long as they meet Canadian content, labeling and packaging requirements. Until now, a firm had to set up shop here if it wanted to sell products containing supply-managed commodities.'
>
> FINANCIAL POST, DECEMBER 19, 1988

food production and consumption. Such a policy allows corporations which dominate the market, rather than elected governments, to make all the decisions and amounts to a loss of national sovereignty. As food production and distribution patterns are globalized, people are effectively discouraged from consuming what they produce, and instead are drawn into the global marketplace as buyers of commodities from other nations and other regions. As farmers, they are forced to judge the value of the food they produce not in terms of nourishment for people, but as a commodity whose value is determined by the market.

CORPORATE DOMINATION OF THE CANADIAN FOOD SYSTEM The structure of Canadian agriculture is such that even though virtually all (97.8 percent) of the assets used in primary production are owned by Canadians, there is a sizable

---

'HOW MUCH LOWER IS LOW ENOUGH?'

Wayne Easter

In simple terms, free trade makes the market the determining factor in all things. Under free trade, any restrictions that may be in place to protect food production, food quality, the family farm, the environment, or rural life in general, will increasingly be viewed as a trade barrier.

The goal that free trade is meant to accomplish isn't a national goal at all. It is meant to establish the domination of a single idea: that what's good for the free market is good for the country. And because we are talking about a global market, we are talking about those players which control that market, the multinationals.

In Canada, our true sovereignty as a nation is being lost as we replace political debate and decision-making for community goals, with the absolute rule of the market.

In no other industry is the evidence of this loss of sovereignty so clear as it is in agriculture. Canada, after 60 years of grassroots struggle by farmers, had some reasonably good policies in some commodity areas. Almost all of these are now being lost or rendered useless under the guise of "competitiveness" and "open borders."

International business has no interest in national goals and is not capable of concern for individuals. If there is a barrier, they want it obliterated, not just adjusted. For example, following the loss of the two-price wheat system, prices in Canada fell from $7 a bushel to $3.50 a bushel.

Yet Ogilvie Mills Ltd. vice-president John Neufeld said recently, "The [flour milling] industry needs a lower price, competitive with that paid by their American competitors for American wheat." The position of the farmer simply does not enter into it. Presently the farmer gets six cents from a loaf of bread selling for $1.39. How much lower is low enough?

Primary industries are especially vulnerable to the logic of the market. That logic demands that capital look for the cheapest possible inputs – labour, raw materials, energy. Yet from a national goals perspective, a strong primary sector is the foundation of a strong economy. Allowing prices for resources to hit rock bottom devastates rural areas, takes money out of the economy, and effectively ships jobs out of the country.

Farmers around the world have to cooperate in designing programs that use agriculture as a foundation for national policy development. We cannot allow it to be treated as an industry to be exploited by the international corporate sector.

We in the National Farmers Union have begun to meet with farmers in the United States and Mexico to explore ways in which we can work together toward our common goal: economic justice for farmers. Without such cooperation, farmers in all countries will be made increasingly subservient to corporate interests.

SOURCE: Pro-Canada Dossier No. 29.

percentage of the food processing, transportation, retailing, and trading sectors which are owned by foreign corporations. In 1987, according to Statistics Canada, nearly 30 percent of Canada's food industry was owned by foreign (mainly American) companies. In 1990, a total of only eighteen food distribution companies controlled the entire Canadian market, according to the *Globe and Mail*'s "Report on Business Top 1000 Companies," July 1991. The larger companies include George Weston Ltd. (which also owns Loblaws'), Provigo Inc., Oshawa Group, Steinberg Inc., Canada Safeway, Great Atlantic and Pacific Tea Company (A&P), and Metro-Richelieu. Their average sales revenue rose 26 percent in 1990 over the year previous, and their five-year average return on capital was 17.1 percent – at a time when farm incomes had plummeted to levels not experienced since the Great Depression of the 1930s. Corporate concentration in this sector is further increased because of the presence of "buying groups" – partnerships formed between two or more distribution companies for the purpose of purchasing from processors.

Similarly, major food processors and manufacturers such as McCain Foods, Kraft, General Foods, Coca-Cola Beverages, Nestlé, HJ Heinz, Campbell Soup Company, and Pepsi-Cola Canada collectively experienced an average 6 percent rise in sales revenue in 1990 and an average five-year return on capital of 16.91 percent.

In contrast, Canadian farm debt now stands at more than $23 billion, and as

MARKETING BOARDS UNDER ATTACK AT TRADE TALKS

Terry Pugh

Canada's system of marketing boards for farm products is under severe pressure on three trade fronts: the Canada-U.S. Free Trade Agreement, implemented in 1989, which has already undercut the regulatory powers of various agencies; NAFTA, which will extend the economic and political leverage of U.S.-based agribusiness transnationals; and the General Agreement on Tariffs and Trade (GATT), which aims to create a global free trade environment.

Revising the rules governing Canada's marketing boards under any of these pacts could spell the demise of thousands of family farms across the country. The most far-reaching impact could come from the current round of GATT talks, where a new arrangement to replace import controls on food products with gradually declining tariffs is gathering steam as a result of a deal between the United States and the European Economic Community. If this "tariffication" scheme is implemented, Canada's national marketing boards, which operate on the basis of controlling surpluses by regulating domestic supplies to meet national demand, would be rendered ineffective. Farmers would no longer be able to receive prices for their commodities which covered their costs of production, because price levels would be based on so-called "world" prices (which are really "dumping" prices for surplus commodities).

The devastating impact of tariffication was brought to the fore at a huge demonstration, involving about 25,000 farmers from across Canada, in Ottawa on February 21, 1992. The farmers, most of whom raise supply-managed commodities like dairy, poultry, and eggs, called on the federal government to reject any GATT deal that sacrifices the boards and leaves producers to the vagaries of an open market controlled by transnational companies.

By nullifying Canada's ability to determine its own national farm policies, the GATT, the NAFTA, and the FTA all contribute to a situation where this country is increasingly dependent on imported food, and may not be able to feed its own people using its own resources.

FREE TRADE, FOOD, AND HUNGER

FARMERS FIGHT BACK This February 1992 protest was a demonstration of farmers' growing anger at Tory policies. Canadian farm debt now stands at $23 billion, and 77,000 farms are considered to be in 'imminent danger' of failing.

PHOTO BY FRED CHARTRAND/ CANAPRESS

many as 77,000 farm operations across the country are considered to be in "imminent danger" of failing because of severe financial difficulties brought on by low commodity prices and high operating costs, according to the House of Commons Standing Committee on Agriculture.

HISTORICAL DEVELOPMENT OF AGRICULTURE IN CANADA While the recent push toward free trade through the Canada-U.S. Free Trade Agreement (FTA), the North American Free Trade Agreement (NAFTA), and the General Agreement on Tariffs and Trade (GATT) is accelerating the trend toward globalization along corporate lines, the historical reality of Canadian agricultural policy is that primary production has always served as a means for the enrichment of the industrial sector. As the late Vernon Fowke, a political economist at the University of Saskatchewan, revealed in his 1947 book, *Canadian Agricultural Policy: The Historical Pattern*, agriculture has always been used primarily for commercial and political ends. In the early years, he points out, it was used as a means of defending territory and trade routes. Later it was the "provisioner of the great staple trades," such as the fur trade. Finally, in the first half of the twentieth century, it provided an investment outlet for surplus industrial capital.

Prior to 1850, attempts by both French and British colonial governments to establish export-based agriculture were less than successful, and virtually all the food grown was consumed locally. The decline of the fur trade and the influx of immigrants created new market opportunities for investment in agriculture. Wheat grown in the St. Lawrence River valley first became a staple export around 1850, and continued to be the major commodity as the agricultural frontier expanded westward. The wheat trade and the opening up of new lands were so closely tied together that the federal Bureau of Agriculture, founded in 1852, was actually an "immigration and colonization agency," according to Fowke. A successful agriculture was viewed by the government around the time of Confederation as one which was constantly expanding, and which therefore required investment and servicing by commercial, financial, industrial, and transportation interests.

Agriculture, particularly in western Canada, became an expanding frontier. As long as that process continued, capital invested in agriculture continued to grow. After World War II, however, the agriculture sector's infrastructure (roads, elevators, railways, etc.) was basically built up, and investment capital increasingly turned to more lucrative opportunities in other industries. A further inflation-fueled expansion period occurred during the 1970s as lending institutions poured capital into the industry on the basis of rising farmland values. The 1980s and 1990s, however, have seen a full-scale retreat by financial institutions from new investments in agriculture, leaving farm families carrying the full burden of accumulated debt built up over the past two decades.

Canadian agriculture has historically been highly integrated into a capitalist market system. In virtually all areas of the country, from the mid-nineteenth century on, the emphasis of agricultural production was on raising commodities for an external market outside the local community. Self-sufficiency has not been a major tradition in Canada, as it has been in other countries such as Mexico.

In general, farm policy in Canada is the result of pressures from the industrial sector – offset periodically by counterpressures from the organized farm movement, which fought to wrest some economic and political control from the major companies. The shifts in national policy from free trade to protectionism and back to free trade reflect the commercial interests of the corporate sector, rather than the needs of family farm-based agriculture.

THE MEXICAN AGRICULTURAL SYSTEM   While Canadian agriculture has historically been extremely dependent on export markets, Mexico's production and distribution patterns have followed a slightly different path. In Mexico, two economies have had an uneasy coexistence throughout the nineteenth and twentieth centuries. An internal economy based on meeting local needs contrasted sharply with an export-oriented cattle and vegetable agro-industry aimed at supplying the American market.

> 'Our problems were created by various levels of government, and government has to help us out ... We had our throats cut by the free trade agreement and they're offering us a Band-Aid.'
>
> KEN PORTEOUS, PRESIDENT OF THE ONTARIO FRUIT AND VEGETABLE GROWERS ASSOCIATION, APRIL 1991

FARM CRISIS, MEXICAN VERSION Integrating Mexico's farms into the continental agro-industry will mean the death of community-owned operations like this, which produce food for local needs.
PHOTO BY ELAINE BRIERE

Up until the 1960s, the majority of Mexicans lived in rural areas and their food systems were largely self-sufficient. Local production of staples like corn and beans was generally adequate to meet local demand, except for the period from 1910 to 1920 during the Mexican revolution. This "peasant agriculture" functioned largely outside the market economy which linked northern Mexico to the United States. In the 1800s, peasant agriculture was predominant, but there were sizable pockets of American investment in giant cattle ranches and vegetable plantations. North-south railway lines linked Texas, California, Arizona, and New Mexico with the northern tier states of Mexico. Exports boomed from 1890 to 1910 – so much so that demands for additional land from the export sector resulted in mass dispossessions of peasants. A decade of struggle by rural Mexicans eventually culminated in the implementation of a system of *ejidos* – publicly held land which was farmed in common by a group of people. Creation of the *ejidos* boosted food production, but in the 1950s and 1960s, agricultural exports gradually assumed a greater role in providing foreign exchange to Mexico, and the government undertook policies aimed at "industrializing" the countryside.

In the period between 1940 and 1980, according to Steven Sanderson (in *The Transformation of Mexican Agriculture*, Princeton University Press, 1986), the role of agriculture changed considerably. "No longer was the agricultural sector primarily designed to produce fresh foodstuffs for the domestic population; it functioned now more as an 'input' sector for agribusiness and trade. Likewise, the main function of agriculture shifted from feeding the rural population in widely varying market and nonmarket relations to feeding the enormous urban populations, who were without access to the means of food production themselves. Basic food production was no longer the principal goal of the agricultural system; it was geared increasingly to support agribusiness processors, retailers, and intermediaries, whether at the international or the national level."

Agriculture's pivotal social importance also declined as more people moved from rural to urban centres. It became a "holding tank for the marginally employed, a buffer for an economy whose structure encouraged the elimination of the peasantry but whose absorptive capacity in wage labor did not permit the transition from peasant to proletarian," according to Sanderson.

In the 1980s, Mexican agriculture experienced a severe crisis as a result of policies initiated in the 1960s. The Mexican government had poured millions of dollars into modernizing export-oriented agribusiness enterprises in an effort to earn foreign exchange. But the value of those export commodities continued to fall as a

---

FOOD WORKERS, FARMERS HIT HARD BY TRADE DEAL

Jim Sinclair

Buying Canadian-grown fruit or vegetables could become a thing of the past.

Fruit and vegetable farmers fear the end of the Canadian industry if the trade deal with Mexico proceeds. Their industry has faced an uphill battle since the FTA signalled the end of tariffs which allowed the industry to survive. Extending the competition to Mexico will simply make matters worse.

"It doesn't sound very impressive to us. We were hurt very badly in the trade deal with the United States," says David Hobson, vice-president of the B.C. Fruit Growers Association. "Large companies see the potential for cheap land, cheap labour, a good climate, and few pesticide regulations, and they will create large commercial orchards."

Tough times for apple farmers have forced them to appeal for a marketing board similar to the ones which regulate production for dairy and chicken farmers. U.S. pressure is threatening to destroy marketing boards at this round of GATT talks.

Vegetable growers are already seeing an increase in Mexican imports of broccoli, strawberries, and cauliflower. This will turn to a flood if tariffs are removed and Mexicans continue to increase food production for exports.

Grape growers have also seen their industry destroyed as a result of free trade. In Ontario, 40 percent of the vineyards have been ripped up, and 70 percent of B.C.'s are gone.

Food processing is being affected by cheap imports and plant closures. "Our industry got hammered," says Doug Kitson, vice-president of Royal City Foods Ltd. "And we don't want to get hammered again."

Food processing is the largest manufacturing sector in Canada, but plants are already heading south. A Bank of Nova Scotia assessment reported that, with the FTA, "major U.S.-owned canning companies will likely move to the United States where excess capacity exists and overall costs are lower."

David Clark, Campbell Soup Co. Ltd. chairman, says free trade has forced the company to close plants, including Ontario chicken plants, mushroom farms, and its Quebec pasta business. This has left four plants in Canada, down from eleven plants five years ago. There is also a trend away from Canadian exports to the U.S. market, and the amount of food imported from the U.S. parent company has nearly doubled.

Protecting farmers and food processing is not just good economics, but an issue of vital national security.

result of global market conditions. Investors pulled out of agriculture in favour of industries like oil which offered higher returns. As export crops like cotton, coffee, wheat, and vegetables displaced domestic staples, the government was forced to import more food in an effort to feed the urban working class. Mexico is no longer self-sufficient in food, resulting in a serious problem of malnutrition and hunger for an increasing number of people.

CULTIVATING HUNGER The shift in Mexican agriculture toward a greater dependence on exports and away from self-reliance is a direct result of its integration into an international market economy. If the NAFTA is implemented, the loss of national sovereignty over food policy will be aggravated, amplifying social and economic inequality.

In the dying weeks of 1991, the Mexican Congress passed legislation effectively dismantling the *ejidos*, freeing roughly one-half of the country's farmland for foreign investment, and putting the livelihood of 3.1 million rural people in jeopardy. Designed to distribute land to farm families when they were first established, *ejidos* allowed land to be passed on to descendants but prohibited sale or rental. *Ejidos* were also immune from expropriation and repossession by government and industry.

The new law prohibits the formation of any new *ejidos* and blocks land from being acquired by existing *ejidos*. Passage of the law was a prerequisite for Mexican participation in the NAFTA, because it effectively killed protection for domestic corn production in Mexico, and opened up a market for U.S. exports.

While the NAFTA is promoted by governments as a vehicle for creating prosperity in the agricultural sector through trade, the reality is that an export oriented agricultural economy greatly increases the probability of hunger and malnutrition. Impoverished and marginalized people are, by definition, excluded from the market because they lack money to buy commodities. Under a free trade regime, the focus of agricultural production is on exports, not on meeting the needs of the domestic population.

Given the fact that half of Mexico's 88.3 million people are already malnourished, that one in seven people in the United States lives in abject poverty, and that half a million Canadians are so impoverished they must rely on food banks to survive, a continental free trade deal is likely to aggravate, rather than alleviate, a growing hunger problem.

Terry Pugh is editor of the *Union Farmer*, a monthly newspaper published by the National Farmers Union. In 1987 he edited the book *Fighting the Farm Crisis* for Fifth House Publishers of Saskatoon.

Special thanks to Annette Desmarais for research assistance in the preparation of this article.

Free Trade and Medicare

Is medicare in worse shape today than it was before free trade? The answer is an unequivocal yes

by Chris Gainor

Three weeks before the conclusion of the November 1988 election that was fought over the free trade deal with the United States, Brian Mulroney was on the defensive. "The simple, unvarnished truth is that medicare, pensions and other social programs are not at risk in the Free Trade Agreement," the Conservative prime minister assured a crowd in Victoria, lashing out at both an NDP television ad and speeches by Liberal leader John Turner that claimed the opposite. Voters' concerns about medicare were threatening the plans of Mulroney and his business backers to advance their right-wing agenda after the election. Mulroney's word wasn't enough to defuse the issue, so the next day, Emmett Hall, the 89-year-old retired Supreme Court judge who is acknowledged as the father of Canadian medicare, appeared before the media to say that he could find nothing in the agreement that affected medicare. To make sure the point wasn't lost in Quebec, Claude Castonguay, the former provincial health minister and future Tory senator, delivered the same message. Relieved Tories, who now could assure Canadians that medicare was safe in their hands, were back on the road to electoral victory.[1]

In the U.S., tens of millions of people face ruin every time illness strikes

To the end of the campaign, both sides stuck to their stories. The pro-free trade forces claimed that medicare wasn't mentioned in the deal, therefore medicare was safe. The anti-free trade side replied that medicare wasn't specifically protected in the agreement, therefore medicare was in danger. They also noted that the agreement did specifically open up provision of health care administration to U.S. corporations.

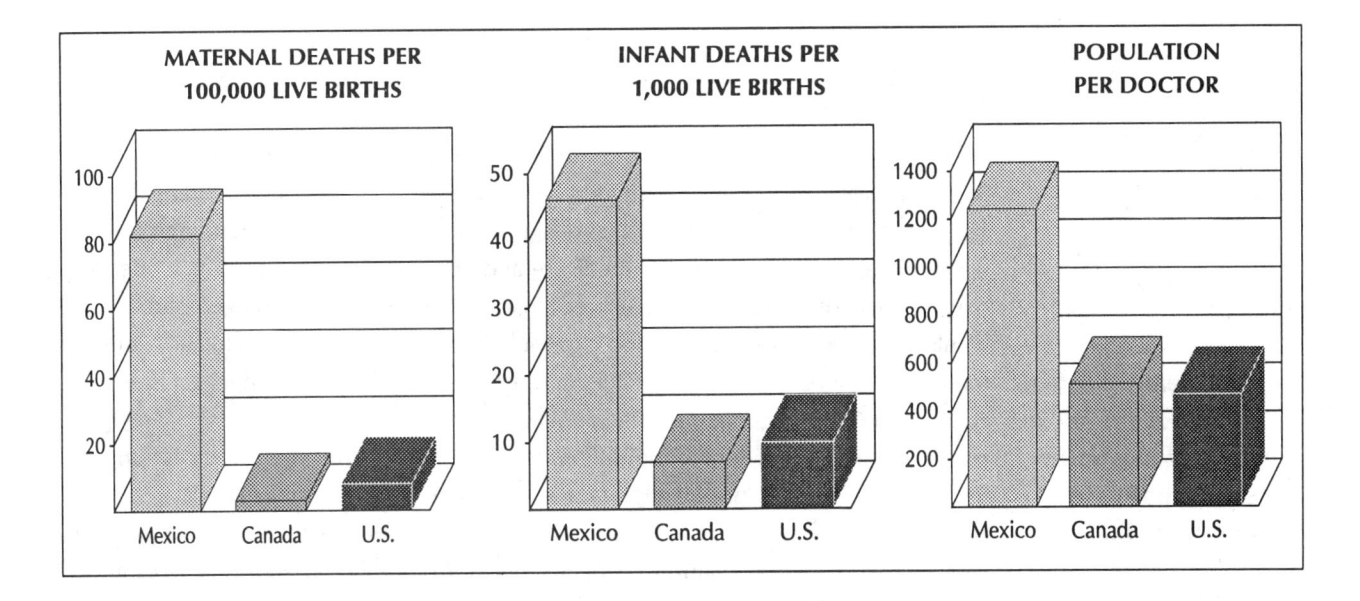

FREE TRADE AND MEDICARE

MATERNAL DEATHS PER 100,000 LIVE BIRTHS	INFANT DEATHS PER 1,000 LIVE BIRTHS	POPULATION PER DOCTOR

BASIC HEALTH INDICATORS The first graph (left) shows the number of women who die in childbirth per 100,000 births. The centre graph shows the number of children who die at birth per 1000 live births. The last graph shows the number of people per doctor in each country.

Now that free trade has been in effect for more than three years, it is time to reopen the debate that many people believe ended when Hall and Castonguay spoke. Is Canadian medicare in worse shape today than in 1988, before free trade? The answer is an unequivocal yes. The free trade deal has a lot to do with the growing problems threatening Canadian medicare, and the proposed three-way deal which would include Mexico in a North American free trade zone would be another blow against Canadian medicare.

Canada's publicly supported health care system is clearly superior to the health care system in the U.S., where the influence of the private sector is much larger. Virtually every Canadian is assured of quality health care without direct financial cost. In the U.S., tens of millions of people face the ruin of their finances and health every time illness strikes, and the number of people in this position grows every day.

CANADA: MEDICARE'S FINANCIAL CRUNCH A few days before the third anniversary of the free trade election, the Canadian Health Coalition linked up five Canadian cities by television to mark a different milestone, the thirtieth anniversary of the passage of medicare in Saskatchewan, the first province to have the system all Canadians now enjoy. The teleconference was not a celebration, because the major topic was not the step forward of 1961, but the crisis of 1991. The coalition, supported by trade unions and health care providers, was in the midst of a battle against the latest move by the Tory government to cut federal funding to medicare.

A decade after it was born in Saskatchewan, medicare became a reality for all

> 'I'm really worried about the social fabric... My father, my grandfather and I fought for medicare and all those things. We don't want to be like the southern States. If Canada ever turns anybody away from a hospital because they don't have any money, I'll go to war. I don't want to be an American. I'm happy to be a Canadian.'
>
> DOUG SWANSON,
> PRESIDENT OF STEELWORKERS LOCAL 480, TRAIL, B.C.

Canadians, largely because of federal legislation under which the federal government split the cost of medical and hospital services with the provinces. Neither level of government was happy with this 50-50 split – the federal government because it could not control costs in provincially controlled programs, and the provinces because they had to account to Ottawa for their spending. In 1977, the Liberal government of Pierre Elliott Trudeau set up a new funding formula which folded together grants for medicare and post-secondary education. Under the new setup, called Established Programs Financing or EPF, the federal government would increase grants according to a formula based on growth in population and the Gross Domestic Product or GDP. In return, the provinces no longer had to account to Ottawa for their health spending.

With a fall in the federal contribution from 50 percent and with the recession of the early 1980s, it did not take long for the pressure to be felt in Canada's provincially run health care systems. Bed closures hit several provinces, and hospital workers faced wage restraints and layoffs. British Columbia turned to user fees and Ontario looked the other way while doctors extra-billed their patients. With the support of Mulroney's Tories, the Trudeau government passed the Canada Health Act in 1984, enshrining the principles of medicare in law, and outlawing extra billing and user fees. The lever, which was successfully used in B.C. and Ontario, was the threat of deductions from EPF payments to any province to match every dollar earned by the government in user fees, or spent by patients on extra-billing.

Before the Liberals left office in 1984, they had unilaterally tinkered twice with the EPF funding formula, setting a poor precedent for the Conservatives to exploit when they took the reins. In spite of promises to do the opposite, the Tories have cut the EPF formula four times, three times since the 1988 election. Increases in EPF are now frozen for the five years starting in 1990, and then the formula will increase at the GDP growth rate, minus 3 percentage points. The latest cut to the EPF formula was contained in Bill C-20, which was passed in late 1991 despite the Canadian Health Coalition's campaign against it, which included the teleconference and a round of public hearings by the House of Commons finance committee. In the fight against the Tories' previous cut to the EPF formula in 1990's Bill C-69, the coalition and its allies pointed out that federal cash payments under EPF would end in most provinces early in the next decade, leaving the Canada Health Act toothless against extra billing and user fees. Instead of restoring the full EPF formula, the Tories cut the EPF formula again with Bill C-20 and included a section in the bill which will allow them to cut federal contributions to other programs such as welfare or equalization if the Canada Health Act is violated. In its brief to the finance committee, the coalition warned that the provinces will fight this part of Bill C-20 in court. Quebec, which refuses to recognize the Canada Health Act, is in the process

FREE TRADE AND MEDICARE

FREE MARKET HEALTH CARE ... means cutting-edge technology and four-star service for the rich, but long waits in older, over-crowded hospitals for those non-rich able to afford health insurance. Millions more in the U.S. don't even have it this good.

PHOTO BY RICKY FLORES/ IMPACT VISUALS

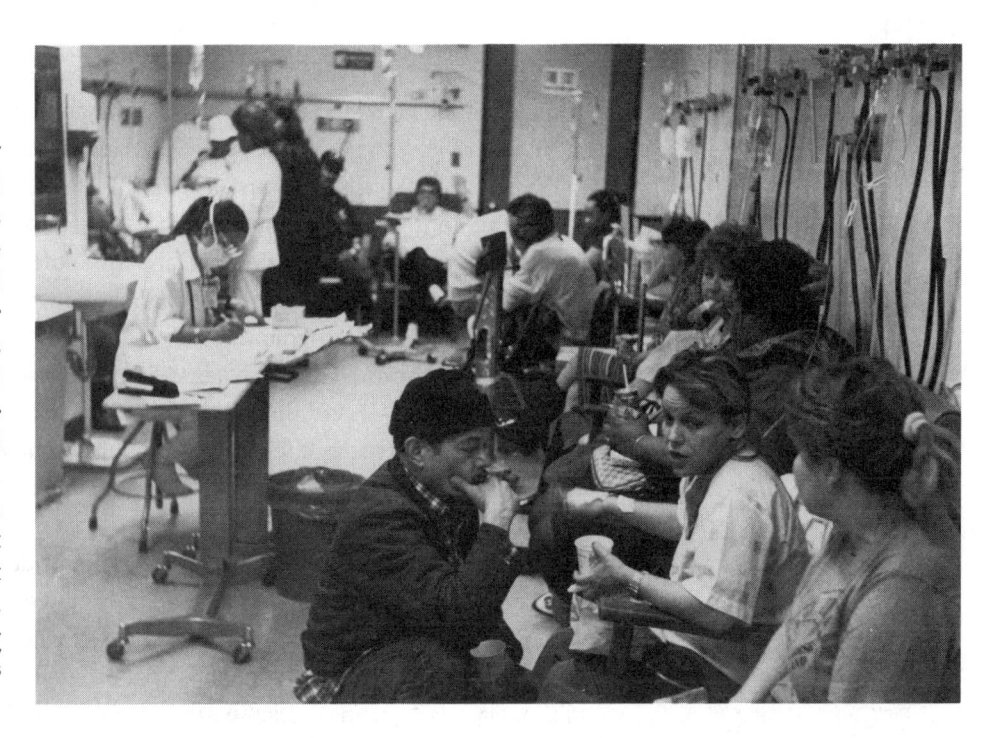

of introducing user fees and appears ready to fight any federal effort to quash them.

So what is behind these cuts in federal funding for medicare, and what are the results? The cuts to EPF are part of a wider Tory and big business agenda of defunding and reducing Canada's social programs. Officially, the cuts to EPF are justified on the grounds of fighting the deficit. The Tories and their allies in business blame social programs for large federal deficits since the 1960s. This belief was exposed as a fraud by a Statistics Canada study in 1991 which showed that high interest rates, and tax breaks for corporations and the wealthy, were to blame for federal deficits, not social programs, which have accounted for a stable portion of federal spending in the last two decades.[2] The Tory argument that provinces are simply being "asked" to do their part to fight the federal deficit is also questionable at best, because cuts in transfer payments account for 46 percent of federal spending cuts, while these transfer payments account for only 20 percent of federal program spending.[3]

Cutting transfer funds between levels of government is a devilishly clever way to destroy social programs. In the same 1985 budget in which Michael Wilson took his first whack at the EPF formula, the Tory finance minister also tried to de-index pensions. The resulting protests by senior citizens seriously wounded the government, a lesson which was remembered by Mulroney and Wilson. When they were re-elected and returned to their agenda of sacrificing social programs in the name of deficit reduction, Wilson targeted cost-shared programs such as medicare, post-secondary education, and the Canada Assistance Plan, which helps fund welfare. By using this route, only provincial premiers and finance ministers would scream instead of thousands of voters. As the simplified explanation in the preceding paragraphs suggests, reductions in transfer funds are much more complicated to explain than a pension cut, and therefore are more difficult to oppose. What appears to be yet another squabble between politicians disguises a direct Tory attack on social programs.

"If there is one responsibility which lies with the federal government, it is to safeguard the key principles set out in the Canada Health Act: universality, accessibility, portability, comprehensivity and public administration. In this connection, the federal government is still as determined as ever to ensure maintenance of these principles in their entirety within the provincial health systems," federal Health and Welfare Minister Benoit Bouchard assured the 1991 meeting of the Canadian Medical Association as his government prepared to ram the Bill C-20 cuts through parliament. This statement, which follows in a long line from Mulroney's "sacred trust" pledge for social programs, was swallowed whole by Canada's media, which tends to blame medicare's woes on rising costs at least as much as on the federal cuts. While it is true that Canadian health care costs are rising at a rate above inflation – a fact that means reforms are needed as

---

AMERICAN STORIES
Chris Gainor

Some Americans do without needed treatment. Others sell their cars, homes, and valuables, and still face the onslaughts of collection agencies sent by their hospitals. Individuals and small businesses face crushing health insurance premiums. Some workers stay in jobs they hate because a job change would cost them their health insurance.

Millions of Americans live with no health insurance, and more live with inadequate health insurance. Many think they are covered, only to receive unpleasant surprises from their insurers. Here are a few stories of Americans who have fallen through what passes for a social net.

Bobby Jean McLaughlin: In a corporate downsizing exercise, the Charleston, West Virginia, woman lost her $6.20-an-hour department store manager job, and with it, her health insurance. Her husband, who worked in a bakery which didn't provide health insurance, was suffering from emphysema, so she took a lump sum payment in lieu of a pension to pay his medical bills. Now her husband is dead, and she earns minimum wage at the same bakery where he worked, trying to make ends meet while paying off a $24,000 hospital bill.

Dana Van Putten: This New York theatrical wardrobe worker and single mother is covered through her union, but she can't afford the $400 a month she would have to pay for a family policy. Her son David was in intensive care for five days after his birth, leaving her to pay bills of $16,195 for his care. "I'll never get that paid off, and I'll never be able to save money to buy a house. What are you supposed to do, go bankrupt?"

Betty Moore: She couldn't find a job in 1970 because health insurers at prospective employers wouldn't cover her due to a heart problem which had already required surgery.

governments cope with limited resources – the Mulroney government's attack on medicare turns the curable cost-control problem into a life-threatening affliction. Dr. Michael Rachlis, one of the leading advocates of Canadian health care reform, points out that the EPF cuts make it much more difficult to make needed changes.

The National Council of Welfare estimates that the four Tory cuts from EPF grants for medicare will cost the provinces $3.8 billion in 1992-93, and a staggering total of $66 billion from 1986 to 1996. Of Ontario's 1991-92 budget deficit of $9.7 billion, $3.7 billion of it is directly due to federal cuts to social programs, and the province projects that the federal cuts will cost it $4.5 billion in 1992-93. The B.C. government reports that Tory cuts to social programs will cost the province $1.1 billion in 1992, and the story is similar in other provinces.

Provincial budgets in 1991 featured tax hikes and service cuts to make up the Tory "offloading" of its deficit. Hundreds of beds were closed and thousands of hospital workers were laid off around Canada, especially in Newfoundland, where 300 nurses lost their jobs and 360 acute care beds closed in a province where federal funds make up almost half of the budget. Provinces are no longer funding services that were once taken for granted, such as drugs and extended health benefits for seniors, certain minor surgery, and eye examinations. Hospital workers who still have their jobs face wage restraints in many provinces, in spite of the fact that more than four-fifths of them are women dealing with systemic wage

---

She set up her own business in Alpharetta, Georgia, and got some help from her husband's insurance. He has left his job, leaving her without coverage and with doctors' bills. Moore is now hoping she can make it through the five years until she is 65 and eligible for public health insurance offered to senior citizens.

David Curnow: This San Diego lawyer was left a quadriplegic after he was struck by an uninsured driver while he was bicycle riding. Doctors and hospitals hounded him for payment of his $250,000 bill when his carrier refused to pay. Eventually the carrier paid, but now he is left with continuing medical bills. He won't be able to get insurance because of his disability, and his job prospects are further limited because of the health insurance question.

Kay Nichols: As a fitness instructor in Gainesville, Florida, 38-year-old Nichols is in good health except for glaucoma, which can cause blindness if not treated. Her employer couldn't change insurers to get a better premium because she would lose her coverage. Insurers won't cover pre-existing health problems, even something that is under control like Nichols' glaucoma. "Maybe I don't want to stay with this company the rest of my life. It makes me worry."

Coila McElroy: When the family of this 94-year-old Arizona woman ran out of money to keep her in the nursing home where she had lived for years, the home put her possessions in plastic bags, and took her and the bags to a public hospital, where a nurse said: "They dumped her. Anybody who knows anything about the elderly understands that a disruption like this is dangerous. But they did it anyway. Because of money."

SOURCES: *PHILADELPHIA INQUIRER, NEW YORK TIMES, CONSUMER REPORTS, ARIZONA REPUBLIC*

discrimination. At the same time, the Tory government in Ottawa looked the other way when Quebec attacked the medicare principle of portability by refusing to sign a medicare agreement the nine other provinces have signed. Now Quebec is about to attack the principles of accessibility and universality with its user fees. Before the demise of B.C.'s Social Credit government and Saskatchewan's Tory government in the fall of 1991, the four western provinces discussed "disentanglement" of cost-shared programs, and changes in medicare that would eliminate universality and open the door to user fees, extra billing, and more privatization. More recently, the Liberal premiers of Newfoundland and New Brunswick have begun to talk about user fees and ending universality. Under the pressure of Tory funding cutbacks, the condition of medicare in Canada is rapidly deteriorating. Many Canadians have feared that the U.S. government would use the countervail provisions of the free trade deal to attack medicare as an unfair subsidy. With the Tories undermining medicare, such an action is unnecessary.

If one accepts that the free trade deal with the U.S. and cuts to social programs are part of one neoconservative agenda, the link between free trade and the attack on medicare is clear. But the link between free trade and the poor state of medicare became undeniable on January 21, 1992, when Ontario Premier Bob Rae announced that federal cutbacks and a recession, which has hit Ontario and Quebec harder than elsewhere because of free trade, meant that Ontario hospitals would be held to a one percent budget increase in 1992 and two percent annually in the two years to follow. Because of the impact of inflation, this means budget reductions. The president of the Ontario Hospital Association predicted that 13,000 hospital workers would be laid off and 3,600 beds closed. Ontario registered a shrinkage of its economic activity in 1990 and 1991 due to high interest rates, the high Canadian dollar, and the freedom the Canada-U.S. Free Trade Agreement gives corporations to move jobs south of the border. It is certain that other provinces will make more cuts to health services and hospital beds in 1992.

The evidence is mounting that free trade has seriously damaged the Canadian economy, and it is now clearly reducing the ability of both federal and provincial governments to raise funds to pay for health and social services. Because Canadian governments see themselves competing with U.S. jurisdictions when setting tax levels for corporations, free trade means that cutting health care services is more acceptable. Free trade's effects on Canada's economic base reduce the money available for social services, while putting more pressure on those services because of high unemployment. Indeed, opponents of free trade say federal cutbacks in

FREE TRADE AND MEDICARE

unemployment insurance and welfare are designed to "harmonize" Canadian income support programs with those in the U.S. as part of the free trade deal. The increased poverty which results will mean even further demands on Canada's health care system. This cycle will grow more vicious under a free trade arrangement which includes Mexico, because more jobs and economic activity will leave Canada.

A FREE TRADE PRESCRIPTION   The question of prescription drugs isn't officially dealt with in the FTA, but that doesn't mean that it isn't an integral part of the deal. Despite denials from the Tory government that drugs were part of the free trade deal, a U.S. summary of the deal, issued at the conclusion of free trade talks in October 1987, mentioned a Canadian promise to pass legislation extending patent protection to pharmaceutical drugs. Two months later, the Tories passed Bill C-22, giving the multinationals seven to ten years' patent protection against generic copies of their drugs. The patent law was a major victory for the multinationals and their supporters in Washington, but it wasn't the total victory the multinationals wanted. That's why prescription drugs and the whole issue of "intellectual property" are bound to be part of a North American Free Trade Agreement.

Pharmaceuticals have been among the more durable trade irritants between the U.S. and its neighbours, Canada and Mexico. The reason is that both Mexico and Canada have permitted compulsory licensing of pharmaceuticals in their countries.

WASHINGTON BELIEVES IN TIERS Profit-oriented health care means two-tier care: one system for those with money, another for the rest of us. Publicly funded facilities which deliver care to the non-rich, such as Sydenham Hospital in New York, are being closed down to help balance city and state budgets.
PHOTO BY LAURIE PEEK/ IMPACT VISUALS

> 'It is simply a fact that, as we ask our industries to compete toe to toe with American industry ... we in Canada are obviously forced to create the same conditions in Canada that exist in the U.S., whether it is the unemployment insurance scheme, Workmens' Compensation, the cost of government, the level of taxation, or whatever.'
>
> LAURENT THIBAULT, PRESIDENT OF THE CANADIAN MANUFACTURERS ASSOCIATION

Compulsory licensing permits companies to apply for a license to manufacture and import generic versions of the patent holder's product during the life of the patent.

Canada's longstanding but narrow compulsory licensing law was widened in 1969, generating an expensive battle on all fronts against it by multinational drug companies, whose levels of profitability are head and shoulders above other industries. The multinationals, many of whose Canadian operations are based in Montreal, have used the English-French issue throughout the battle against compulsory licensing. In 1983, the federal Liberal government was feeling the heat in this tender spot, so they launched an inquiry into the matter. The Eastman Report, which found that compulsory licensing had little impact on the profitability of the multinationals, landed in 1985 on the desks of the new Tory government. Eastman found that in 1983, Canadian consumers saved $211 million in a pharmaceutical market that totalled $1.6 billion. But the Tories set about to give the multinationals much stronger protection in Bill C-20 than Eastman recommended. The Reagan administration put pressure on the Mulroney government throughout the free trade talks,[4] and Mulroney, having led the Tories out of the Quebec political wilderness, was sensitive to the fact that the multinationals had politicians from every part of the Quebec political spectrum lined up behind them. The multinationals promised that drug prices would not rise above inflation, that research spending in Canada would rise, and that 2,000 new jobs related to pharmaceutical research would be created in Canada by 1995. In his recent study for the Canadian Centre for Policy Alternatives, Dr. Joel Lexchin found that while the price increases for drugs under patent have fallen below inflation since 1987, price hikes for other pharmaceuticals have not, and the lack of generic competition has removed the effect of price competition on new drugs. Research spending by the multinationals has risen, but most of this spending has followed the tradition of funding clinical studies of existing drugs and of drugs similar to existing products; it is certainly not producing the exciting breakthroughs promised by the multinationals. Lexchin projected that the new jobs created would fall below the targets promised by the multinationals, and added that hundreds of manufacturing jobs have been lost in this industry in Canada.[5]

Throughout 1991, Canadian television viewers were bombarded by television ads from the multinationals, boasting of their research innovations. The reason was a promised cabinet review, late in the year, of the future of drug patents in Canada. On January 14, 1992, Michael Wilson, now trade minister, announced that his government would endorse a proposal, made at the talks for a new General Agreement on Tariffs and Trade, that called for full 20-year patent protection for pharmaceuticals, in line with existing practices in the U.S. This announcement means that the goal of the multinationals is in sight. Although Wilson's announcement is officially related to GATT, the link to free trade is also clear. Because Bill C-22 wasn't a total capitulation to the multinationals, Washington kept the pressure on Ottawa by putting Canada on a special trade "watch list."

Mexico has felt similar pressure from its powerful neighbour. Washington fought compulsory licensing in Mexico with the "watch list" and the withdrawal of preferential tariff treatment for Mexican chemical products in 1987. The pressure worked, and now Mexico is in the process of extending the patent protection for pharmaceuticals to 20 years. Although Washington is winning the pharmaceutical war without a new free trade deal, intellectual property rights are the subject of one of the negotiating groups in the NAFTA talks. Strong intellectual property rights provisions in NAFTA or GATT will allow multinational corporations to defend monopolies and drain royalties from Canada, Mexico, and elsewhere.[6]

Strong intellectual property rights assist large corporations and discourage innovation and economic development where they exist, as the pharmaceutical industry demonstrates. The link between patents and innovation is very tenuous,

---

GETTING SICK IN THE U.S.A.

Judy Haiven

New Year's Day 1990, 10 p.m. The phone rings. "Mrs. Haiven, drop everything and come to the hospital immediately. Your husband has had a serious heart attack. He's critical."

Course of treatment: Monitoring in the cardiac care unit, followed by several days on the medical ward. Tests assigned: blood work, electrocardiogram, X-ray, ultrasound, angiogram, exercise stress test, and others. Prescribed: Medication to ease cardiac function and to "thin" blood. Prognosis: The patient seems to be doing well and will be discharged to a cardiac rehabilitation program and placed on relevant medication.

Charge to patient: $0.00. The costs wil be paid by the provincial government medical insurance. This is Canada, after all.

I had seen American friends burdened with unending payments on uninsured medical bills. I had listened to stories of seniors deprived of their savings to pay for chronic care. I had watched TV shows about patient "dumping" after the most cursory emergency treatment. I shuddered as I wondered what it would have been like if Larry, my husband, had been hospitalized in the United States.

I didn't have long to wait to find out. The doctors gave their blessing to a brief holiday in a warmer climate, and we flew to Southern California in February to stay with our friends Connie and Mike. But we cut short a visit to Sea World when Larry complained of chest pains. When the pains persisted, I called 911. "I sure hope you have insurance for down here," whispered Connie, as the ambulance blared down the street toward Scripps Memorial Hospital.

Fortunately, it wasn't a second heart attack. But by the time the cardiologist determined this, Larry had spent four nights in the hospital, including one in intensive care, receiving virtually the same tests and medications as in Canada. For the hospital stay, specialists' fees, private lab work, and the ambulance, the charge was $12,590.34 (over $15,000 Canadian). Everything had been itemized, right down to the sample-sized tube of toothpaste ($5.25), the aspirin pill ($4.14), and the laxative ($17.04), which Larry didn't take.

I knew that a similar course of treatment in Canada would be "free" to the patient. But I wondered what it would really cost the health system as a whole. I consulted the authorities and learned that Larry's treatment in Saskatoon had cost the system $3,500 (U.S.).

SOURCE: 'Mediscare,' *Mother Jones*, March/April 1991

and research by the multinationals tends to be biased and limited in favour of drugs with the greatest potential profit. A large proportion of the multinationals' research is based on developing "me-too" drugs. As well, the basic research that does produce breakthroughs is usually based in the home countries of multinational firms. The multinationals have won a victory over home-grown generic drug industries in Canada and Mexico. The Canadian generic industry, which has so far weathered the storm caused by Bill C-22, is worth $400 million, employs 2,300 people, and also does its own research and development.

Prescription drugs are becoming a hot issue as provincial governments struggle to contain health care costs. Individuals are feeling the pinch as drug entitlements are cut and deductibles increased by provincial prescription drug programs, which are used mainly by seniors and the poor. The B.C. Royal Commission on Health Care and Costs reports that between 1985 and 1989, direct drug costs rose annually at an average rate of 13.7 percent above inflation. Part of the reason is price increases by the multinationals and the lack of competition in this industry. As well, multinationals spend huge amounts of money on promotion – 17 percent of their sales revenues, according to the Eastman report. The drug companies' promotional spending in 1984 worked out to $4,500 for each physician in Canada. Evidence is mounting that many Canadians suffer from overuse and over-reliance on pharmaceutical drugs prescribed by physicians whose main source of information on these products is the pharmaceutical drug industry.[7] The effort to reform the place of drugs in treatment of illness will not be assisted by boosting the power of multinational drug companies through free trade deals.

MANAGING MEDICAL PROFITS The flashpoint for much of the medicare – free trade debate in 1988 was a provision of the free trade deal which makes the management of hospitals and other health care facilities open to corporations from both countries. At the time, Hawkesbury and District General Hospital in Ontario was in the sixth year of having its management provided by American Medical

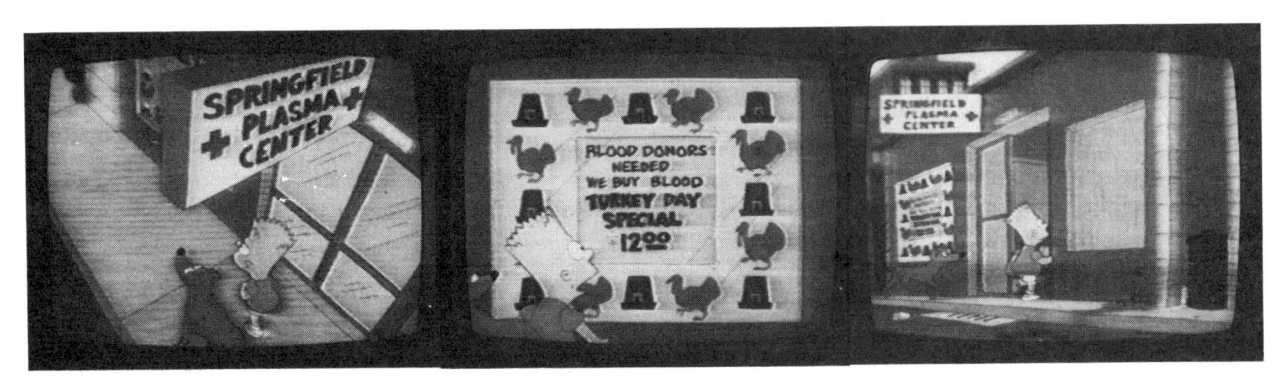

KINDER, GENTLER HEALTH CARE Bart Simpson takes advantage of a uniquely American institution – a private cash-for-blood donor clinic. The U.S. health care system is becoming a major issue for U.S. voters, who don't like the way it compares to the Canadian model.

> 'I give you the assurance that I gave my mother, and that I would give my mother if she were on the blower to me right now... 'Ma, your medicare is okay, your pension is okay, everything is protected.' What free trade is going to do is give Canada more money so we can do more for all of you. And God bless you all.'
>
> BRIAN MULRONEY,
> 3 NOVEMBER 1988

International, one of three major corporations which control three quarters of "for-profit" hospital beds in the U.S. At the time, the push was on from right-wing governments and big business for more privatization of public services, including those in health care.

In part because of the lack of solid data on trade in this area, the record on health management so far is ambiguous. For example, AMI quietly left Hawkesbury in 1990, five years before its contract was due to expire. The big three in U.S. hospital corporations – AMI, Humana, and the Hospital Corporation of America – have not made any major incursions into Canada since the free trade deal took effect. But contracting out of management and other services continues to grow in Canada. Extendicare, the health care subsidiary of the Canadian multinational Crownx, owns long-term care facilities used mainly by the elderly in all parts of Canada, as well as in the U.S. and the United Kingdom. Extendicare manages hospitals in Olds and Athabasca, Alberta, the extended care wing of the Queensway General Hospital in Toronto, and the Hoyles-Escasoni long-term care facility in Newfoundland. Versa Services, another Canadian multinational, provides food services to Canadian hospitals. The Canadian subsidiary of the U.S.-based Marriott Corporation is also providing housekeeping services in Canadian hospitals, such as St. Paul's Hospital in Vancouver. Governments in B.C. and Alberta have compelled hospitals to contract out laundry work to companies such as the Alberta-based K-Bro Linen Systems. Psicor Inc., which provides equipment and operators for the heart-lung machines needed in open heart surgery, has its first contract outside the U.S. in Toronto. Other U.S. companies offering technical health services are also looking north, and services such as medical transcription are being contracted out and done outside Canada.

The limited use of private hospital management in Canada is probably related to the fact that there is virtually no proof that private management is more efficient in Canada or the U.S., unless "cream skimming" of easy-to-treat cases is employed by the private facilities.[8] The quality of contracted-out management and services is under constant fire. For example, contracted-out food services in smaller centres means local merchants are bypassed and patients eat prepackaged food instead of fresh food.

Many of the changes taking place in Canadian hospitals today are related to the growing numbers of hospital administrators and their increasing use of methods developed in the private sector. Hospital administrators now call themselves CEOs and vice-presidents of corporate services, and give themselves six-figure salaries to match. They contract out services more, and are now bringing in quality circles and other "team" concept programs designed to weaken unions and get more work out of hospital workers. Hospitals are experimenting with amalgamation. For example, the Toronto Hospital Corporation was formed from the Toronto Western and Toronto General hospitals. Nursing care in hospitals is being redefined in terms of tasks rather than care, ignoring and de-emphasizing the human and nurturing aspects of nursing.[9] Such redefinitions of other hospital work have cut off hospital workers from patients, contributing to union militancy in health care. Hospitals have set up foundations to tap donations from wealthy friends through lavish balls and from poorly paid staff through raffles. One result of this corporate ethos is clear: hospital costs continue to rise without a corresponding increase in the quality of care.

U.S. AND MEXICO: HEALTH CARE NIGHTMARES   One year before the 1992 U.S. presidential election, an unknown Democrat named Harris Wofford defeated George Bush's former attorney-general for a U.S. senate seat in Pennsylvania in what pundits called a shocking upset. Wofford overcame his opponent's overwhelming early lead, by calling for Canadian-style public health insurance. (Significantly, opposition to a NAFTA was another key plank in Wofford's platform.) Wofford's win followed reports from the General Accounting Office of the U.S. Congress and the *New England Journal of Medicine* which detailed the relative efficiency of Canada's public health insurance system compared to the U.S. private system. But the crucial factor is that growing numbers of Americans are falling through the growing cracks of the U.S. system.

The predictable riposte from Bush, his Republican allies, and the U.S. insurance business features twisted facts and horror stories about waiting lists for certain procedures in Canada. The battle being waged in the U.S. goes far beyond Bush's bid for a second term as president. It is also about the $175 billion Americans pay in health premiums every year and the billions made by U.S. physicians, along with the right-wing ideology that private services are always better than public services.

> **One result of the corporate ethos: hospital costs continue to rise without a corresponding increase in quality of care**

Until the mid-1960s, the U.S. and Canadian health care systems were virtually identical, and they cost the same. But in 1965 and 1966, the U.S. opted to leave all but the poor and elderly under private health insurance while Canada chose universal public health insurance. Today, the U.S. health care system is the most expensive in the world, gobbling up more than 12 percent of GDP. Canada's system, while still more expensive than other countries, accounts for only 9 percent of GDP. Per capita costs are significantly higher in the U.S. than Canada, but all Canadians have health coverage, while 34 million Americans – one in eight – have no health insurance, and another 50 million have inadequate health insurance. For example, five million

UNHEALTHY OUTLOOK Mexico spends considerably less on health care for its citizens than do Canada and the U.S. Under a NAFTA, this disparity would increase pressure on the Canadian government to get out of the health care business.
PHOTO BY ELAINE BRIERE

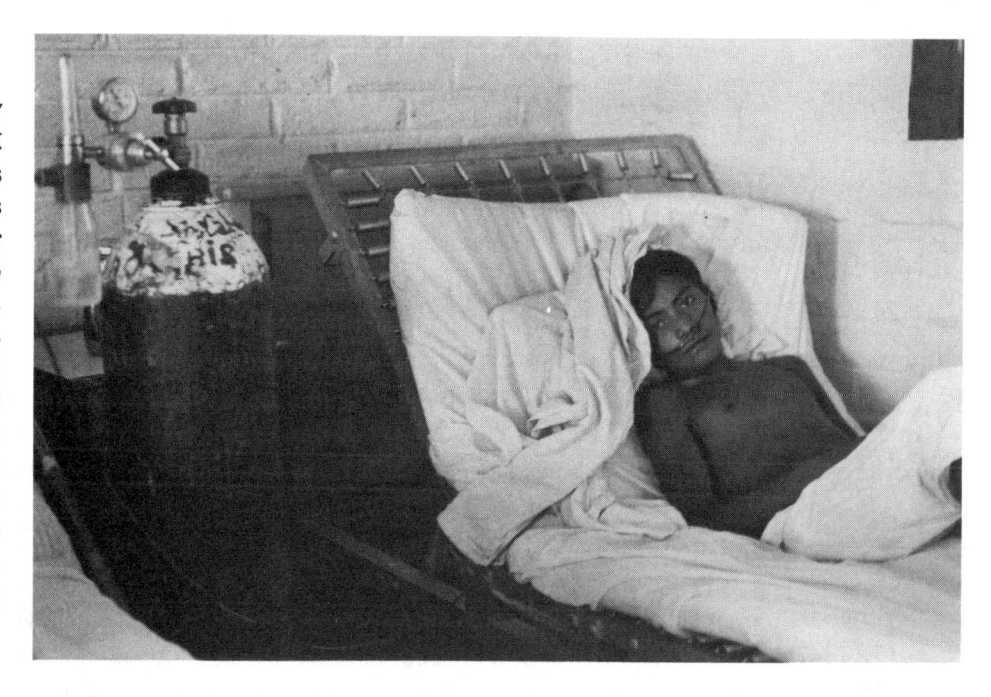

women of childbearing age have insurance that doesn't cover costs related to maternity. Most private insurance in the U.S. is provided by employers, but more than half of the uninsured are working, and their numbers are rising as soaring premiums cause smaller businesses to reduce or end health insurance, or cut pay to cover annual premium increases of up to 50 percent. In a 1984 survey, 37 percent of large U.S. employers were found to pay their employees' full premiums. Four years later, that figure had fallen to 24 percent.[10] Three-quarters of U.S. strikes in 1989 had health insurance as a major issue. Many previously insured Americans lost their coverage when their companies reorganized, laid them off, and then claimed bankruptcy. Chrysler chairman Lee Iacocca estimated in 1989 that health insurance added more than $700 to the price of each U.S. car, compared to $223 for Canadian-built cars. When it was set up, the publicly funded Medicaid covered 70 percent of Americans living below the poverty line. Now the figure is 38 percent, and many of those people have difficulty getting treatment or a hospital bed because Medicaid fees are so low. Canadian stats for life expectancy and infant mortality are significantly higher than those for the U.S., and now the lack of proper health insurance is being related to the reappearance of tuberculosis and other preventable public health problems in the U.S. These facts, and the growing numbers of middle-class Americans who are losing their health and wealth, have made U.S. health care a major political issue.

Even though polls show an overwhelming majority of Americans want to change

> 'Health care costs have risen *90 percent* while *insurance premiums* have risen *360 percent*! And not only are corporations cutting benefits, more and more are cutting the entire plan so that the number of workers covered by health care has dropped 20 percent in just 10 years. In 1987, 30 percent ($128 billion) of all health care costs in the U.S. were paid *out of pocket* by patients themselves! These shocking statistics have led unions to make national health care reform a top priority. How we envy our Canadian brothers and sisters.'
>
> JOYCE MILLER,
> VICE-PRESIDENT,
> AMALGAMATED CLOTHING
> & TEXTILE WORKERS

to public health insurance, the path to reform faces many obstacles. The American Medical Association, which opposes public health insurance, spent $5.3 million in the 1988 U.S. congressional elections. The following year it gave campaign money to 348 of the 535 members of the U.S. Congress. American Family Corp., the fifth largest seller of health insurance, is eighth on the U.S. election commission's list of top corporate campaign contributors, ahead of such giants as Boeing, Citicorp, and Ford.[11]

The hundreds of health insurance providers in the U.S. need an army of salespersons and bureaucrats to run the system. Health administration costs in the U.S. are estimated to be 117 percent higher than in Canada. Between 1983 and 1987, U.S. health administration costs rose 37 percent in real dollars, while in Canada they declined. The same study estimated that between $69 billion and $83 billion could have been saved in 1987 if U.S. health administration was as efficient as Canada's.[12] "If the universal coverage and single-payer features of the Canadian system were applied to the United States, the savings in administrative costs alone would be more than enough to finance insurance coverage for the millions of Americans who are currently uninsured," the General Accounting Office report stated. Clearly, the private U.S. system is much less efficient and effective than the public Canadian system. Therefore, it can be said that the stakes in the fight over medicare in the U.S. go beyond the political fortunes of Republicans or even the billions of dollars wasted in sales and administration. This battle goes right to the heart of conservative ideology: the idea, never supported by facts, that private business can do a better job than government. The battle in the U.S. will likely go on for years, and conservatives in Canada are gutting Canada's system to help their American allies win.

Mexico provides a handy warning to Canadians of what could happen. The Mexican government that is promoting policies such as free trade has also slashed public spending on health care, despite the fact that health care is provided for in the Mexican constitution. The budget for health services such as public hospitals and clinics fell from 4.7 percent of Mexican public spending in 1980 to 2.7 percent in 1989. The consequence of this is massive growth in the use of private health insurance in Mexico.[13] Like the U.S., Mexico has a two-tiered health system, and like the U.S., the population of the lower tier is growing rapidly.

Although there is no written provision ordering Canada and Mexico to harmonize their health care systems with the bloated, expensive, and unfair U.S. system, right-wing forces in both countries are making sure that the work is well under way. North American free trade will increase the pressure on both Canada and Mexico to cut public health programs, and the price could be our health.

1. Graham Fraser, *Playing for Keeps*, McClelland & Stewart, Toronto, 1989, pp. 328, 329, 352, 353.
2. H. Mimoto and P. Cross, "The Growth of the Federal Debt," *Canadian Economic Observer*, June 1991, Statistics Canada, Ottawa.
3. Ministry of Finance and Corporate Relations, British Columbia, "Federal Offloading: A Media Briefing," January 23, 1992.
4. Joel Lexchin, *Pharmaceuticals, Patents and Politics: Canada And Bill C-22*, Canadian Centre for Policy Alternatives, Ottawa, February 1992, pp. 1-5.
5. Lexchin, pp. 6-10.
6. John Dillon, "George Bush's war on [affordable prescription] drugs," *Action Canada Network Dossier*, July-August, 1991, pp. 13-14.
7. Michael Rachlis and Carol Kushner, *Second Opinion: What's Wrong with Canada's Health Care System*, Harper & Collins, Toronto, 1989, pp. 99-112.
8. Greg L. Stoddart and Roberta J. Labelle, *Privatization in the Canadian Health Care System: Assertions, Evidence, Ideology and Options*, Health and Welfare Canada, October 1985, pp. 9-28.
9. Pat Armstrong and Hugh Armstrong, *Health Care as a Business: The Legacy of Free Trade*, Canadian Centre for Policy Alternatives, May 1991, pp. 6-12.
10. "The Crisis in Health Insurance," *Consumer Reports*, August 1990, p. 535.
11. "The Crisis in Health Insurance, Part 2," *Consumer Reports*, September, 1990, pp. 609-610.
12. S. Woolhandler and D.U. Himmelstein, "The deteriorating administrative efficiency of the U.S. health care system," *New England Journal of Medicine*, May 2, 1991, pp. 1253-8.
13. Guillermo Anguiano Rodriguez and Manuel Garcia Urrutia, *The Free Trade Agreement, the Social Cost of Its Viability, the Social Cost of the Economic Opening*, Frente Autentico del Trabajo, 1991.

Chris Gainor is a communications officer for the Hospital Employees' Union. He is also coordinator of the Health Care Advocates of B.C. and serves on the board of the Canadian Health Coalition. As a journalist for the Vancouver *Sun* and *The Medical Post*, he covered health care issues for several years.

PART 3
Fighting Back

Fighting Free Trade, Canadian Style

The Action Canada Network has emerged as a national coalition fighting the free trade agenda

by Tony Clarke

In the days following the 1988 federal election on free trade, representatives of the country's major labour unions and social organizations came together for a post-mortem at the Action Canada (then Pro-Canada) assembly in Ottawa. The big question was whether this would be the last assembly of the Pro-Canada Network. After all, the network was initially organized around the common demand for a federal election on the U.S.-Canada free trade deal. While it was clear that the network had lost the election battle to defeat the deal, the delegates declared that we had won something else instead, namely, the creation of a progressive social movement in Canada. The delegates resolved to continue as a national coalition for the purpose of mobilizing public opposition to the corporate free trade agenda and promoting alternative economic and social policy directions for the country.

The building of a broad-based coalition like the Action Canada Network is unique in this country's history. To be sure, hundreds of coalitions of popular groups have been organized around numerous public policy issues in the past. But these coalitions have generally been organized around single issues; they normally dissolve once the issues are addressed. We have also had regionally based coalitions like the Common Front in Québec in the mid-1970s and the B.C. Solidarity Coalition in the mid-1980s. What we have not seen before in this country is a national coalition like the Action Canada Network, which is organized for democratic social change on a broad set of policy issues related to the basic economic and social structures of the country.

The FTA became a catalyst, bringing diverse groups together in a common cause

FIGHTING FREE TRADE, CANADIAN STYLE

WHAT, ME WORRY? The Pro-Canada Network was instrumental in building opposition to free trade during the 1988 election. More and more often as the campaign wore on, Brian Mulroney had to face hostile crowds like this one in Surrey, B.C. A majority of Canadians voted for parties opposed to the deal.

PHOTO BY DAN KEETON/ PACIFIC TRIBUNE

A major reason lies in the nature of the Free Trade Agreement (FTA) itself. It is important to remember that the FTA became the centrepiece of a political strategy designed to restructure Canada's economy and society for the "tough, new world of global competition." The FTA, coupled with privatization and deregulation measures, was used to radically transfigure the economic and social face of Canada. People from diverse sectors and regions of the country were directly or indirectly affected by the corporate free trade agenda that was being unleashed upon the country. In effect, the FTA became a catalyst for bringing diverse groups together in a common cause. Without the FTA, the movement might not have taken shape.

Thus, the Action Canada Network (ACN) has emerged as a national coalition of labour unions, social organizations, and community groups committed to fighting the corporate free trade agenda. In addition to the leading private and public sector unions in the country, the ACN is composed of women's groups, farm associations, nationalist groups, anti-poverty organizations, environmental groups, church networks, senior citizen associations, aboriginal nations, cultural associations, peace networks, student organizations, and professional groups (e.g., teachers, nurses). One way or another, all these constituencies are affected by the FTA. At the same time, the ACN consists of regional coalitions made up of similar constituent groups in each province. And, through Common Frontiers, formal working relationships have been established with similar coalitions in Mexico and the United States.

WHAT'S THE BIG DEAL? More than a quarter of a million copies of this pamphlet, designed to counteract the uncritical pro-free trade message of the for-profit media, were distributed across Canada during the 1988 election.

As a national coalition, the ACN has developed a dynamic organizational model. Three times a year, delegates representing their member organizations come together from across the country in the ACN assembly to map out action strategies. As the main decision-making body of the ACN, the assemblies follow a consensus model in setting priorities. Task forces have been set up to work between assemblies on the major program priorities (e.g., continental free trade, constitutional reform, and solidarity campaigns). The Action Canada *Dossier* keeps member groups and their constituencies regularly informed about the Network's main issues and activities. In the past year, the ACN has been reorganized to reflect a more binational structure, which gives Québec-based groups more freedom and self-determination in developing strategies related to their needs.

Over the past five years, the ACN and its member organizations have demonstrated a capacity to mobilize public opposition to the corporate free trade agenda. In the case of the FTA, for example, public opposition grew from 34 percent in October 1987 to 53 percent in November 1988 at the height of the federal election campaign. This shift in public opinion occurred, despite a

> 'The Canada-U.S. Free Trade Agreement limits Canada's democratic ability to use capital and resources for worthy national purposes and our ability to use our democratic and economic institutions to more adequately care for each other as Canadians.'
>
> UNITED CHURCH OF CANADA GENERAL COUNCIL, 1988

predominantly pro-free trade media, largely because of the popular education that took place in a variety of constituencies across the country. Using basic methods of grassroots communication (i.e., women speaking to women, workers to workers, farmers to farmers, etc.) plus popular education tools like the mass distribution of a cartoon booklet in the country's major newspapers, a groundswell of public opinion formed. Similarly, when the Mulroney government introduced its Goods and Services Tax (a free-trade-driven tax), the ACN joined with the Canadian Labour Congress and other member groups to mobilize 2.5 million people on a single weekend (April 7-9, 1990) to say "No to the GST" and "Yes to Fair Taxes" through ballot boxes in the work place and community centres.

This movement, however, has also had its shortcomings. In terms of resources, for example, there is often an imbalance between what labour unions and the social organizations are able to provide. While the unions continue to provide the bulk of the Network's funding, it is important to ensure that financially strapped social organizations are able to make a creative contribution and effectively participate in decision making. At times, tensions still surface between national and regional bodies or between large, more hierarchical organizations and community-based groups. Perhaps one of the most serious shortcomings is the ACN's limited capacity to make full use of its communication networks. Through its member groups, the ACN has the potential to communicate its message to well over half the adult population of this country. This potential has only been partially realized.

The labour movement, of course, has been an indispensable factor in the building of the ACN as a national coalition, yet its real potential has not been fully exercised. The labour movement, more than any other component, has the material resources and human energies required to turn the ACN into a more powerful coalition for democratic social change in this country. However, labour has been plagued by internal political disputes over participation in coalitions. While major advances in support of coalitions have been made recently in many parts of the labour movement, there are still significant pockets that either ignore or resist this agenda. These, and related factors, have put constraints on the capacities of the labour movement to give clear and strong political leadership in challenging the corporate free trade agenda through coalitions at regional and national levels.

Furthermore, the ACN has not yet been able to fully develop an effective working relationship with progressive political parties at the federal level. To be sure, consultations on issues and policies are held, on a more or less regular basis, with the New Democratic Party, for example. But much more needs to be done to build an effective working relationship around the development of policies and strategies related to the corporate free trade agenda. This is crucial, especially in the current period leading up to the next general election. Here, a comprehensive plan for the abrogation of the FTA along with an alternative economic program will be of strategic importance.

As we look ahead, 1992-93 will be a critical year in the struggle against the corporate free trade agenda. Public opposition to the FTA is bound to intensify further as communities continue to suffer from plant shutdowns, farm bankruptcies, and social program cuts. The GATT negotiations are expected to reach a new agreement this year, one that will more than likely reinforce the negative provisions of the FTA. This is also the year for the completion of the NAFTA negotiations on a

MEMBER GROUPS OF THE ACN

Action Canada Network (Alberta)
Action Canada Network (B.C.)
Action Canada Network (P.E.I.)
Alliance of Canadian Cinema, Television, and Radio Artists
Assembly of First Nations
Canadian Auto Workers
Canadian Brotherhood of Railway, Transport, and General Workers
Canadian Environmental Law Association
Canadian Federation of Students
Canadian Labour Congress and affiliated provincial federations of labour
Canadian Paperworkers' Union
Canadian Peace Alliance
Canadian Teachers' Federation
Canadian Union of Postal Workers
Canadian Union of Public Employees
Cape Breton Coalition for Economic Justice
Centrale de l'enseignement du Québec
CHOICES: A Coalition for Social Justice
Communications and Electrical Workers of Canada
Confederation of Canadian Unions
Conféderation des syndicats nationaux
Council of Canadians
Ecumenical Coalition for Economic Justice
Graphic Communications International Union
International Ladies Garment Workers' Union
Inter Pares
Latin American Working Group
Metro (Halifax-Dartmouth) Coalition Against Free Trade
National Action Committee on the Status of Women
National Farmers Union
National Federation of Nurses' Unions
National Pensioners and Senior Citizens' Federation
National Union of Provincial Government Employees
Newfoundland Coalition for Equality
One Voice Seniors' Network
Ontario Coalition for Social Justice
Organized Working Women
OXFAM Canada
Playwrights Union of Canada
Public Service Alliance of Canada
Rural Dignity of Canada
Saskatchewan Coalition for Social Justice
Solidarité populaire Québec
Transportation and Communications International Union
United Electrical, Radio, and Machine Workers of Canada
United Fish and Allied Workers Union
United Food and Commercial Workers
United Steelworkers of America

continental free trade deal to be ratified by the U.S., Canada, and Mexico in early 1993. It therefore looks like free trade will, once again, be a major issue on the national political agenda, as Canadians prepare for another general election in 1993.

In response to these events, the ACN should be in a position to develop a political program and strategy leading up to the 1993 general election. The centrepiece of this program should be a plan of action for the abrogation of the FTA (and, by implication, withdrawal from NAFTA). To gain support for abrogation, the public needs to know how the FTA can be terminated, what steps can be taken to counter potential forms of U.S. retaliation, and what measures can be used to continue Canada's trade relations. This abrogation program, in turn, must be accompanied by a set of alternative economic strategies designed to help Canada remain an independent nation state in North America. These alternatives should include an economic development program, a social development plan, and a continental development strategy for the 1990s.

What is required in the coming year is the building of a new political consensus around this program and strategy. The same process that was originally followed in building opposition to the FTA in various constituencies must be pursued again. Commitment to this program and strategy must be rekindled in sector after sector and region after region – with women, factory workers, farmers, poor people, senior citizens, environmentalists, public service workers, students, educators, people in the churches, and others. The ACN has a major role to play in consolidating popular support for this kind of alternative program to the corporate free trade agenda.

The next federal election could be the last chance we have to effectively dismantle the corporate free trade agenda. Over the past three years, the economic and social disintegration triggered by the FTA has been tearing this country apart, piece by piece. The addition of NAFTA, which is largely based on a model of competitive poverty, will further accelerate this process of national disintegration. Moreover, the current attempt to entrench the corporate free trade agenda in the constitution has set off new alarm bells. The question before us is whether or not Canada will actually survive the decade of the nineties intact as an independent nation state on the northern half of this continent. In short, this country simply cannot afford another four years under a right-wing regime. For these reasons, our attention must now shift to electoral politics.

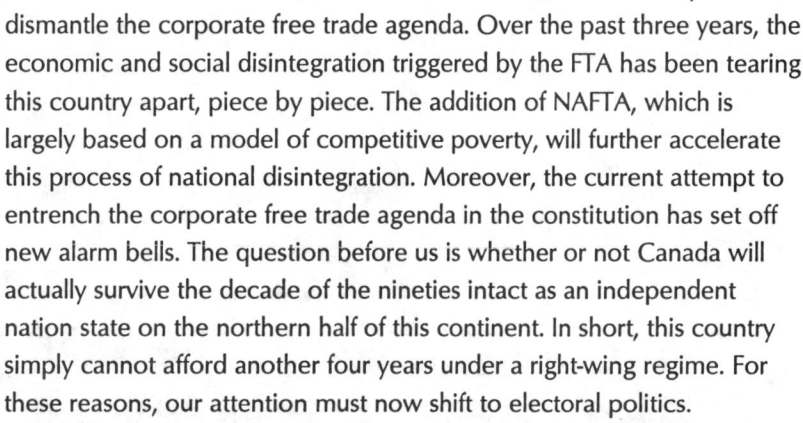

Yet, the 1993 election will be quite different from that of 1988 or any other in recent history. Instead of the traditional three-party race, there will be at least five or six parties in the running, two of which are regional strongholds. At the same time, the polls consistently show that the electorate is very volatile. Under these conditions, it is quite likely that no one party will emerge from the 1993 election with a sufficient plurality (i.e., 148 seats) to form a majority government. While it is too early for firm predictions, the prospects of a minority government are real. In this kind of electoral climate, coalition politics becomes the name of the game.

The danger here is that the 1993 election could result in the formation of a right-wing minority or coalition government committed to the task of carrying out the corporate free trade agenda. Every effort must be made to prevent this course of events. In a period of coalition politics, the ACN must be prepared to do whatever is possible to lay the ground for the election of a progressive minority government with a mandate to dismantle the corporate free trade agenda and institute an alternative, people's agenda. This means, in effect, that the electorate must be faced with a fundamental choice between two diametrically opposed visions or directions for Canada's future: the continuation of the corporate free trade agenda or the implementation of an alternative democratic agenda.

In the months leading up to the 1993 federal election, the ACN and its member groups need to become more active in building public support for an alternative democratic agenda. The program of abrogation and alternatives identified above contains some of the basic elements. Resources must be prepared for popular education and action, to help people understand the destruction caused by the FTA, the dangers of a NAFTA, and the ways in which the free trade deal itself could be terminated. Similar resources and tools are needed to show how Canada, under a progressive government, could go about the task of implementing an alternative agenda for economic and social development, based on democratically managed trade options rather than corporate free trade.

At the same time, campaigns need to be organized around some key symbolic issues for public education and action. For example, public campaigns organized around plant closures, health care, foreign takeovers, agriculture marketing boards, water exports, unfair taxes, generic drugs, cultural enterprises, and environmental safeguards could highlight the negative impacts of the corporate FTA-NAFTA agenda. Conferences, workshops, and media events could be organized to build up public support and confidence in key sectors of our society concerning the main components of an alternative democratic agenda. These actions could be further supplemented by electoral initiatives, such as organised "drops" in selected ridings, with popular tools designed to help voters make clear choices between parties wedded to the corporate free trade agenda and those committed to a democratic alternative.

To be effective, this pre-election campaign strategy will require a major infusion of organizational commitment and resources on a variety of fronts. The wide range of constituent organizations that comprise the ACN should each be encouraged to prepare popular education and action resources for their members and utilize their own communication networks to spread the message. To assist the regional coalitions of the ACN, resources will be needed to put together teams of field organizers for work on local campaigns across the country. The labour movement, supplemented perhaps by some community sector organizations, should be encouraged to make a substantial commitment of financial resources for these purposes. In addition to training and fielding organizers for local campaigns, these resources should be used to strengthen coalition building in each region or province.

The shift to a more strategic focus on electoral politics calls for closer working relationships with political parties who are in tune with the ACN's agenda. The NDP is the only political party that has taken a clear position on abrogation of the FTA and NAFTA (the Liberals favour renegotiation of the FTA, which is unacceptable). The NDP's economic and social policy program appears to be similar to positions adopted by the ACN and most of its member organizations. As the 1993 federal election approaches, steps must be taken to encourage the NDP to give more dynamic leadership on these issues. Efforts should be made to organize consultations with the NDP related to campaign issues, policies, and strategies. At the same time, given the realities of coalition politics and the prospects of a minority

TAKING IT TO THE STREETS The No Big Deal Players staged a little street theatre at an April 1989 anti-free trade demo in downtown Vancouver to dramatize the forces behind free trade.

PHOTO BY
DAN KEETON/
PACIFIC TRIBUNE

> 'This is a good country, a strong country, a decent country. We should keep it that way. We can't reverse the decision of Nov. 21, at least not immediately. But we must work to keep free trade from turning Canada into a replica of the U.S. The fight for Canada isn't over. It has only just begun.'
>
> DON McGILLIVRAY, SOUTHAM NEWS COLUMNIST, DECEMBER 1, 1988

government, measures must be taken to test whether other parties, or factions of parties, are prepared to support the movement for an alternative democratic agenda.

It should also be noted that any ACN-organized campaigns on continental free trade would be carried out in collaboration with our counterparts in Mexico and the United States. Through Common Frontiers, the ACN participates in joint strategy meetings, on a regular basis, with Mexican and U.S. coalition representatives. In the coming year, these discussions will focus on developing a trinational analysis of the NAFTA texts, organizing common action events around the trilateral ministerial negotiations on the NAFTA, and stimulating public debate about free trade issues in forthcoming electoral events (e.g., the 1992 U.S. presidential primaries, 1993 federal election in Canada, 1994 presidential elections in Mexico). The ACN anticipates that its campaigns for abrogation of the FTA (and NAFTA) and alternative approaches to continental development and trade will be publicly supported by popular coalitions and even some political parties in Mexico and the U.S.

In pursuing these strategies, we must not lose sight of some of the broader and deeper dimensions of the struggle against the corporate free trade agenda. The FTA and NAFTA are the staging grounds for a corporate free trade zone throughout the southern hemisphere. Under the Bush administration's Enterprise for the Americas Initiative, countries throughout Latin America will become part of a continental economic bloc dominated by Washington. In effect, a new "Fortress America" is being built to counter the threats to U.S. economic competitiveness posed by the formation of the European Economic Community (dominated by Germany) and the Pacific Rim (dominated by Japan). For these reasons, it is important that links be forged with popular movements that are challenging this corporate free trade agenda elsewhere in Latin America.

Moreover, it is important to recognize that the Enterprise for the Americas Initiative is but the latest attempt on the part of the United States to fulfill its long-standing dream of Manifest Destiny in the hemisphere. But there is a new twist to the dream. Whereas American superiority and way of life was the original vision behind the dream of a Manifest Destiny, it is now the freedom and power of the transnational corporations that form the new vision. Expanding the corporate free trade zone to include the rest of Latin America simply extends the playing field in which transnationals are free to make profitable investments without interference or regulation by nation states. The new Manifest Destiny gives transnationals the power to rule nation states and thereby undermine democracy.

This brings us back to the heart of what it means to "fight free trade – Canadian style." In essence, this is a struggle for both nationhood and democracy. As long as the corporate free trade agenda is in place, we will have little chance of surviving as an independent country. As long as this corporate agenda is allowed to continue unabated, we have little chance of regaining democratic control over our economic and political future. Our last, best hope lies in the building of a dynamic political movement for democratic social change.

Tony Clarke is co-chair of the Action Canada Network. The ACN can be contacted at 904-251 Laurier Avenue West, Ottawa, ON K1P 5J6. The phone number for the national office is 613-233-1764.

Fighting Free Trade, Mexican Style

by Fronteras Comunes/CECOPE
Translated by Nick Keresztesi

As the presidential candidate for the ruling PRI (Institutional Revolutionary Party) in 1988, Carlos Salinas de Gortari insisted that our country was not interested in forming part of a North American common market. Four years later his government spares no effort to ensure the signing of a free trade agreement with the United States and Canada.

The about-face is not surprising. During our 62-year history of one-party rule, presidents routinely decreed whatever policies they chose, uninhibited by democratic practices. The previous government had already paved the way to economic integration by unilaterally reducing duties and signing trade accords with both countries. Government representatives initiated secret talks with U.S. counterparts practically from the moment Salinas took office. North American Free Trade (NAFTA) has become the centrepiece of the administration's economic and political survival strategy. The profound social and economic transformations free trade would bring to Mexico are being met with growing resistance as Mexicans search for sound development alternatives to the neo-liberal economic model, and struggle to construct a political process that is truly democratic – one that would allow for clean elections and would liberate social organizations from state control. Left and right opposition agree that these are indispensable elements for any resolution of the grave and urgent problems facing the nation.

> **The NAFTA has become the centrepiece of Salinas' economic and political survival strategy**

FIGHTING FREE TRADE, MEXICAN STYLE

CAUGHT IN A SQUEEZE
The CTM's control of Mexican labour is under attack. While new independent and democratic unions are challenging it from below, the PRI is finding the CTM less useful than it used to be, and is promoting a new model of unionism to back its neo-liberal program.

PHOTO BY
ELAINE BRIERE

REVERSING THE REVOLUTION "In 1992 Mexico will put an end to its revolutionary past," the British newsmagazine, *The Economist*, wrote about neo-liberal policies that are undermining the principles for which our grandparents fought one of the world's bloodiest civil wars: the Mexican Revolution of 1910-1917.

Modern Mexico inherited from the revolution a constitution that guarantees our sovereignty over national territory and resources. It grants the state wide-ranging powers to direct economic development, and guarantees fundamental social rights, such as the right to work, to education, to health care.

The expropriation of foreign holdings in key resource and infrastructure industries like railways, public utilities, and banking, stimulated the development of national industries and prosperous agricultural production. The 1938 expropriation of the foreign-controlled petroleum industry by President Lázaro Cárdenas was an attempt to make Mexico's vast oil reserves serve national development objectives, and has become a symbol of national pride.

Also emerging from the post-revolutionary turmoil was a profoundly anti-democratic political process that has allowed a single party to dominate political life and control government ever since. The PRI fattens itself from the public trough and has become indistinguishable from the state.

During periods of economic growth, the system succeeded in consolidating

MAYDAY, MAYDAY
Workers have an official place in the corporatist Mexican state of the PRI. Unions are tolerated, if they align themselves with the government, and May Day is a national holiday. But as usual, the reality for Mexican workers does not match the ideal.

PHOTO BY
ELAINE BRIERE

popular support by allocating considerable resources to guarantee a minimum level of well-being to the population. The government ensured access to land, and provided credits and subsidies to small farmers, free basic education and public health services, and subsidies for housing and basic foodstuffs. However, the collapse of oil prices, combined with sharp increases of international interest rates at the beginning of the 1980s, threw the nation into economic and political crisis, exposing the underlying social poverty and the fundamentally undemocratic nature of our system.

Miguel de la Madrid assumed the presidency in 1982 amid profound crisis. He attempted to restore government credibility by attacking corruption. The director of Petroleos Mexicanos (PEMEX – the state-owned oil monopoly), the chief of police of

FIGHTING FREE TRADE, MEXICAN STYLE

> The March 4, 1992 edition of THE ECONOMIST included an article on 'Mexico's house-trained unionists.' It said that, without Fidel Velasquez, general secretary of the CTM, 'Mr. Salinas's government could scarcely have forced through a successful economic stabilization programme, built on a fall in average real wages of almost 50 percent since 1982.'
>
> THE ECONOMIST, MARCH 14, 1992

Mexico City, and other civil servants were jailed for their provable and ostentatious corruption. He tried to satisfy the demands of international creditors by launching a program of severe "structural adjustment." Policies like currency devaluations, trade liberalization, privatization of state companies, income-devastating inflation controls, and drastic cuts in public spending deepened the crisis, rather than resolving it.

This was only the beginning. In 1988, after the most disputed presidential elections in recent history, Salinas de Gortari aggressively pursued the same policies. In only three years his government has shed important state companies, re-privatizing the banks and selling Telefonos de Mexico, the state telephone company, for example. Yet the Salinas strategy goes further. It extends legal and constitutional guarantees to foreign corporations, protecting their interests against any changes a future government might want to make.

One of the most far-reaching changes is constitutional reform permitting private ownership of agricultural lands, until now reserved for community use. Critics warn that this paves the way for agribusiness to dominate Mexican farm production, causing the dislocation of millions of campesinos.[1] Reforms to the intellectual property rights law extend the time limits for patent protection, and permits patenting software and biotechnology.

Reforms like these, applauded by transnational capital, weaken democratic control over significant areas of national interest. They have already brought greater social disparity and growing concern for our future as a country.

THE DEMOCRATIC AGENDA No theme generates more debate and discussion in Mexico today than that of democracy. Internationally acclaimed Peruvian novelist and conservative politician Mario Vargas Llosa scandalized Mexico's elite by calling our political system the "perfect dictatorship." Opinion from across the political spectrum agrees that economic modernization must be accompanied by democratizing the political system. Yet the dominant group within the PRI seems intent on pushing through profound structural reforms without democratizing the political process.

Discontent focuses on the systematic disrespect for the vote. Sophisticated computer-based fraud augments traditional dirty tricks to ensure that growing opposition does not translate into electoral defeat for the PRI. Fraudulent practices, once accepted as part of our folklore, provoked serious political crises in the states of Guanajuato, San Luis Potosi, and Tabasco, where angry citizens forced the resignation of "elected" PRI governors in the 1991 mid-term elections. The token recognition of a few opposition victories, unimaginable five years ago, has not satisfied the clamour for truly clean elections.

At the root of the conflict is an authoritarian political system inspired by a corporatist vision of social control. Post-revolutionary society was organized into three sectors: workers into unions, peasants into campesino organizations, and community groups into associations. These sectors became the foundation of the PRI, and through them, the PRI filtered surplus and managed participation in public life. Social policy was negotiated among these sectors within the party structure, limiting public debate and participation of groups outside the PRI. The leadership of these sectors are high-ranking PRI members who use their positions more to enforce government policy than to represent their members' interests. Loyalty is maintained by co-opting members and repressing dissenters. Leaders cross over into government posts and benefit from state contracts as though they were running their own companies.[2]

These once powerful sectors are losing influence as Salinas seeks to replace the decentralized, interventionist state with one that administers an economic and social system ruled by the free market. Salinas has initiated programs to weaken sectoral groups both inside the PRI and within society at large. Key to this is the transformation of the PRI from a party of powerful sectors into a party of private citizens.

The recently re-elected Secretary General of the Confederation of Workers of Mexico (CTM), the largest labour central, 92-year-old Fidel Velasquez, stands squarely opposed to Salinas' efforts to isolate the CTM from its real power base, the PRI and the state. The CTM has effectively maintained labour peace during the last 15 years when wages lost 60 percent of their value, unemployment soared, and living standards plummeted. It has repressed dissatisfied members, manipulated labour tribunals, and violently crushed attempts to set up independent, democratic unions. In return, the CTM seeks continued participation in the governing apparatus. But the Salinas administration identifies the very factors which have permitted the PRI to maintain its hegemony for over half a century as obstacles to its survival.

> **Salinas is trying to clean up corruption and appeal directly to the electorate in order to buy back their vote**

Salinas has nurtured a different model of trade unionism and new forms of labour relations in key sectors of the economy: education, telecommunications, and electricity supply. Unions in the latter two are the driving force behind a new coordinating body, FESEBES (Federation of Workers of Public Goods and Services Enterprises). The Telephone Workers' Union (STRM), the leading union in FESEBES, differs from the authoritarian CTM. The STRM is not corrupt, is more democratic, and its leadership has credibility among its membership. Support of the FESEBES

FORD HAS A BETTER IDEA Ford and the CTM 'union' collaborated to crush workers resisting wage rollbacks, speedups, and layoffs imposed in 1988 at this assembly plant near Mexico City. In a 1989 confrontation at the plant, one worker was shot to death and another nine were wounded by CTM goons.
PHOTO BY NICK KERESZTESI

unions is important to the Salinas "modernization" scheme.

Another Salinas tactic to erode the power of the organized sectors within the PRI has been to deny them access to the public resources they use to exercise patronage. The most visible of the new programs, called Solidaridad, redirects a large part of the budget for basic services like water, sewage, housing, and food, bypassing regional governments and further concentrating control in the office of the presidency. Salinas is trying to clean up corruption and appeal directly to the electorate in order to buy back their vote.

GROWTH OF AN INDEPENDENT POPULAR MOVEMENT Since the 1920s, important movements of campesinos, workers, teachers, students, and urban slum dwellers have risen up in defense of their interests. But for the most part, the government has successfully isolated and neutralized its opposition. In some cases, movements were violently snuffed out, like the 1968 student protests when government troops massacred hundreds of unarmed peaceful demonstrators.

The 1980s saw a new kind of social protest. The government's strategy of shifting the cost of the economic crisis to middle and lower classes, compounded by its gross ineptness in responding to the natural catastrophe of the 1985 earthquake, sparked the rise of a more integrated and coordinated social movement wary of government and party efforts to co-opt it.

WHO IS THAT MASKED MAN? Mexico's growing pro-democracy movement includes a super-hero in its ranks. Superbarrio, an intrepid crime-fighter who opposes poverty and injustice wherever they raise their heads. This popular image is catching on. Here 'The Ecologist' joins a community group protesting pollution in their neighbourhood.

PHOTO BY NICK KERESZTESI

Response to the earthquake was characteristically self-interested and riddled with corruption; the government was apparently more concerned with reassuring tourists and foreign investors than organizing rescue and relief operations. Generous international relief aid was pocketed and soldiers patrolled streets to protect private property, leaving victims buried in rubble.

But the population responded with energy and selflessness. Community groups, organized first as search and rescue brigades, continued to work after the immediate emergency response, pressing for housing, water, and other services over the longer term. These organizations insisted on their right to exist independent of corporatist PRI structures, and did not incorporate themselves into other, traditional opposition groups. Instead, they maintained their independence and developed novel ways of pressing for their demands. The most famous of these is the image of Superbarrio, a kind of comic super-hero who struggles on behalf of residents of poor and working-class neighbourhoods.

FREE TRADE COMES TO MEXICO The job of introducing Mexicans to the "benefits" of free trade fell to Canadian Prime Minister Brian Mulroney on a state visit to Mexico in March 1990. He praised the Canada-U.S. Free Trade Agreement for creating jobs and stimulating the Canadian economy. A few days later, U.S. sources revealed that our government was seeking a free trade agreement. The news, denied at first by official sources, was corroborated when President Salinas "suggested" to the Senate that it carry out public hearings on "Mexico's trade relations with the world." After two days of testimony from government officials, the business community, and researchers, the PRI-dominated Senate (60 PRI members and 4 PRD members) concluded that free trade was both necessary and urgent.

Salinas accepted the recommendation and publicly requested the Bush administration to initiate talks toward a free trade treaty. Following old customs, declarations supporting free trade began to be issued by all kinds of PRI-linked interest groups: business organizations, "official" trade unions, the media, and prestigious intellectuals. Insisting on secrecy, the government has divulged almost nothing about the form or content of the negotiations. An advisory council of supportive businesses, unions, and specialists passes for public consultation. Spending millions on publicity to portray free trade as the solution to all our problems, the government permits no obstacle to impede its headlong drive toward a NAFTA.

OPPOSITION GROWS The fast pace of negotiations and absence of information about their process or content (U.S. media continue to be the best source of information on the Mexican negotiating position) have slowed public response to Salinas' economic integration plans. Only gradually did North American free trade assume the centre of national attention.

By mid-1990 a number of forums, conferences, publications, and newspaper articles began to raise important questions about free trade's impact on Mexico. Promises that increased foreign investment will create jobs were met with warnings about the risks posed to national sovereignty and to control over natural resources and the environment. Groups of small and medium-sized businesses – pork producers, household appliance manufacturers, textile manufacturers, and some service industries, among others – began to raise concerns about negative consequences on their sectors. Many have demanded special treatment. Numerous campesino organizations[3] have demanded that basic grains and dairy products be exempted, and that there be delays of 15 to 20 years before the removal of protective tariffs on other produce. Campesinos are finding that rural life is deeply challenged by NAFTA-inspired constitutional reforms which threaten to destroy communal land holdings and promote the sell-off of prime agricultural lands to multinational agribusiness.

The principal political parties have been slow to develop positions on free trade. The leadership of the second strongest electoral force, the conservative National Action Party (PAN), has had to confront the contradiction between its support for neo-liberalism and the opposition to NAFTA expressed by groups of nationalistic businessmen who form a substantial part of PAN membership.

> **The liberty maquiladoras have enjoyed to pollute the region could be extended under NAFTA**

The Democratic Revolutionary Party (PRD), the principal electoral force on the left, strongly opposes the treaty. Cuauhtemoc Cárdenas, the PRD leader who appears to have been cheated of victory in the 1988 presidential election through electoral fraud, presented his alternative Continental Trade and Development Initiative in a speech to the 1990 B.C. Federation of Labour convention. For the PRD, the struggle against free trade is inextricably linked to the struggle for an equitable economic development and a democratic society.

Women's organizations from the three countries have met to analyze the impact of economic integration on women workers. In February 1992, for example, a trinational meeting was held where more than 120 women discovered that policies which cut back social services, deregulate and privatize state industries, and erode job security are common to all the countries.

Environmentalists were quick to identify the dangers of free trade to the U.S./Mexico border zone environment. Groups argue that the liberty which maquiladoras have enjoyed to pollute the region could be extended under NAFTA. Their concerns are being echoed on both sides of the border by residents and local governments who joined forces to protest toxic waste dumping in March 1992.

LABOUR AND NAFTA Unions have various responses to the NAFTA initiative. The "official" labour movement, led by the CTM, endorses the deal, but insists that there be no deterioration of labour legislation, the right of association, the right to collective bargaining, or the right to strike.

A different position is presented by the major unions in the FESEBES. They support NAFTA, but seek a parallel social charter to ensure that Mexican salaries and working conditions rise to U.S. and Canadian levels. Recently, the STRM signed a trinational accord with sister unions in Canada and the U.S., an important step in developing regional union relations.

The small but active labour movement independent of PRI ties has played a critical role in fighting the neo-liberal agenda and has been central to the formation of broad-based coalitions challenging NAFTA. Labour centrals like the Authentic Front of Labour (FAT), and union coordination structures like the Unified Union Front (FSU), were the first to raise criticism of free trade and initiated the earliest contacts with Canadian organizations opposed to free trade. They continue to lead the development of an articulate and unified social response to free trade in Mexico.

MEXICAN ACTION NETWORK ON FREE TRADE A crucial element in developing a critical perspective on free trade came from learning about the Canadian experience under the Canada-U.S. Free Trade Agreement. In October 1990 a key exchange between 30 Canadian organizations and 60 Mexican groups inspired the formation of the Mexican Action Network on Free Trade (RMALC). This coalition, officially launched in April 1991, has become an important voice pressing for

HUMAN RIGHTS PROSPECTS DIM UNDER NAFTA

Nick Keresztesi

Mexico's poor human rights record is not part of the official NAFTA negotiations, but human rights groups in Mexico feel that the Salinas administration is under pressure to "clean up its act." Mariclaire Acosta, president of the Mexican Commission for the Defense and Promotion of Human Rights, points out that "every time Salinas meets Bush, something spectacular happens in Mexico." Just four days before Salinas went to Washington in 1990 to initiate free trade talks, the National Commission for Human Rights was created. Close to the date of another meeting, the mystery surrounding the assassination of Norma Corona, a human rights lawyer, was cleared up. "Last time they met, 60 anti-narcotics officers were disciplined." The list goes on.

Ms Acosta rates Salinas' human rights record as "very bad, violations have not diminished with his administration." Over 100 cases of political assassinations have been documented since 1988, including two close advisors to Cuauhtemoc Cárdenas. Amnesty International reports that 80 percent of all prisoners have been tortured. Anyone could be a target for fundamental rights violations. Human rights abuses are endemic to the power structure and the system of political control. The authorities have impunity and without free and fair elections, people have no way to hold them accountable.

"Neo-liberal policies have already had a negative impact on human rights," says Acosta, "by making the impact of market forces stronger than ever on people, it takes away whatever minimal control they have over their resources and their lives." She predicts a great deal of violence in Mexico's future under NAFTA, especially "in the rural areas, when campesinos see their communal lands given up or lost."

Mexican human rights groups have participated in the struggle around free trade, but have tried to keep human rights out of the NAFTA negotiations. Arguing from a perspective North Americans find hard to understand, Acosta says, "We don't want to achieve short-term gains on the human rights front that diminish Mexican sovereignty. We do not want some act of the U.S. Congress to determine how human rights are dealt with in Mexico." Instead, the Mexican strategy is to work through international conventions governing human rights, like those of the United Nations and the Organization of American States. "The U.S. is the only UN member not to sign rights accords," says Acosta. "Perhaps one day the U.S. will ratify the international agreements. That is our long-term hope."

Based on an interview with Mariclaire Acosta, March 23, 1992.

democratic participation in devising economic development strategies. It has grown to represent more than 100 independent unions, campesino and women's organizations, non-governmental organizations, environmental and community groups, academics, and other representative social groups.

RMALC represents the most successful attempt to unify a wide range of social organizations. RMALC seeks to promote public debate on the social impact of NAFTA, and to coordinate political actions to influence the government regarding commercial relations and economic integration. Important to the work of RMALC is strengthening relations with networks and social organizations working on similar themes in the U.S. and Canada.

By studying the impact of neo-liberal policies on member groups and sharing their analysis, RMALC is developing alternative proposals. RMALC supports expanded international trade, including with the U.S. and Canada, but condemns NAFTA for serving transnational business interests at the expense of social and economic development for Mexico. RMALC opposes the secretive nature of the negotiations which prohibit input from sectors that will be directly affected. The textile industry, for example, will be decimated by foreign competition, yet has no effective input into the treaty.

The maquiladora job creation model, at the centre of the Salinas economic integration project, is rejected by RMALC members. The same policies that attract maquiladora investment have de-industrialized the rest of the economy. Over the past 25 years, maquiladoras have created 500,000 jobs, while many times that number of better paying manufacturing jobs have been lost from the economy as a whole. High productivity in maquiladoras has not stimulated wage increases: in fact, average maquiladora pay is less than the average national industrial wage.

> **The textile industry will be decimated by foreign competition, yet has no input into the treaty**

While the government promises that free trade will resolve Mexico's severe economic crisis, RMALC notes that the most pressing problems are not even on the table. One example is foreign debt payments, which consume a huge portion of the public purse. RMALC argues that economic development is impossible without a resolution to the debt crisis that substantially reduces the wealth flowing from Mexico to the international banks. Another important issue is the problem of Mexican migrants working in the U.S. They have no rights and are targets of police harassment. Any treaty dealing with long-term economic relations must address the rights of migrant labourers.

Rather than recognizing the fundamental inequalities of the three economies,

FIGHTING FREE TRADE, MEXICAN STYLE

FRIENDLY FASCISM The smiling faces of these Mexico City policemen belie a record of corruption and political repression. Mexican officials are eager to keep human rights out of NAFTA talks, which is fine by their U.S. and Canadian counterparts.
PHOTO BY ELAINE BRIERE

NAFTA assumes that they are equal. RMALC asserts that instead of equal treatment, Mexican economic development requires preferential treatment, much like the European Community allowed its lesser developed members: longer periods for tariff reductions, protection of key sectors, and assurances that standards rise to the highest existing levels rather than drop to the lowest. RMALC rejects a free trade deal that damages Mexico the way the Canada/U.S. deal has damaged Canada.

DEBATE OVER A SOCIAL CHARTER The role of a social charter in improving working conditions, social benefits, and environmental protection generates lively debate in Mexico. Some opinions support NAFTA on the condition that a parallel charter be attached. Others support trinational efforts to develop such a charter, but insist that no social charter can fix the flaws of this NAFTA initiative. A trade and development pact that is based on democratic social and economic rights must be negotiated. Others note that Mexican social and labour legislation already is in many ways superior to that in the U.S. or Canada; the problem is that Mexican laws aren't enforced. International charters and agreements are meaningless as long as Mexicans have little power to enforce those that already exist. Still others propose that the question of social and labour rights and their enforcement are a Mexican issue and must not become subject to decisions made in Washington or Ottawa.

> 'We are running late. Another type of agenda is also being constructed, much more rapidly than we could have imagined. This other agenda is not aimed at creating a new continental relationship, but at subordinating both of our countries to our common neighbour – the United States. Our goal is to join forces with you . . . to build the right kind of relationship among our three nations, not the wrong one.'
>
> CUAUHTEMOC CÁRDENAS, PRD LEADER, TO THE B.C. FEDERATION OF LABOUR CONVENTION, NOVEMBER 30, 1990

TRINATIONAL ACCOMPLISHMENTS The silver lining in the dark cloud of NAFTA is the opportunity it provides for relationship building among social organizations in the three countries. Our first meeting with Canadians opened our eyes to the potential impact of free trade. Since then, many valuable exchanges have enabled social organizations from the three countries to share analysis and work toward developing common responses to the corporate agenda.

Perhaps the most significant of these meetings was held in October 1991, in Zacatecas, Mexico. RMALC hosted the Action Canada Network and networks from the U.S. at a meeting held parallel to the one the three governments were holding a few blocks away. Representatives of 150 organizations hammered out a joint declaration, based on common analysis and identifying joint demands. Delegates tried to deliver the Zacatecas Declaration to their country's official negotiators. Only the Canadian minister for international trade, Michael Wilson, emerged from the secret talks to receive the statement; the Mexicans and Americans had to settle for third-level bureaucrats. But perhaps because of the international attention focused on the event and the Mexican government's desire to project a positive image internationally, Mexico's trade secretary, Jaime Serra Puche, did agree to a future meeting with RMALC. The mutual respect that made the Zacatecas Declaration possible is important for the continued success of trinational exchanges.

The Zacatecas meeting was important for RMALC because of the public exposure it received in the Mexican and international media, and for the strong representation it drew from different parts of Mexican society. The presence of distinguished political leaders such as Cuauhtemoc Cárdenas and Salvador Nava, unified PAN/PRD opposition candidate for governor of San Luis Potosi state, brought the struggle for democracy into the forefront. Without real advances toward democracy, Salinas de Gortari's free trade scheme means nothing more than greater inequality and injustice for working people.

CONCLUSION It would be misleading to say that the majority of Mexicans oppose NAFTA. But an increasing portion of Mexican society criticizes its terms and the concessions being offered to achieve it. It is clear that the opposition in our three countries cannot, in isolation, reverse the neo-liberal trend, but if we work together we strengthen our own national goals, and advance our common agenda for fair trading relations that contribute to the economic development and well being of our countries. In Mexico the primary struggle is to shed an authoritarian, anti-democratic political structure and replace it with a participatory, democratic society that will enable economic development to benefit every Mexican.

The new relationships of mutual respect among social organizations in our three countries have already borne fruit. Women's groups, environmentalists, and trade unions have broken new ground in mutual understanding and coordinated efforts to develop a common social agenda. Sector-by-sector solidarity must be continued if we are to find viable alternatives and effective means to make capital respond to our democratic values.

As Latin Americans we cannot forget that NAFTA is just part of the U.S. Initiative for the Americas plan which sets its sights on integrating the whole hemisphere under the same kind of anti-democratic and pro-transnational capital terms. New relations of mutual solidarity which have grown over the past two years among popular organizations from Canada and the U.S. must be extended to include the rest of Latin America. Together, we must develop a strategy to take our future in our own hands.

1. Campesino refers to people who earn a subsistence livelihood by selling agricultural products produced by their own labour.
2. A case in point is Fidel Velasquez, General Secretary of the Confederation of Workers of Mexico (CTM) for more than 50 years, who has also been a senator twice and a deputy a number of times. He has accumulated a considerable personal fortune in shady business dealings.
3. Members of CAP (Permanent Agrarian Council), a national federation of campesino organizations, some of which are affiliated to the PRI.

Fronteras Comunes is a working group created in 1989 to promote analysis of free trade and development alternatives. It is a founding member of the Red Mexicana de Accion Frente Libre Comercio (RMALC) and works actively to build solidarity between Mexican and Canadian social organizations.

CECOPE, the Centre for the Coordination of Ecumenical Projects, is a national non-governmental organization which supports projects dealing with health, housing, human rights, refugees, and maquiladora workers.

Fighting Free Trade, U.S. Style

The fight for fair trade in the U.S. has been taking place behind the scenes – until now. The election year is bringing it out in the open

by Mark Ritchie

Although the fight for fair trade in the U.S. has been occurring for some time now, it is generally a fight which has taken place behind the scenes and out of the public eye. It has only been within the past three years that public awareness, education, and interest group empowerment has enabled the launching of serious opposition to government and business interests dominating the arena of trade negotiations.

Beginning with the Canada-U.S. Trade Agreement (FTA, often referred to as CUSTA in the U.S.) negotiations in 1988, organized opposition in the U.S. came primarily from the raw materials sector, including agriculture, timber, non-ferrous metals, coal, uranium, and from independent oil and gas producers. In addition, effective lobbying by the auto and maritime industries succeeded in eliminating provisions of the agreement that could have harmed these industries. But beyond these economic sectors, there was little awareness or concern expressed by other political forces such as the women's movement, environmentalists, or consumers. Without this broader participation, efforts to stop the FTA in the U.S. remained essentially invisible, and the negotiations received minimal media coverage.

Most groups did not see any connection between trade and the environment

Outside of Washington, D.C., the most extensive public education efforts were organized by the Institute for Agriculture and Trade Policy based in Minneapolis. The Institute held training seminars on the FTA around the country, produced reports and analyses on the impacts of the treaty on specific economic sectors, and organized workshops with U.S. and Canadian experts to stimulate discussion and debate among public interest groups.

FIGHTING FREE TRADE, U.S. STYLE

Although there was a high degree of interest from grassroots organizations, there was very little response from most of the Washington D.C.-based groups. For example, the Institute organized a seminar in Washington on the environmental impacts of U.S.-Canada free trade. The seminar featured Steven Shrybman, counsel for the Canadian Environmental Law Association and author of one of the most comprehensive ecological critiques of the FTA. Invitations were sent to all major environmental groups and followed up by phone calls and personal visits to encourage participation. Most groups, unfortunately, reacted with indifference, arguing that they did not see any connection between trade and the environment. A few groups like the National Toxics Campaign, Friends of the Earth, Greenpeace, and Clean Water Action expressed an interest, but no organized effort emerged at this time.

In sharp contrast to the reactions of most environmentalists, many family farm organizations could see the potentially negative implications of the FTA. A number of progressive farm leaders, including Howard Lyman of the National Farmers Union and David Senter of the American Agricultural Movement, worked with leaders from raw materials sectors to pull together a Fair Trade Caucus in the House of Representatives under the leadership of Congressman Wes Watkins (D-OK). This caucus became the source of serious opposition to the FTA.

GATHERING STORM
Slow to build, opposition to free trade within the U.S. has been gaining force since the Mobilization on Development, Trade and Labor Education was formed early last year. This demo, outside a Seattle hotel where Michael Wilson, Carla Hills, and Jaime Serra Pucho were meeting to agree on the broad outlines of the NAFTA, took place in August 1991.

PHOTO BY SEAN GRIFFIN/ PACIFIC TRIBUNE

The only interest group to win a battle during the course of the FTA negotiations was the maritime industry, which successfully lobbied for exemption from the final agreement thanks to effective action by key leaders such as Senator Breaux (D-LA) and Congressman Moakley (D-MA).

Beyond maritime, however, almost all other concerns were ignored. Given the strong political power of President Reagan, the final vote in Congress wasn't even close. The only significant opposition came from upper midwest farm states.

> **Powerful constituency groups discovered that they had been 'stabbed in the back'**

The public outcry against the FTA in the U.S. came too late to amount to a serious national campaign, but the public education and organizing that has taken place on this issue since 1988 has laid the groundwork for much more successful efforts to influence both the North American Free Trade Agreement (NAFTA) and the General Agreement on Tariffs and Trade (GATT) negotiations.

First, a broad range of activists became aware of how their local or state level work on a variety of issues could be seriously affected by trade agreements. For example, it became clear that the many important environmental victories that had been won over the past couple of decades were being targeted by the Reagan Administration for overturning or weakening through these negotiations.

Second, a number of powerful constituency groups had received promises from Reagan administration officials that they would not be affected by these talks. After the negotiations were completed and the agreement accepted by Congress, they began to read the small print. They then discovered that they had been "stabbed in the back." This feeling of betrayal was especially common among some of the more conservative business groups, who had believed that their financial support for the Republican Party would be repaid by their being protected from harm in the FTA.

Farm groups, many of which were vehemently opposed to the FTA, had their worst fears confirmed. For instance, U.S. wheat growers found that although Cargill and other grain companies could import Canadian wheat into the U.S., resulting in lower prices, they were prohibited from shipping their wheat north into Canada. The excuse given by the administration was that U.S. government expenditures on agriculture were greater than those of the Canadian government.

Furious at this obvious discrimination, North Dakota's Secretary of Agriculture Sarah Vogel pressed for the actual figures. What she discovered was that the U.S. Department of Agriculture (USDA) had purposely inflated these figures by including in their list of so-called government expenditures such items as 4-H Clubs, State Fairs, and even farmer-paid inspection fees.

By the time most groups had become aware of the real impact of free trade, it

FIGHTING FREE TRADE, U.S. STYLE

was too late to turn back the clock on the FTA. However, these groups were now on notice and much better prepared when negotiations began on the GATT.

In 1986 and 1987, the Institute for Agriculture and Trade Policy began holding a series of GATT training sessions around the country which culminated in the formation of a national coalition – the Fair Trade Campaign – to influence the outcome of these talks. Founding groups included national unions such as Oil, Chemical and Atomic Workers Union (OCAWU), farmers groups such as the American Agriculture Movement and Farmers Union Milk Marketing Cooperative, church groups such as the National Council of Churches, and consumer and environmental groups such as the Community Nutrition Institute (CNI) and the National Toxics Campaign (NTC).

What is important about the overall trade campaign is the broad coalitions which are growing out of this work. In nearly twenty states, coalitions including labour, farm, consumer, small business, church, environment, and Third World solidarity groups have come together to address both the NAFTA and GATT. For many groups, this is the first time they have

RUST IN PEACE Abandoned factories now dot every part of the American landscape. Scenes like this are forcing U.S. labour to come to grips with the global capital trends which underlie the recent push for free trade.

PHOTO BY JIM WEST/ IMPACT VISUALS

ADDING UP MEXICAN FREE TRADE

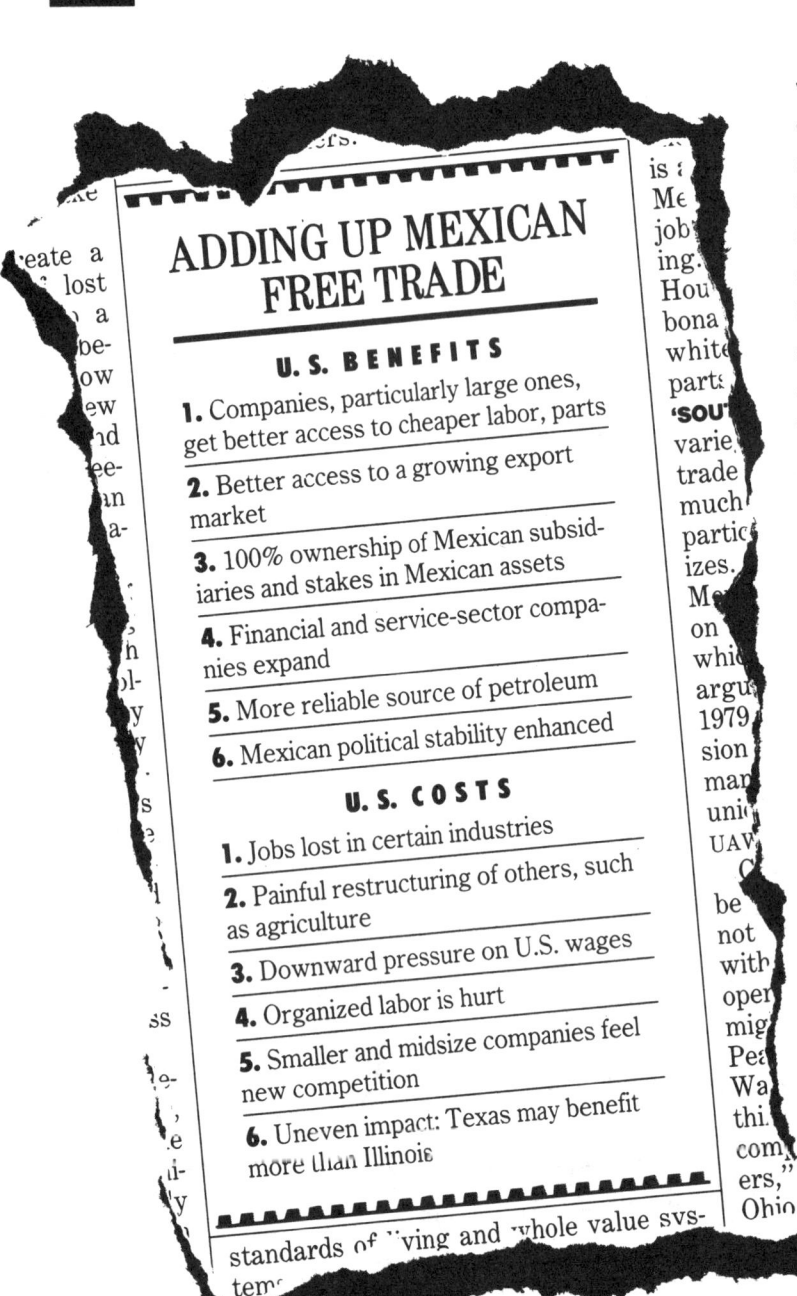

U.S. BENEFITS

1. Companies, particularly large ones, get better access to cheaper labor, parts
2. Better access to a growing export market
3. 100% ownership of Mexican subsidiaries and stakes in Mexican assets
4. Financial and service-sector companies expand
5. More reliable source of petroleum
6. Mexican political stability enhanced

U.S. COSTS

1. Jobs lost in certain industries
2. Painful restructuring of others, such as agriculture
3. Downward pressure on U.S. wages
4. Organized labor is hurt
5. Smaller and midsize companies feel new competition
6. Uneven impact: Texas may benefit more than Illinois

TELL IT LIKE IT IS This item from BUSINESS WEEK shows clearly the winners and losers under continental free trade.

---

worked together. These coalitions, based on economic interest, are turning out to be more stable and potentially long lasting than many others. Looking over the border into Canada, this seems to be the same experience coming out of the earlier FTA battles. Although it is too soon to judge the success of these coalitions in the long-term, a serious commitment by major groups within each sector may provide this long-term success.

INSIDE WASHINGTON Although the number of specific economic sectors were beginning to voice their concerns about the GATT talks during the summer of 1987, most of the non-economic issue groups inside the Washington D.C. beltway continued to ignore the GATT until 1990. The first significant breakthrough inside Washington came at a gathering of consumer and environmental groups called by the National Wildlife Federation to discuss the potential impacts of the GATT. The two speakers at this event were Herman Daly from the World Bank and Mark Ritchie of the Institute for Agriculture and Trade Policy.

A great deal of concern was generated by this event, leading to a follow-up meeting attended by a wide range of D.C.-based consumer and environmental groups. Participants at this second meeting agreed to form the Ad Hoc Working Group on Trade and Environmentally Sustainable Development. For the first time, many of the Washington D.C.-based groups began to understand what many Canadians had come to know during the FTA negotiations: free trade can be a disaster for environmental and consumer protection.

FIGHTING FREE TRADE, U.S. STYLE

> 'Economics and the recession will be key issues in this presidential election year, and hence the free-trade agenda is brought center stage. We can win on this issue, and we can build the coalitions that will help transform this country in the future.'
>
> RON BLACKWELL, AMALGAMATED CLOTHING AND TEXTILE WORKERS UNION

At a kick-off press conference for the Ad Hoc Working Group on Trade and Environmentally Sustainable Development, consumer interest leaders called GATT one of the primary tools multinational corporations use to overturn the victories won by citizen's groups. Although the Ad Hoc Working Group concentrated primarily on GATT during its first year in existence, President Bush's announcement of his intention to extend the FTA to include Mexico through the NAFTA forced much of the emphasis to change.

At one of the Ad Hoc Working Group meetings in the summer of 1990, the video "Dirty Business," which portrayed the ecological and employment impact of Pillsbury's Green Giant plant's move from California to Mexico, made the issue of free trade more dramatic. The Ad Hoc Working Group began to meet every week, alternating between discussions on GATT and NAFTA.

Eventually these two discussion groups evolved into two separate entities. The discussion on NAFTA, for example, eventually incorporated a number of new groups concerned with other issues such as human and labour rights, and took the name of the Mobilization on Development, Trade and Labor Education (MODTLE).

On January 15, 1991, the Ad Hoc Working Group held its first public event on the NAFTA – a briefing on Capital Hill. At a similar briefing held only one year earlier on GATT, only 50 people showed up. This time, in spite of the fact that January 15 was the deadline given to Iraq to withdraw from Kuwait, over 400 showed up. A national cable television network known as CSPAN covered the event live and rebroadcast it at least two more times. Such a response was overwhelming.

The reasons why there was such a tremendous interest in the U.S.-Mexico proposal compared to the GATT is not clear, but it was probably a combination of the steady growth in overall awareness of trade issues, as well as the close proximity of Mexico, which made the issue much more real and concrete for a lot of people. For whatever reason, the NAFTA became the major factor in the ongoing organizing around trade issues in the U.S. The Fair Trade Campaign, which continued to lead the fight on these issues at the grassroots level outside Washington, became increasingly active on NAFTA issues along with their work on GATT.

Fair Trade coalitions sprang up all over the country, including one very active group in the Minneapolis and St. Paul area of Minnesota. This group pulled together the first national conference on NAFTA on a bitter cold Saturday in March 1991. The United Auto Workers (UAW) union at the local Ford truck assembly plant had formed ties with the independent trade union at the Ford Motor Plant in Matamoros, Mexico. The local UAW brought up representatives from this plant, who joined with people from Canada and at least 10 different states in the U.S. to start the first attempt at coordinating trinational actions to influence these talks.

One of the most exciting outcomes of this early meeting was a pledge of

NAFTA? NO THANKS! Democrat Harris Wofford is a big reason why George Bush wants to play down the NAFTA during an election year. Running on an anti-free trade platform in Pennsylvania, a state hit heavily by capital flight and closing factories, Wofford won a 1991 U.S. Senate race against heavily favoured Richard Thornburgh, Bush's personal candidate.

PHOTO BY HARVEY FINKLE/ IMPACT VISUALS

assistance by U.S. and Canadian groups to the independent union organizing efforts in Mexico, which included the monitoring of human rights violations during union elections at the Ford plant in Matamoros, Mexico. In addition, groups attending this conference agreed to support a boycott of the Pillsbury Company to support the union in Watsonville, California's Green Giant plant which relocated to Mexico, displacing workers and avoiding the U.S.'s more stringent environmental and labour laws. A picket line at the Pillsbury plant headquarters in Minneapolis brought the first serious media coverage to the campaign.

During the spring of 1991, national organizing around GATT and NAFTA took another significant step forward. In Washington D.C., Ralph Nader's Public Citizen watchdog group began to take on a more important role in organizing the fight to deny President Bush the fast track negotiating authority he needed to complete both the NAFTA and GATT. The fast track authority essentially gives a blank check to Bush by denying Congress the right to amend any final agreement. Supported by aggressive pressure at the grassroots level, Senator Hollings (D-SC) and Representative Dorgan (D-ND) led major congressional fights against the fast track. Although it appeared that they would successfully halt it, a final blitz by the White House succeeded in convincing a few D.C.-based environmental groups that their concerns would be addressed if they would support the president. Administration

FIGHTING FREE TRADE, U.S. STYLE

efforts also succeeded in convincing House Majority Leader Representative Gephardt to support fast track. This last minute support by Gephardt and a handful of environmental groups gave Bush the slim majority he needed to win the right to the fast track negotiating authority.

Although Bush won the battle over fast track, the fight succeeded in achieving a new level of cooperation between concerned farmer, labour, environmental, and consumer groups. Immediately after the fast track fight, this coalition became the Citizen's Trade Watch Campaign, led by Public Citizen's Lori Wallach. The Citizen's Trade Watch Campaign became the most important force behind trade issues inside the Washington D.C. beltway.

During the summer of 1991, there was widespread organizing against the NAFTA, including counter-events wherever U.S. trade negotiators showed up for public hearings or conferences. Carefully coordinated media work at every public event was an effective tool, helping to create a network of skilled Fair Trade Campaign organizers throughout the country. Craig Merrilees, a media consultant for the National Toxics Campaign, was brought into the Fair Trade Campaign to help in this aspect of the effort.

These efforts primed both media and national organizers for the biggest trade news story of the year, which broke in August: the tuna/dolphin ruling at GATT which broke the trade issue wide open nationally.

Up until this point, the suspicion that trade agreements would be used to lower environmental protection laws was seen as extremist and alarmist by many members of Congress. The tuna/dolphin ruling by GATT, however, turned out to be the "smoking gun." GATT ruled that the U.S. law, the Marine Mammal Protection Act – used to protect dolphins by blocking tuna imports from Mexico and other countries that use fishing methods that kill dolphins – was illegal by GATT definition and demanded that the act by repealed.

Fast track gives a blank check to Bush by denying Congress the right to amend any final agreement

The ruling sent shock waves through Congress. Representative Ron Wyden (D-OR), a strong supporter of the president's push for fast track, stated in a hearing on the tuna/dolphin ruling that he was changing his position and encouraged others to follow suit. From this point on, it became possible for fair trade advocates to mount a new attack on fast track.

House Majority Leader Gephardt (D-MO) had been very heavily criticized by labour and farm groups for his support of Bush on fast track. In an attempt to win back their support, Gephardt passed a resolution in the House of Representative stating that if the NAFTA or GATT talks failed to protect the environment or worker's rights, for instance, he would personally lead a fight to amend or kill the agreement. Fair trade organizers took him at his word and began to press him on this commitment. Citing the tuna/dolphin decision, they argued that the handwriting was on the wall and that he needed to lay the groundwork for a fight to repeal fast track and to amend or kill both the GATT and the NAFTA. In a letter to U.S. Trade Representative Carla Hills, Gephardt outlined a long list of concerns he had with the direction of both the GATT and NAFTA talks, and restated his intention to either amend or kill any agreement that did not meet these specific conditions.

At the same time, Senator Riegle (D-MI) began to circulate a resolution calling for the lifting of fast track on all non-tariff issues related to NAFTA. Eventually, the Gephardt letter was incorporated into a congressional resolution co-authored with Representative Waxman (D-CA) and co-sponsored by dozens of committee chairs.

In early November, Democratic Senator Wofford defeated George Bush's personal candidate for the Pennsylvania Senate seat, former Attorney General

---

WHAT'S LEFT ON WALL STREET?
Rolf Maurer

Activists resisting the corporate agenda already know that the best sources of information on the enemy include the business media. Publications like *The Economist*, *Business Week*, and the *Wall Street Journal* can be disconcertingly honest when writing about the world of capital – they'll often brag about things that the *Globe and Mail* or the *New York Times* would blush to report.

Unfortunately, these publications are so informed by the values and priorities of the multi-national corporations (MNCs) they report on, that most of us need a strong stomach to get through them on a regular basis.

Fortunately, there is one publication that will give you business news without all the pro-business cheerleading. The *Left Business Observer*, an eight-page newsletter published out of New York every six weeks or so, is one of the few publications on business or the economy which has been running articles critical of the NAFTA and GATT. "'Free trade' is a veil for the transformation of the globe into a free-fire zone for the MNCs," is LBO's take on the matter. Now, you won't find *that* sentiment expressed in the *Financial Post*!

LBO publisher Doug Henwood and his small staff have produced several articles on trade topics in recent issues. Issue 49 (November 4, 1991) featured a lengthy article, "Talking trade," about trends in international trade and how MNCs stand to benefit from them. "In an MNC-dominated world, national interest is obsolete, as are conventional statistical measures of imports and exports," the article states. "If you redefine exports as the foreign sales of U.S. MNCs, whether shipped from the U.S. or from overseas affiliates, and redefine imports as purchases by U.S. residents from foreign firms, whether imported from abroad or bought from their U.S. branches, then the 1986 trade deficit of $135 billion becomes a $23 billion surplus. Of course, this is of little help to U.S. workers, but it means plenty to the management and stockholders of MNCs." The same issue contained a smaller article reporting on the ongoing NAFTA negotiations.

"Trade, free and unfree," in Issue 50 (December 16, 1991), examines the reasons George Bush wants to "fast-track" the NAFTA through the U.S. Congress. Accompanying it was another sidebar reporting on the latest from the NAFTA and GATT fronts. Issue 51 (February 10, 1992) contained another NAFTA/GATT update.

A sub costs US$20 a year ($50 for institutions and the rich). The LBO can be reached at 250 W. 85th Street, New York, N.Y. 10024-3217.

Richard Thornburgh. Wofford campaigned heavily against free trade, using powerful television commercials to attack the Bush administration proposal for free trade with Mexico, particularly addressing the loss of jobs that would occur. These ads were an important factor in Wofford's success in overcoming a 44 percent deficit in the polls.

Wofford's astounding success was interpreted by the White House as a referendum on the Free Trade Agreement. Bush concluded that the NAFTA was very unpopular and politically damaging, and decided to slow the talks down until after the presidential election in November 1992. Though NAFTA now seems to be on the back burner, it, along with the GATT, will be major electoral issues. Republicans Patrick Buchanan and David Duke are challenging President Bush in the presidential primary and are also raising the trade issue as one of their top criticisms. Clearly, the fight for fair trade in the U.S. will continue to build.

Mark Ritchie is president of the Institute for Agriculture and Trade Policy, a non-profit and non-partisan research organization in Minneapolis, Minnesota. Since the late 1970s, he has been active at a national and international level to widen public awareness of the economic, social, and environmental challenges facing rural America.

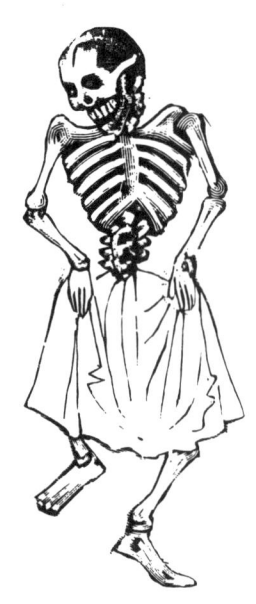

Women Fight Back

Women from Mexico, the U.S., and Canada are meeting to talk about the free trade deal and how it will affect them

by Denise Nadeau

"La mujer luchando y al mundo transformando!" Women fighting to transform the world! Raising her fist, and with strength shining in her eyes, the Mexican woman shouted this slogan of Mexican women activists. It was the end of Regina Avalos Castaneda's address to the International Solidarity Night at the 1991 British Columbia Federation of Labour Convention. As the audience leapt to its feet in response to her call to resist the North American Free Trade Agreement, there was no doubt that the message of the devastating impact of NAFTA on the lives of Mexican and Canadian women was beginning to be heard.

> **The experience of our Mexican sisters sheds light on our own experience of free trade**

Regina Avalos Castaneda and Georgina Rangel Martinez were two Mexican women who had been on a tour to B.C., sponsored by the B.C. Federation of Labour Women's Committee and Women to Women Global Strategies. There were a lot of "firsts" about this tour. It was the first time either of them had been north of Mexico ("el Norte"), and for Regina it was the first time she had left her country. It was also the first time the two of them had worked closely together. The coming together of the Urban Popular Movement's Women's Committee and labour women has been very recent in Mexico. It is partly the result of an initiative fostered by Mujer a Mujer, a Mexican-based women's organization that has been linking U.S., Canadian, and Mexican women affected by the restructuring of the global economy since the late 1980s. It was also the first time that community women and union women in B.C. have come together to sponsor a joint tour on free trade. With the realization that we are "all in the same boat" as our Mexican and American sisters has come a sense of urgency to share, learn, and work with each other.

The experience of our Mexican sisters sheds light on our own experience of free trade. Regina and Georgina made it clear that the signing of NAFTA is not a beginning for the Mexican people. For them it will be the final stage in the entrenchment of a process of continental economic integration that started as early as the mid-1960s with the beginnings of the Border Industrialization Program, later known as the maquiladora program, on the Mexican-U.S. border. The effect of NAFTA will be to lock the Mexican people into the devastating changes to their economy that have resulted from the structural adjustment programs imposed on them by their government in response to the IMF, the World Bank, and private bank creditors in the last 10 years. It is becoming clear that these same forces and policies have also been at work in Canada in the last decade, creating unemployment and poverty among Canadians.

THE MEXICAN EXPERIENCE Regina had been a factory worker for 20 years. She worked at Tootsie-Pop, a U.S. firm, placing 7,000 suckers an hour into holes on a conveyor belt moving to a machine that wrapped the suckers. One day, leaving the factory after a 9-hour shift with only a 30-minute lunch break, she was run over by a car at the factory gates. It took her three years to recover and she now lives on a small disability pension. For the past four years she has worked as the organizer for CONAMUP, a nationwide popular movement that represents the interests of the millions of unemployed, underemployed, and displaced who live in the outlying "colonias" and "barrios" of the large urban centres. She is also a member of the Mexico City Valley Women's

REGINA AVALOS CASTANEDA AND GEORGINA RANGEL MARTINEZ Regina (right) spent 20 years of her life making Tootsie Pops before a car accident ended her 'career.' Now, she is an organizer for CONAMUP. Georgina (top) has been a trade union activist for 17 years.
PHOTO BY NORM GARCIA/IWA

Regional Committee of CONAMUP, founded in 1983 to struggle for the specific demands of women within the larger urban popular movement.

Georgina has been working with women in the labour movement for the past 17 years. As a member of the Independent Union of the Workers of the Autonomous Metropolitan University she has been an activist for women's rights in the trade union movement. Mujeres en Accion Sindical (Women in Union Action) is a cross-sectoral group which provides workshops on working women's issues in the sectors which are the most affected by continental integration – the garment, telecommunication, and health care sectors.

The experience of Regina and Georgina gives us an overview of the working lives of the majority of Mexican women. Women work in both the formal and informal economies in Mexico. In the formal economy, ten million Mexican women receive salaries or wages; of these, 80 percent earn no more than $100 a month. Only one million women are unionized. Unions do not necessarily guarantee higher wages; a primary school teacher makes $100 a month, a hospital cleaner $100, a nurse $120, and a doctor $300. A social psychologist with a masters degree makes $320, while a university teacher with a doctorate makes $800 a month.

There are also 20 million Mexicans who work in the informal economy, without security or benefits. The majority of these are women. Seventeen million Mexicans live in extreme poverty. As there is no welfare in Mexico, people live by begging on the streets or by finding or creating whatever work they can. Women survive through economic activities like selling tortillas, pens, and hairclips on the street, washing and ironing clothes at home, doing domestic work for others, or by doing "homework" for factories, e.g. clipping and tying tiny copper cables for $50 per 5,000 for the electronics industry, or sewing piecework for the garment industry.[1]

Structural adjustment programs imposed by the IMF since 1982 have forced real wages to fall by 60 percent. School teachers, nurses, and factory workers are now joining the informal economy, selling merchandise in the street or doing "homework" after their first job is over. Many women work 12 to 16 hours a day, as well as having the responsibilities of home, just so they and their families can survive.

The structural adjustment and economic liberalization policies imposed by the IMF were embraced by the de la Madrid and Salinas de Gortari governments as the only way to pay off the interest on Mexico's massive foreign debt while still guaranteeing access to IMF loans. However, not only were there drastic losses in real wages, but also rampant inflation and devaluation of the peso. Official unemployment has risen and continues to rise (from 8.5 percent in 1982 to 17.9 percent in January 1991.)

Privatization and cutbacks in social spending have been introduced, resulting in collective agreements being rolled back. Vacation pay, daycare, and leave for

> 'Thirty percent of women of child-bearing age have been sterilized, many without their knowledge or consent, or as a requirement to receive government services or aid. Five percent are receiving injections of Depo-Provera, a cancer-causing contraceptive that has been banned in the U.S. and Canada. Cervical-uterine cancer is the fifth most common cause of death among Mexican women. Resources provide for only 20 percent of women over 25 years of age to have periodic pap smears.'
> THE GUARDIAN (NEW YORK)

women to look after their sick children, are all now threatened. In education, public services, and health, a new system of bonuses is being imposed. These bonuses for "productivity" and "good behaviour" (the meaning of which is decided by the boss) create an atmosphere of tension and competitiveness in the workplace.

Another major cost-cutting measure linked to structural adjustment that has severely affected women has been the reduction in basic food subsidies. Subsidies for rice, sugar, corn, and beans have been cut. Gains won by the Women's Committee of CONAMUP, like the free breakfast program for 25,000 children, have been lost or undermined.

Many women are the sole breadwinners in their families. Either as single women or single parents, or as women with partners who cannot contribute to the family financial support or who migrate "el norte," these women are forced to work at whatever they can find. Even women in extended family units – living with husbands, sisters, brothers, etc., which is quite common – have to work to contribute to the combined household earnings. Some women have no choice but to work as

---

WOMEN IN THE MAQUILADORAS
Deborah Bourque

In the maquiladoras, women face even harsher realities than their male co-workers.

Women comprise 68 percent of the entire maquila workforce. Except in heavier industry, employers tend to prefer hiring women – the younger the better. One employer in an electronics plant we visited claimed "women work with more dexterity, adapt easier to repetitive work, and are more punctual." The reality is that employers know that women are very often reluctant to do anything, such as union organizing, to risk losing their jobs when they have children to support.

In Mexico, there is no unemployment insurance. "If you are laid off," a union official told us, "you lose the right to live." And repercussions from employers are not restricted to firing. We met one woman who was driven from her home village and forced to leave her son behind because of actions taken against her by her employer for her organizing efforts.

The burnout rate is such in the maquiladoras that workers often last only five to ten years, only to be replaced by younger workers. The legal working age is 16 but employers and unions routinely turn a blind eye to this legal requirement. "About 10 percent of the workforce is underage," Enrique Lomas, a Mexican labour activist, told us. We talked with a group of young women who, when asked their ages, answered in unison "dieciseis" (16). They were obviously much younger and some told us they had been working in the maquila plant "for more than one year."

Women in the maquila plants face serious sexual harassment on the job and are subject to discipline and discharge for resisting managers' sexual advances. Maquila employers have been known to host what are referred to as "Friday night rape parties" for supervisors, involving female workers. Rapes are also frequently reported when women must travel late at night from their jobs.

Women routinely face dismissal on becoming pregnant. In some factories women are required to show proof to staff doctors that they are menstruating. And despite legislation which provides that a pregnant woman will be moved to other work if her health or the health of the fetus is endangered, pregnant women continue to be forced to work unprotected with toxic chemicals. This chemical exposure often results in birth defects, we were told by women trade unionists.

SOURCE: Pro-Canada Dossier No.29

migrant labourers, travelling to the border-zone maquiladoras, or into the U.S., illegally or on contract to U.S. factories like Tootsie-Pop Chicago which uses short-term Mexican labour because "the women will cause less trouble than American workers," as Regina pointed out.

The maquiladoras are presented nationally and internationally as the place where the economy is growing. The maquiladoras function as a free trade zone. Free trade zones are a growing international phenomenon. In 1975 there were 31 zones in 18 countries. In 1986 there were 500 zones in 70 countries.[2]

Maquila work is labour-intensive and boasts cheap labour as its main asset. It involves assembly-line production in industries like electronics, fibre, footwear, electrical products, plastics, knitwear, and toys. In free trade zones throughout the world, maquila work has been represented as work ideally suited for women, requiring patience, manual dexterity, and docility. Presenting assembly work as consistent with traditionally ascribed female gender roles and characteristics has served to legitimize the employment of women, who are then paid lower wages.

By hiring young women, who are usually politically inexperienced and often recruited from the informal economy, management is able to impose appalling conditions. In Mexico these range from mandatory pregnancy testing, three-month contracts, no health and safety regulations, and wages that begin as low as 55 cents an hour, to continual sexual harassment on the job. Women in maquiladoras are either without unions, fired if they start one, or automatically become members of a company union that is set up by management to protect the employers from legitimate unions.

What further impact would a North American Free Trade Agreement have on Mexican women? The Salinas government is streamlining economic and social policies to make the Mexican investment climate more favourable for multinationals. In the fall of 1991 and winter of 1992, several constitutional amendments were introduced that will greatly affect the poor and working classes of Mexico, and in particular, the lives of women and their children. The following constitutional provisions have been changed and/or undermined:

> **The Women's Committee is fighting to maintain and expand basic food programs**

❏ The right to free, secular, public education. The Mexican government is now encouraging private and, in particular, church schools.

❏ The protection of *ejido* lands, collective plots that guarantee peasants land. As the proposed privatization of the *ejido* goes through, 2.7 million peasants and their families will be displaced, adding to the ranks of as many as 6 million small property owners, landless, and labourers who will be displaced by free trade.[3]

❏ The Federal Labour Law, which guarantees the right to health care, maternity

UGLY PATTERN
Textile and garment workers have been front and centre in anti-free trade efforts, and no wonder – Canada has lost more than 80,000 jobs in those industries since the Free Trade Agreement was signed.

PHOTO FROM THE FISHERMAN

leave, a seniority system, pension retirement plans, and job security, and the right to belong to unions, strike, and bargain collectively. While many of these provisions are not actually enforced in Mexico, the fear that the law may be struck entirely, as it was in Colombia in December 1990, has workers realizing that free trade comes at the cost of attacks on unions and cutbacks to workers' benefits.

For urban poor women, structural adjustment programs and free trade have brought cuts in basic food subsidies. To soften the impact of economic restructuring and to undermine popular resistance, Salinas has created a new government organization called PRONASOL, a "solidarity" program, to help the poor. Before the August 1990 elections, milk and tortillas were given out to the people to get their votes. PRONASOL has since introduced a series of popular consultations as a means of getting consensus for its charity program. Handouts and limited funding for projects like community kitchens and the breakfast programs are now being used as a way to undermine the community control that CONAMUP had gained in the last few years.

The Women's Committee is fighting to maintain and expand basic food programs like the children's breakfast program and a subsidized tortillas program (*tortibonos*), as well as to provide milk stores and gas distribution in the poor neighbourhoods. But it is also engaged in political education and training so that women can resist the charity onslaught of the government and move toward neighbourhood control of living conditions.

The garment industry in Mexico is already reflecting the impact of free trade. The garment maquila process – involving cutting in the north, sewing in Mexico, and exporting – was tailored to the loopholes opened by the U.S. customs and commerce regulations #806 and #807. NAFTA will remove the necessity of this process and allow for a more effective integration of the industry across national borders. The Mexican consulate has already approached manufacturers in Toronto as part of a strategy of setting the stage for a new "trinational" garment industry which will involve joint ventures between Mexican, U.S., and Canadian capital. In August 1990, government "sew-mobiles" were touring the poor peripheral neighbourhoods of Mexico to prepare women to work in the new factories which the government will be installing in areas of high unemployment.[4]

Mexican women activists are anticipating similar drastic changes in other industries. The telecommunications industry is being privatized, deregulated, and transnationalized. Telmex, the government phone company, was sold to Southwestern Bell and France Telecom. 10,000 to 13,000 women's jobs are threatened by the takeover and the introduction of digital technology.

As jobs are lost with the restructuring of domestic industries – many of which will shut down completely as they are unable to compete with U.S. imports flooding the market – Mexican women are being told it's better to work at home and to work part-time. For women, the trade agreement will accelerate and legitimize changes that are already occurring.

THE CANADIAN EXPERIENCE   The Mexican women were not alone in wanting to make international links. B.C. women activists are aware to what extent structural adjustment and the global restructuring of capital have been affecting Canadian women for the last ten years. As a First World country, we have not seen or experienced the difficult conditions that our Mexican and other Third World sisters have. The Free Trade Agreement, signed with the U.S. in January 1989, has suddenly pulled Canadian women into the dynamic of global restructuring.

As part of the B.C. tour, Women to Women Global Strategies took Georgina to a local unionized garment factory. The majority of workers there were women doing piecework and making $7.50 an hour guaranteed, with benefits. The machine operators, most of whom were men, made between $9 and $11 an hour. This shop had been through many changes in the last few years, its ownership passing from

> 'Transnational corporations arrange to have labour supplied to their Mexican operations through a company which warehouses young women and men in barracks. In one of the barracks, we found sixty women living in one room sleeping in bunk beds spaced one meter apart. The living quarters had no windows to the outdoors. A supervisor's office sits next to the living quarters, allowing for surveillance of the women. For these accommodations, workers pay a day's wages per week.'
>
> SISTER SUSAN MIKA, PRESIDENT, COALITION FOR JUSTICE IN THE MAQUILADORAS

WOMEN FIGHTING BACK

INFORMAL ECONOMY
Women make up the majority of the informal economy, where people survive selling food and other products on the streets, or doing piecework at home.

PHOTO BY ELAINE BRIERE

Levi's to Wrangler to the present U.S.-based multinational VF Corporation. VF had made a considerable profit in the last two years but was beginning to lay off some employees and was pressing for concessions during contract negotiations in order to make bigger profits. With 5,000 jobs lost in the B.C. garment industry in the last two years, workers are feeling the pressure to accept rollbacks as companies threaten to move to Mexico. The manager at the shop we visited told Georgina he was learning Spanish so he would be ready to move.

The union business agent told us that only 2,000 garment workers are unionized in B.C. Of the 10,000 non-unionized workers, the majority work in non-union shops with no benefits at minimum wage. Recently, underground sweatshops have been opening up, and at least 3,000 home servers are doing piecework in the lower mainland of B.C. without benefits or minimum wage. What we see in B.C. is a strategy of increasing layers of subcontracting as a way of reducing costs. At the same time, some of this labour-intensive work is being sent to Mexico. In both countries, women are being exploited.

The garment industry has been a major employer of women (90 percent of the workers are women), specifically immigrant and visible minority women who are the majority. While the industry has become more automated, there are labour-intensive jobs that can't be automated. To make a profit, companies try to keep costs for this labour-intensive work low. The Canadian garment industry has been particularly hard hit by free trade – 80,000 jobs have been lost since the agreement with the U.S. went into effect. Since the 1980s the industry has experienced steady job loss as free trade zones in Asia produced lower-priced imports. The FTA hastened this process, and the city of Toronto lost a third of its industry between 1988 and 1990.

The shifts in the garment industry reflect the major restructuring of work and, in particular, women's work in Canada. In the 1980s, many of the new jobs held by women were in low-paying, high-turnover jobs concentrated in clerical, sales, and service industries. The majority of these jobs are not unionized and are part time. Many women's jobs in Canada are now in the lowest-paid service sector – waitressing, tourism, chambermaids, and fast foods – where salaries for women dropped by 10 percent between 1981 and 1987. The majority of women in these industries also have been relegated to an on-call, part-time labour force.

With the recession of the early 1980s and the election of the Conservatives, who decided to follow neo-liberal policies, employers and corporations followed suit to reduce costs and lower wages. The overall strategy involved going to the Third World for labour, building a two-tiered employment structure at home, and attacking workers and their rights. Organizations are being restructured to create a small core of full-time employees and a larger circle of peripheral workers. Technology has become a tool in this strategy of downsizing and creating a more "flexible" workforce which can only find work on a casual and part-time basis.[5]

Clerical employment has been particularly hard hit by restructuring. In the 1970s, clerical work increased by 60 percent. In the 1980s it has changed from one of the fastest growing occupations to one of the slowest, and continues to be an area of high unemployment and underemployment for women. Recent advances in computer and communications technology have contributed to the loss of clerical jobs. Long before free trade came into effect, clerical, data processing, and accounting jobs were being contracted out and/or transferred to American head offices. The Canadian Independent Computer Services Association estimated that by 1988, 200,000 managerial, administrative, clerical, and computer-related office jobs had been transferred to the U.S. With the FTA removing restrictions on the movement of information and services, another 150,000 office jobs will be moved to the U.S. by 1993. The potential loss of clerical jobs alone is 241,500 jobs.[6]

CAREER OPPORTUNITIES
This issue of TWIN PLANT NEWS depicted the maquilas as a great place for women to work. Women do make up most of the maquila workforce, but almost all are unskilled teenagers making even less than their male co-workers.

Offshore data processing is also on the rise. Confederation Life has a Barbados office. A walk through the Yellow Pages in Vancouver revealed a data processing brokerage firm that was shipping out work to processors in Peru.

Women in the public sector have been among the first affected by this economic restructuring. As part of their agenda, the federal and many provincial governments adopted policies of reducing public expenditures by cutting jobs and restricting wages and benefits. The public sector was one of the first to go to part-time work. With privatization, many women's jobs have disappeared.

Another area where women have been hard hit by the Free Trade Agreement and other policies of the corporate agenda is the health sector. Bill C-69 and Bill C-20 will reduce federal payments for education and health from 40 percent to zero by the year 2000. This will further accelerate the process of privatizing services and contracting out. Major job losses are beginning to be felt, with the added perils of health risks for women and their families. For example, pap smears from Vancouver are now being processed by piece rate in northern Washington State. The pressure produced by piecework, as opposed to fixed, wages increases the risk of errors.

Cutbacks in social spending have increased the feminization of poverty in Canada. The cuts in unemployment insurance coverage affect fish processors and other types of seasonal workers. The cutbacks in federal contributions to the Canada Assistance Plan, which funds welfare and social assistance, are serving to keep welfare rates alarmingly low. Prices have risen, not fallen with FTA, largely because of imposition of the GST.

The decline in full-year, full-time employment over the last decade means that women cannot earn enough to support themselves. The average income of a single mother who worked full-time in 1990 was $24,923. In contrast, women who worked part-time (49-52 weeks) earned $12,099; women who worked part-year (less than 49 weeks) made $5,449. Eighty percent of minimum wage earners are women. Earning minimum wage places both single women and single mothers far below the poverty line, which nationally is $13,485, and for a parent with two children, $25,467. A single woman with a minimum wage of $5 an hour will earn $9,880 a year. (Child Poverty Task Force, 1991).

> The women who work in the maquiladoras of Reynosa, Mexico, 'earn among the lowest wages on the globe at the same time the border's maquila boom and inflation continue to drive up the price of food, children's clothing and schoolbooks, and other necessities. "If your kid needs new shoes, it's a crisis," says Maria Cruz Mendoza, a single mother of two. "If you have to buy clothes for them, you go to the second-hand market.'"
>
> AUSTIN-AMERICAN STATESMAN, DECEMBER 16, 1990

The North American Free Trade Agreement will entrench an acutely polarized labour market. In this market, a small number of core workers, largely white, will co-exist with a large contingent of peripheral workers. Most of these part-time workers will be women, the majority, immigrant and visible minority women. The core workers will be multi-skilled, technologically trained workers; the majority of these will be men. It is important to note that the divisions between core and periphery are and will continue to be along class and race lines as well as gender. In fact, educated women are benefitting from restructuring, while uneducated working-class and non-white women and men are definitely not.

A recently documented shift in the make-up of the workforce in the maquila zones in Mexico has raised another question. In 1975, 85 percent of the workers were women; in 1990, 60 percent were women, indicating a rise in the proportion of male workers. What is not clear is whether this represents a temporary situation limited to the transfer of capital-intensive industries to the maquila zones, or whether women will be forced out of their jobs by men displaced from traditional industries.

RESISTANCE: ORGANIZING FOR ECONOMIC CONTROL "La deyda no es del pueblo/El pueblo no lo pidio/Que no se hagan pendejos/El PRI se lo chingo" The debt doesn't belong to the people/The people didn't ask for it/Don't be fools/The PRI stole the money.

We were on our way to Victoria to talk to anti-poverty and solidarity groups. Georgina and Regina were using the ferry time to share some of the slogans that the women use in marches, demonstrations and sit-ins.

The use of popular cultural forms like slogans to tell "the real story" of what is happening to the people is a common tool of resistance among Mexican women. We were amazed at these stories of resistance of our Mexican sisters, and at their militancy and energy in fighting changes which can seem so overwhelming and immobilizing to us. We got much inspiration from these women who, with fewer resources to work with, were working to build a new solidarity both nationally and internationally. We also learned that Mexican women, as well as American women along the U.S./Mexican border, were looking at strategies that move beyond the workplace into the neighbourhood and were using methods of organizing that have a strong cultural dimension.

The refusal-to-shoulder-the-debt slogan is shouted by the women of the Urban Popular Movement when they are in demonstrations outside the government offices. They may be demanding free breakfasts for school children, subsidized tortillas and milk, control of community food distribution centres, or protesting cutbacks in subsidies. The membership of CONAMUP is 85 to 95 percent women, and these women are a formidable force when they press their demands. In the last

FREE TRADE JOBS
Young women like these make up the majority of maquila workers. They can look forward to mandatory pregnancy testing, three-month contracts, no health and safety regulations, and starting wages of 55 cents an hour. Unrestricted sexual harassment is also common.
PHOTO BY ALEXANDRA DAGG

few years they have focused on two demands as key to organizing women: the reduction of the high cost of living, and an end to violence against women.

The Women's Committee of CONAMUP provides an example of the new models of resistance that are developing amongst women in the face of economic restructuring. The recent cutbacks in government subsidies to basic foods have resulted in massive demonstrations by the Urban Popular Movement. Besides struggling with the government, the Regional Women's Committee has started health centres and clinics; given training workshops in health care, herbal medicine, and nutrition; created consumer co-ops so peasants can sell their products directly to the city dwellers; and created sewing co-ops and Popular Kitchens run completely by the women. The women have also organized workshops, marches, and demonstrations on violence against women, and have created "commissions of honour and justice" to respond to and stop violent attacks on women by men.

CONAMUP uses a form of neighbourhood organizing which links workplace, community, and family issues. By focusing on the high cost of living they have brought thousands of women out to demonstrate against the government. On one march, 60,000 women banging pots with spoons marched to the Zocalo (the central square in Mexico City). They use tactics like occupying offices of newspapers that don't give coverage to their issues, or occupying the front steps of government offices of the officials with whom they want to negotiate. They hang clotheslines around the building, set up cooking

> **WHERE COMPUTERS COME FROM**
> 'In one job you measure the width of capacitors,' says Gloria, an electronics worker in a maquila factory. 'On each tiny piece you take five or six measurements, making the same motions of your wrist all day long. Eventually the workers get a growth on their wrists and then they have to have an operation.'

stoves, and "turn their children loose" until someone comes to negotiate.

In these actions CONAMUP uses powerful cultural symbols like motherhood to show the strength of the women. The character of "Superbarrio" (Super Neighbourhood) complements this. Superbarrio is a masked and caped popular wrestling figure who often appears at marches and negotiations, transforming the superman character into a figure representing the strength of the people.

The tactic of organizing women around neighbourhood rather than workplace lines has also emerged in the southern U.S., especially along the border area. Because the turnover in maquila and border factories is so high, it is more effective to organize these women in their communities. Mujer Obrera in El Paso, Texas, has been organizing women on both sides of the border since 1981. Originating in response to the terrible conditions of Mexican and Chicano garment workers, it has established food co-ops, health clinics, a workers' centre with ongoing classes in workers and women's rights, literacy, and self-defense, as well as providing crisis services to respond to domestic violence. In June 1990, Mujer Obrera women chained themselves to sewing machines and staged a hunger strike to protest a factory's closing without meeting its payroll. Their action resulted in a state law being passed that made nonpayment of wages a crime. In May 1991, Mujer women walked out of four factories and put up picket lines demanding basic workers rights. Mujer Obrera has started to develop alternative economic strategies at the community level.

Fuerza Unida, based in San Antonio, Texas, was formed in January 1990 after the closing of the Levi Strauss plant which employed 1,500 workers. Levi transferred its operation to Costa Rica where it pays workers $2.50 a day rather than $7 an hour. Since 1985, Levi Strauss has closed 35 plants in the U.S. Fuerza Unida formed three weeks after the January closing. It now has 650 members and has organized a national boycott of Levi's products, carried out hunger strikes, and filed a class action suit against the company. As well, it has initiated a national campaign against U.S. garment plant shutdowns. Now the members are looking into worker co-ops and setting up a displaced workers centre.

Other U.S. women's organizations organizing in low-wage industries against plant closures and non-enforcement of workers rights are: Asian Immigrant Women Advocates in Oakland, the Green Giant workers of Watsonville, California, and the North Carolina Poultry workers. All these organizations have seen the number of jobs in their industries fall drastically with free trade zones and free trade agreements. (In the garment industry, over 800,000 women's jobs have been lost in the U.S. in the past 20 years.) Women in these organizations are trying to define what conditions and laws will encourage industry to stay, what options they can develop if companies relocate, how to improve wages and working conditions, and how to get adequate salaries for women doing human service work. As well, they are providing leadership training and challenging racism. All are looking at creating community-based economic alternatives for their members.[7]

The other new model that has developed in response to the impact of economic restructuring is that of cross-sectoral women's groups with international links. Mujer a Mujer (MAM), based in Mexico City and in San Antonio, Texas, is a pioneer of this form. A collective of Canadian, American, and Mexican women, MAM links women in common sectors across borders in order to foster a common global analysis of local issues and to develop common strategies and common actions. In February 1992, MAM co-sponsored, with Mujeres en Accion Sindical, a trinational conference of Women Workers on Continental Integration. This conference brought together women from the U.S., Mexico, Canada, and the Mexico-U.S. border region, as well as representatives from Central and South America. This conference resulted in the Ville de Bravo Declaration which outlined the basic social and labour rights that women want guaranteed in any form of continental integration. Participants also laid the groundwork for future trinational cooperation in specific sectors, as well as for a trinational fact-finding tour of the maquiladoras, skills and information exchanges, and ongoing research on new

> **Levi Strauss transferred its operation to Costa Rica where it pays workers $2.50 a day rather than $7 an hour**

methods of organizing. The women left the conference also committed to having the Ville de Bravo Declaration endorsed and acted on by coalitions, unions, popular groups, and political parties.

Women to Women Global Strategies has recently formed in B.C. to do education, research, and cultural work around the issue of the impact on women of global restructuring. Also cross-sectoral, it is working to offer a gender perspective on the fight against NAFTA and the corporate agenda, as well as to reach women who are not being reached by existing organized movements resisting free trade. A similar committee has formed in Toronto. As well, in Toronto a coalition of community, women's, and labour groups has formed to mount a campaign for increased protection for garment workers.

> Anti-poverty activists have organized women around economic issues, linking these to the FTA and NAFTA

Nationally a Global Strategies sub-committee has formed within the National Action Committee on the Status of Women (NAC) to address the impact of free trade and continental integration on women's work and lives. A NAC-sponsored Women and Work project, developing in different regions of the country, helps women analyze and organize around how their paid work and home lives are being changed by restructuring and free trade.

Anti-poverty activists have also been organizing women around economic issues and linking these to the FTA and proposed NAFTA. An example is End Legislated Poverty's successful campaign for government-funded, non-stigmatizing lunch programs in schools as a mobilizing step in the fight against the growing impoverishment of women and their families. Like the Regional de Mujer in CONAMUP, ELP links the struggle for basic needs, adequate food, adequate welfare rates and minimum wage, and full employment, with the struggle against the corporate agenda and free trade. ELP also has experimented with more popular organizing tactics – bringing children to government lobbying sessions, presenting street theatre, and doing "corporate agenda" popular education workshops with poor women and their allies.

Women are adopting new forms of organizing, partly because of the failure of more traditional approaches to organizing which occurred in the 1980s. The emphasis on male workers, trade unions, the state, electoral processes, and political parties excludes the realities and struggles of large numbers of unorganized women. This, coupled with the lack of democratic practice in unions, has led women to reach outside their unions and ally themselves with other women's organizations who are struggling for human rights and justice for women and their children.

CHALLENGES TO CANADIAN WOMEN Canadian women need to look more closely at new models of organizing being developed in the U.S. and Mexico, where women have been feeling the impact of global restructuring longer. We also need to find the common basis of unity amongst workers in the three countries as well as with women in Central and South America whose countries are being drawn into the free trade vortex. We have to explore how we can express international solidarity. As Cecelia Rodriguez, a former organizer of Mujer Obrera, said, "The women of La Mujer Obrera have done a tremendous job, but they will only have a future if women in other parts of the country [continent] connect with them. How different the ending of 'Thelma and Louise' would have been if hundreds of other women had come to their rescue."[8]

1. *Correspondencia*, December 1990, p. 9.
2. Noel Watson, *Evaluating the Net Economic Benefits of Free Trade Zones in Theory and Practice: Applied to the Kingston Export Free Trade Zone in Jamaica*. Simon Fraser University Ph.D. dissertation, 1988, p. xiii.
3. John Dillon, "Ethical Reflections on North American Economic Integration," draft paper, 1991 Ecumenical Coalition for Economic Justice, p. A.5.
4. Linda Yanz, "Heading South: Restructuring in the Garment Industry," October 20, 1991.
5. Marcy Cohen and Margaret White, *The Impact of Computerization and Economic Restructuring on Women's Employment Opportunities*. Final Report, Labour Canada Technology Impact Program, 1989, p. i.
6. *Ibid.*, p. 39.
7. Kalima Rose, "Women Are Stirring the Pot," *Equal Means*, Vol. 1, No. 1, Winter 1991, pp. 5-8.
8. Felicia Ward, "Something Has Crossed Over in Me and I Can't Go Back," *Equal Means*, Vol. 1, No. 1, Winter 1991, p. 11.

RESOURCES AND REFERENCES

Cohen, Marcy and Margaret White, *The Impact of Computerization and Economic Restructuring on Women's Employment Opportunities*. Women's Skills Development Society, 1989.

Correspondencia (the quarterly of Mujer a Mujer), send $20 U.S. to Mujer a Mujer, P.O. Box 12322, San Antonio, Texas 78212, U.S.A.

Fuentes, Annette and Barbara Ehrenreich, *Women in the Global Factory*. South End Press, 1983.

Kopinak, Kathryn, "Living the Gospel Through Service to the Poor: The Convergence of Political and Religious Motivations in Organizing Maquiladora Workers in Juarez, Mexico, " in *Race, Class, Gender: Bonds and Barriers*, edited by Jesse Vorst, et al. Garamond, 1991.

Miller, Susan. *Common Fate, Common Bond: Women in the Global Economy*. Pluto, 1986.

"Review of the Situation of Canadian Women." *NAC Reports*, February 1991.

Ward, Kathryn. *Women Workers and Global Restructuring*. Ithaca Press, ILR, 1990.

Denise Nadeau is a member of Women to Women Global Strategies, the NAC Global Strategy Committee, and the Christian Task Force on Central America. She has been doing popular education work on global restructuring and economic justice, with women's and church groups, since 1987.

(This article was written with input from Marcy Cohen, Lin Bueckart, Linda Yanz and Elaine Burns.)

Solidarity, Not Competition

Workers must seek allies across national borders in order to stop 'free' trade

by Fern Valin and Jim Sinclair

In the 1990s, many Canadians find themselves in a world that has come to resemble a child's "dot picture." Global corporations with no commitment to any one country appear to be the only entities with the resources and power to join the dots together, drawing their world vision clearer with each passing day. Workers and their countries become powerless in this picture, relying on the hope that one of these corporations will connect them with the new "global factory," keeping the illusion of progress alive.

When all the dots are finally connected, money, goods, and raw resources will flow freely without any constraints or social responsibilities at all. Governments, borders, and democracy simply complicate the smooth running of the free market.

"Our ultimate aim is a world where technologies can move freely, where goods and services are exchanged without impediment, where investments flow where they can most productively be used," said Prime Minister Brian Mulroney.

The global corporations, a few with head offices in Canada, won a major victory when Mulroney pushed through the free trade agreement with the United States in 1988. The agreement opens the door to unrestricted foreign ownership, curtails the right of government to stop the export of our unprocessed resources (oil, natural gas, lumber, fish, water), and provides open access to our markets for U.S. corporations by removing tariffs. For workers, the result has been disastrous. Manufacturing jobs are disappearing as corporations

> **Globalization is being embraced by Canadian corporations who see its benefits for the balance sheet**

SOLIDARITY NOT COMPETITION

MAKING CONNECTIONS During the 1980s, hundreds of Canadian trade unionists visited Central America. Here, a demonstration is held by Canadians in front of the U.S. embassy in Nicaragua.

PHOTO FROM LAWG ARCHIVES

"restructure." The latest count shows 400,000 workers have lost their jobs. Millions of other Canadians live in fear as corporations and governments tell us daily that, in the "New World Order," we must adapt to globalization, free trade, and world competition. For working people, these words inevitably precede demands for wage cuts, flexibility, cuts in social programs, and, in more and more cases, the closure of plants. Within two years of Canada's falling to free trade, U.S. president George Bush announced that Mexico would be the next conquest on the way to creating a free trade zone "stretching from the Port of Anchorage to Tierra del Fuego."

At the turn of the century, a similar free trade proposal was rejected by Canadian business, but today globalizaton is being embraced by Canadian corporations who see its benefits for the balance sheet. A perfect example is provided by Northern Telecom, a "Canadian" corporation which is a world leader in telecommunications. In 1991 it declared profits of more than $500 million. Ten years ago this would have prompted workers to gear up to win their fair share at the bargaining table. Not any more. Although the number of Telecom employees has grown from 35,000 to 63,000 in the last decade, 1,000 unionized employees in Canada have lost their jobs since the free trade deal was signed. Worldwide, growth was 834 percent, but that was mostly in cheap labour zones like Asia, Latin America, or Mexico. Today only 21 percent of the workforce carry union cards compared to 41 percent 10 years ago. Business is profitably booming for everyone but the workers.

At bargaining tables across Canada, workers face bleak choices. Private sector workers are told to take cutbacks or lose the jobs to the United States or Mexico. Public sector workers are told there's no money for wages unless there are layoffs. This kind of blackmail has become a powerful employer tool for lowering wages and living standards for workers.

If Canadian workers were to see themselves and their families in the corporate crystal ball, the view would be a shock. Canada in the year 2000 will have virtually no manufacturing base, no medicare, few public services, bankrupt governments, and millions of unemployed. Raw resource exports of logs, fish, water, etc., low-paid service jobs, and increased environmental degradation will characterize the economics of the country. U.S. social critic Noam Chomsky describes this vision as the "Third Worldization" of the north, and it is already underway.

But this bleak picture does not have to become reality.

MAKING THE CONNECTIONS How do Canadian workers rebuild collective power, maintain a sustainable and healthy economic system, and reclaim the

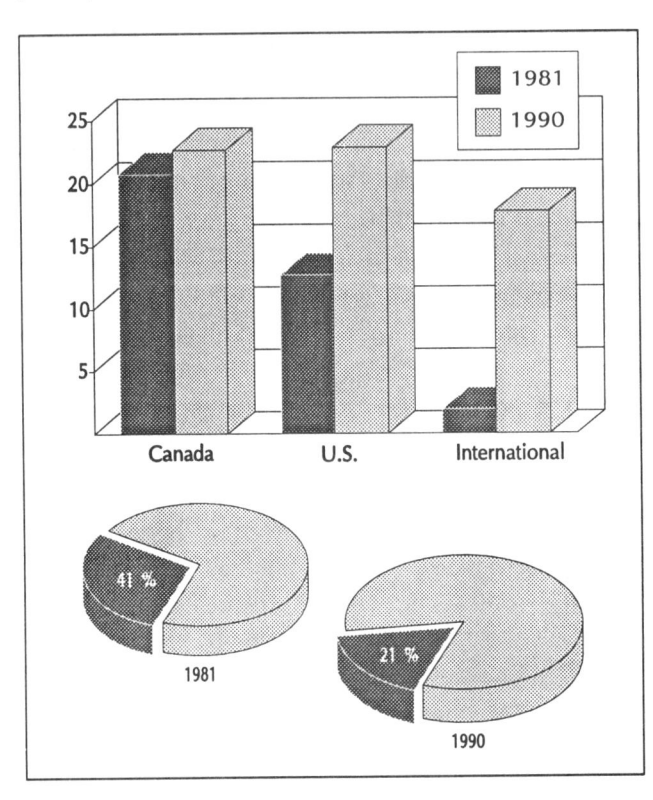

PROUDLY CANADIAN? During the 1980s the 'Canadian' multinational Northern Telecom moved many of its operations to low-wage, non-union plants outside North America. The graph (left) shows the number of Nor Tel employees (in thousands) in Canada, the U.S., and abroad in 1981 and 1990. As a result, the proportion of NorTel workers who are unionized has fallen from 40 percent to 20 percent of the workforce (pies).

sovereignty of the country?

The initial steps must include the rejection of not only free trade, but also the entire argument for open borders and increased competition between workers, both in Canada and with our sisters and brothers to the south. For workers, competing with each other for the attention of capital means we become bidders at an auction where the final price is the destruction of our living and working conditions and our environment. It is not Mexican or American workers who are the enemy, but an economic and political system which pits us against each other in our fight for a decent life.

Contrary to the dominant corporate view, workers are not powerless to act. The alternative to "competitive poverty" is for Canadian workers to fight for a strong, progessive country and to build new forms of solidarity with our counterparts in the south. Fortunately, our history is full of examples where solidarity, and not competition, has won out.

Without solidarity, unions would never have been formed, strikes would not have been successfully fought, nor decent contracts won. Strong collective action extended to the streets and the ballot box, where it was instrumental in forcing governments to play a major role in the economy, at times to the benefit of workers and their communities. Programs such as medicare, unemployment insurance, and public education are the result of this type of struggle. At its roots, solidarity is the rejection of a society where individual wealth takes precedence over the well being of the group as a whole.

This type of solidarity didn't stop at the border. During the last two decades, the changing international scene helped to deepen our experiences and understanding of solidarity. In the case of South Africa and Central America in particular, thousands of Canadian trade unionists found themselves in direct contact with workers on the front line of a life-and-death struggle for sovereignty and self-determination.

In the case of Nicaragua after 1979, there was a vibrant and dynamic young leadership in the government, which challenged the U.S. agenda for the region. The trade union movement grew dramatically, and Nicaraguans were clearly better off than their counterparts in other southern countries. Both these developments – a strong government which favoured workers, and an active union movement linked to a strong popular movement including women, youth, and campesinos – made it possible for dramatic change to take place. An increase in public services such as medicare, transportation, and free education, nationalization of the banks and some industries, controls on the export of capital, and land reform, began to challenge a century of poverty and exploitation. For Canadian trade unionists visiting Nicaragua, it was not difficult to relate to their struggle for a better society, given our tradition of fighting for social justice and an end to poverty in Canada. Here were people, surrounded by dictatorships and under invasion by U.S.-backed contras, creating an alternative vision to the corporate view of the world. The spirit and sacrifices we witnessed in Nicaragua sent many of us home with a new commitment to solidarity.

Unfortunately, the growing solidarity movement with Nicaragua found little support from the leadership and staff of the Canadian Labour Congress. The Congress, which represents more than two million workers in Canada, allied itself with a small anti-government union in Nicaragua, with links to the contras.

Despite this, many unions took the lead, creating new forms of solidarity. Links were often facilitated by groups such as the B.C. Trade Union Group, Saskatchewan International Labour Program, Latin American Working Group and various trade union activists in all parts of Canada. Canadian trade unionists visited unions in Nicaragua, then strengthened their relationships by inviting Nicaraguans to visit Canada, arranging tours for them from British Columbia to Newfoundland.

Returning trade unionists brought news from Nicaragua that challenged the media's version of the revolution and the U.S. backed contra war. Because this alternative view came from their own sisters and brothers' first-hand experiences,

---

MAQUILADORAS BOOM IN GUATEMALA

Jim Sinclair

Many large clothing corporations are passing up the maquiladora zones of Mexico in favor of the maquiladoras in Guatemala. Here workers earn between $1 and $2 a day compared to $3.50 to $4.00 a day in Mexico.

In the past five years, the number of clothing plants in Guatemala has mushroomed from five to more than 200. They now employ 40,000 workers, mostly women, and produce exports valued at $100 million.

Fueled by Korean, U.S., and Guatemalan money, Guatemala's maquiladoras produce goods that are being sent to the United States, mostly to brand-name firms including Levi's, Gitano, Liz Claiborne, Guess, Van Heusen, Sears, and K-Mart.

Workers are on the line for up to 60 hours a week, often until midnight, and then they are locked in their factory overnight so they can begin work again early the next morning.

A combination of government and company repression ensures that union organizing is kept to a minimum. Recent unionization attempts by 500 workers at two plants owned by Phillips-Van Heusen, a large U.S. shirtmaker, have resulted in bribes, firings, and death threats.

Union supporters report that one of PVH's personnel managers has issued death threats, stating, "Everyone involved in the union is going to die," and "If you join the union you will be killed."

Although the company dismissed the threats, workers took them seriously after a member of their executive committee was shot and nearly killed. The government has failed to recognize the new union.

Ironically, Mexico has already announced its intention to extend free trade to all of Central America in the near future.

SOURCE: Stephen Coats, "Made In Guatemala – Union Busting in the Maquiladoras" *Multinational Monitor*, November 1991.

SOLIDARITY NOT COMPETITION

> When he announced that his Canadian-based auto parts company was opening a plant in Mexico, Frank Stronach said, 'Profit means money. Money has no heart, no soul, no conscience, no homeland.'
>
> FRANK STRONACH, MAGNA INTERNATIONAL

the message carried a great deal of credibility. Many unions turned words into material aid and, with the help of CUSO and OXFAM, created projects such as health and safety training, union education, and daycare centres, or provided fish boats, gear, and expertise. This work contributed to the formation of international solidarity committees in some unions. Tools for Peace blossomed into the largest solidarity organization ever built in Canada – a coalition of churches, unions, community organizations, and solidarity groups that raised more than $10 million in aid. The slogan "When they win we win" came to reflect the view that, although we live in different realties, our fates are increasingly tied to one another.

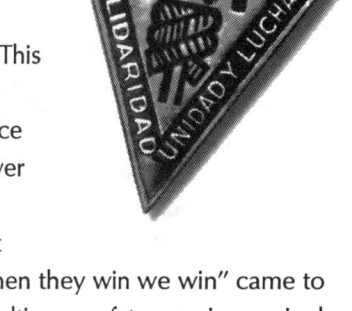

For many Canadian unions, Nicaragua opened the door on the region. Union delegations travelled to such places as Guatemala and El Salvador, and discovered that death squads and military repression were used to break unions. As in Nicaragua, workers in these countries were deeply involved in a political process which had at its roots the reclaiming of their country from foreign domination and the creation of a new society based on the needs of the majority.

As the eighties drew to a close, a new and clearer picture of the need for solidarity began to emerge. What we in Canada saw as isolated attacks on our living and working conditions, Central Americans and Mexicans described as part of the "neo-liberal agenda." As Canada moved closer to the free trade election in 1988, it made perfect sense for these solidarity groups and unions to turn their attention to Mexico. Prior to the election, a tour was organized to the maquiladora zones, where Canadians saw first hand what free trade did to Mexico's border zone. It was this shift to building solidarity with Mexico which led to the founding of Common Frontiers, a group which expanded to take a lead role in the fight against the NAFTA.

THE WORLD GETS SMALLER Free trade has changed the relationship between Canadians and workers in the south in a fundamental way. Prior to free trade, we were workers facing a common enemy, but the ability of corporations to use us against each other was curbed by government intervention in such areas as imports, foreign investment, and labour laws. With Mexico in the equation, international solidarity has moved from the convention floor to the bargaining table. The superexploitation of Mexican workers earning $3.50 a day is now openly used as a threat to undermine our wages and working conditions. Mexican workers, in turn, are threatened by the use of Guatemalan workers earning $1 a day.

The alternative is not to cut ourselves off from each other, but to confront the

FREE TRADE SPINOFF
NAFTA is forging new links between grassroots organizations. This October 1990 meeting in Mexico City brought together labour and community groups from Canada and Mexico.
PHOTO BY JIM SINCLAIR

underlying structures which create this competition and keep all working people impoverished, with little power. The loss of 25 percent of our manufacturing industries, and the destruction of our food production system, are tied directly to free trade and to U.S. demands at the GATT negotiations. By the same token, the historic underdevelopment of Third World countries is the direct result of international trade arrangements, both formal and informal, which accelerate the flow of money and resources north. The recent Human Development Report of the United Nations says the net flow of money from poor countries to rich countries reached $50 to $60 billion in 1989. Foreign debt for Third World countries has grown from $17 billion in 1972 to $1 trillion dollars in 1990.

Massive foreign debt – largely the result of capital flowing out of countries like Mexico and of large hikes in interest rates – has a crippling effect on the ability of governments to respond to the needs of people. The International Monetary Fund and the World Bank, both controlled by the United States, are now forcing these governments to implement "structural adjustment programs" aimed at restructuring their economies. These programs include such measures as devaluing the currency, cutting social services, privatizing state-owned enterprises, and laying off literally millions of workers. Brazilian labour leader "Lula" (Luis Ignacio Siliva) describes the restructuring as the new war against the Third World: "I will tell you that the Third World War has already started – a silent war, not for that reason any less sinister. This war is tearing down practically all the Third World. Instead of soldiers dying, there are children; instead of millions of wounded, there are millions of unemployed; instead of the destruction of bridges, there is the tearing down of factories, schools, hospitals and entire economies."

Hand in hand with the cutbacks is an ever increasing dedication of land, labour power, and resources to create export economies which service this debt. This

SOLIDARITY NOT COMPETITION

> 'We are about to become the only country in recorded history to reverse the traditional evolution from under-development to a manufacturing economy.'
>
> PETER C. NEWMAN

comes at the expense of local needs. Nowhere is this clearer than in Mexico's maquiladoras, which attract foreign capital because of low wages, few pollution controls, and virtually no taxes. Profits and products are all exported, and the result is Third World slums, with no services of any kind, surrounding the new factories. The final insult is that the difference between low Mexican wages and what companies used to pay Canadian and American workers to produce the same products, is some $12 billion annually. This is a direct subsidy to global corporations from Mexican workers.

Rather than solving the crisis for the Mexican people, extending free trade will entrench this type of "development." The result will be increased poverty, unemployment, and dependency.

THE CHALLENGE BEFORE US The challenges facing us are huge. The free trade agreement began dismantling the country we know as Canada in the midst of profound global reorganization. It occurred at the same time as the Eastern European communist model crumbled, with the subsequent declaration of the official end of the "cold war."

In Central America and other areas of the Third World, the hopes and strategies of liberation movements also underwent profound changes. No longer able to determine their countries' future without intervention of the most extreme sort, liberation movements sat down at the table and began to negotiate an end to the civil wars in their countries, making a place for themselves in the electoral process. The Nicaraguan experiment ended at the ballot box, a "democratic" result of the illegal contra war and the effects of the U.S. embargo on the economy and population. The Mexican elite, not liking the results of their 1988 elections, simply changed the outcome. Goliath clearly had won.

At home, Canadian unionists were more and more able to identify an experience we shared with our sisters and brothers in the south. We could no longer protect our economic, political, and cultural sovereignty under free trade, nor could we have confidence in our nation's long-term economic viablity. Our common enemy was never more apparent, and the critical need for sharing information, strategies, and struggle now became the challenge.

WHAT NOW? We are entering a new era of struggle and the path ahead is uncharted. To search for long-term solutions, we must enter into a different kind of dialogue and struggle, one which brings us into common cause with the south, and they with us.

The Mexican opposition to continental free trade has become critical to building our understanding of the task before us. The Common Frontiers project, a coalition effort of solidarity groups, trade unions, churches, and social organizations bound together to fight the continental free trade agreement, has been instrumental in making the connections.

Workers and unions will have to give international solidarity a high priority if we are to protect our wages and working conditions. Connections between unions in Canada and their counterparts in other countries are critical. This has started to happen. Unions representing workers at many Northern Telecom operations have already met and carried out joint actions, including solidarity during strikes. This is not always easy. Northern Telecom's anti-union policies have ensured most new plants have no unions, but labour organizations from Asian and Latin American countries are participating. Autoworkers in Canada, the United States, and Mexico have opened up communications and started making commitments for joint action. At a recent Canadian Paper Workers Union convention, delegates vowed to form alliances with workers in the U.S. and Mexico. Solidarity exchanges between unions and workers must be supported and developed far more in the coming years. As our past work shows, nothing can replace first-hand experience in building solidarity.

Education about the effects free trade and the global economy have on workers must be increased as well. Challenging this "New World Order" will require a much higher understanding of global economics and corporate power.

At the very top of the labour movement, there must be a realization that the cold

---

SOLIDARITY VIA MODEM

Larry Kuehn

The global corporations do it. And so can we: stay in touch with the information we need electronically.

Two technological developments are bringing activists together on a daily basis – even if they are across the continent, or thousands of kilometers away in another country.

Computers are getting cheaper, almost by the day, as well as getting more powerful. And a single microcomputer can now run a bulletin board connected to an international network of social activists.

In Canada we have Solinet, the national labour network run by CUPE, and available to the entire labour movement. Hundreds of union officers and staff sign on to share information about issues. Call Marc Belanger at (613) 237-1590 to join Solinet

One Solinet conference maintains a lively discussion about the impact of the free trade agreement on Canada – and the economic alternatives.

Through the Association for Progressive Communications (APC) network, we can also reach trade unionists in Latin America, Africa, Asia, and Europe. PeaceNet in the U.S., GreenNet in Britain, Worknet in South Africa, and several systems in Latin America can be reached though Canada's system, WEB (call (416) 596-0212 to join).

Conferences on the APC network provide important connections for labour and social activists on free trade, the environment, and many more issues.

Challenging global capital requires us to use the global communications systems that are now available to us.

war is over and that major shifts are necessary if labour is to play a significant role in building new forms of solidarity. Rather than blocking the obvious desire of workers and unions to open the doors to solidarity, the Canadian Labour Congress must play a key role in paving the way for increased activity at the membership level, and to ensure that energy and commitment are organized to take up this challenge.

To be successful, labour solidarity must not only stretch across geographic borders; it must also reach out to others in the community and make the connections necessary to strengthen our fight. Coalitions within Canada, such as the Action Canada Network – where workers are joined by farmers, women's organizations, native groups, groups seeking equality, and community organizations – are critical to building alternatives to the corporate vision. In the 1990s it is human solidarity, not just labour solidarity, that is critical to any successes we achieve. The experiences of our southern sisters and brothers in building popular movements are very important to our work in Canada.

In the short term, labour and popular movements must fight to stop the extension of the free trade agreement to include Mexico, and demand the abrogation of the Canada-U.S. agreement. For Canadian workers, this is the only way to set the stage for the defeat of the Tory government in the next election. This task is absolutely urgent if Canada is to survive. For our sisters and brothers in Mexico and Latin America, the defeat of the free trade deal would signal a new stage in the global fight to reclaim countries and communities.

In the long term, we must build solidarity based on the mutual respect for the sovereignty of our nations and on our collective fight for national and international development strategies aimed at meeting the basic needs of all people. This must include the right of national governments to enforce strict controls on the flow of capital, and the right to develop national energy, industrial, social, cultural, and agricultural policies to meet the needs of its citizens. In this context, our borders must again become barriers against the exploitation of our people and the environment by global corporations, but must not become walls to block the true sharing of resources and ideas between equals in a common struggle for survival.

Jim Sinclair is an organizer for the United Fishermen and Allied Workers' Union in Vancouver and an executive member of the Trade Union Group.

Fern Valin is a member of the Latin American Working Group.

> 'Perhaps the best response to Globalization, however, is not to let it terrorize us. We are being told that, more and more, we will have to let the market make the decisions. Perhaps our best answer is: Thank you very much, but we'd rather make those decisions ourselves. While this may sound flip, the truth is that anything else amounts to a surrender of what little control we've managed to gain over our lives.'
>
> LINDA McQUAIG
> AUTHOR OF THE QUICK AND THE DEAD

The Road Back

Abrogation of the FTA will bring cries of outrage from business, but remaining in the deal threatens Canada's future

by Maude Barlow

It is distressingly easy to make the case that the Canada-U.S. Free Trade Agreement is a failure. The Mulroney government has given up trying to defend it, blaming American "thugs," in Simon Reisman's inimitable language, and not the deal itself or how badly it was negotiated, for its breakdown.

What is going to be more difficult is undoing the damage of this policy, and weathering the inevitable conflict that will arise over whether or not to terminate the agreement. Any question of abrogation will inevitably lead to cries of outrage and dire warnings of impending economic armageddon from the business community. The threat of American retaliation, real enough, will be used as a battering ram to frighten an already recession-chastened populace into fearful submission.

Even among those opposed to the free trade deal, however, there will be disagreement. Many are already arguing that by the next election, the free trade road will be too far travelled to turn back. Businesses have made decisions based on free trade, they point out, and our economies have merged so deeply in the years since the deal was signed that unscrambling the interlocking pieces is not possible. Besides, some say, politically speaking, this isn't a popular position to take. While a healthy majority of Canadians now say that free trade was a mistake, breaking our word in an international deal isn't very "Canadian" and would be hard to sell.

Free trade turns over to the market decisions that have been shared by government

To assess this question, it is important to remember how Canada was formed politically and economically, and how fundamentally the FTA alters our system of

IT'S UP TO YOU Canadians will face a federal election in 1993. The fate of the country will ride on the outcome.

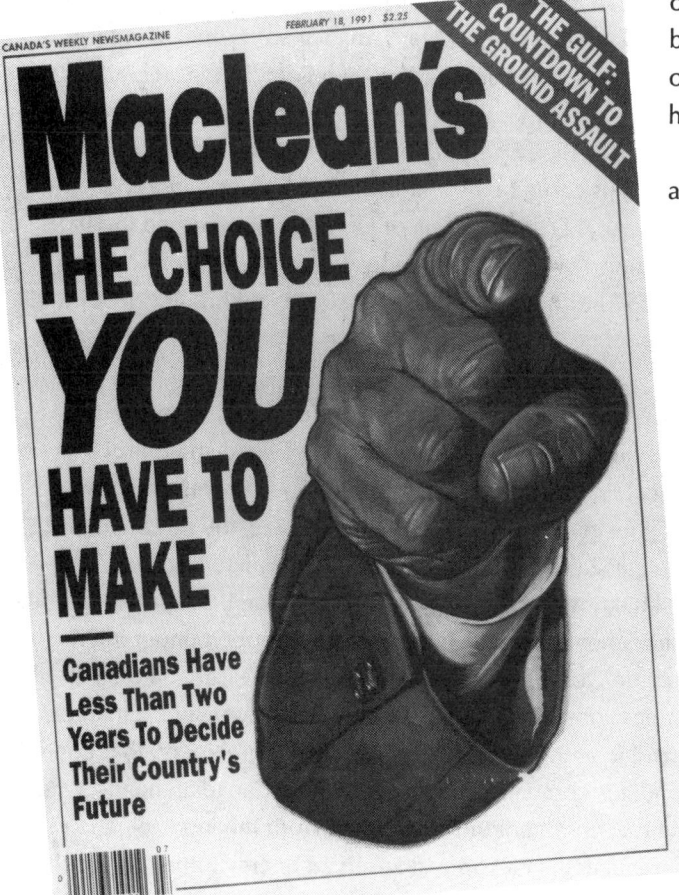

government and our sovereign ability to choose our own economic path. Our ancestors chose to build a different kind of society on the northern half of the continent, and generations of Canadians have nurtured this society and its values.

The histories of Canada and the United States are very different. Because our country is so geographically vast and environmentally harsh, and because we had such a sparse population, mostly strung out along the U.S. border, we had to develop a distinct economic model of sharing for survival. We entrusted our government to develop a mix of public and private enterprise to provide affordable services. This economic system not only served to foster a distinct way of life but also prevented us from being absorbed into the United States. To have permitted the marketplace to dictate all economic decisions would have doomed the country.

Canadians have, therefore, a history of not only trusting government to work in the interests of all Canadians, but also of expecting government to take an active role in the distribution of wealth and opportunities, the search for equality, and the development of Canadian culture and values. The purpose of free trade is to turn over exclusively to the market what have been decisions shared by government. As we harmonize our economy with that of the U.S., our very existence is threatened. Essentially, the policy options once held by government in this country have been dramatically reduced by this deal, and the institutions that served to maintain our sovereign identity are being destroyed.

There are many examples of our governments, federal and provincial, buckling to the free trade deal by changing current laws and practices or by curbing their behaviour once in office. Following are just a sample:

THE GOODS AND SERVICES TAX The GST is a free trade driven tax. It was required to replace the multi-billion dollar annual loss of government revenue as tariffs are phased out under the deal. It also replaced revenues from the old

> 'It would be reasonable for you to give it [free trade] three years in any event because there's not likely to be an election for four years.'
>
> JOHN CROSBIE, MINISTER OF TRADE, KICKING OFF THE FREE TRADE DEBATE IN PARLIAMENT, DECEMBER 22, 1988

Manufacturers' Sales Tax, and we were told that it was necessary in order to remove the tax differences between Canadian and American corporations in the new level playing field economic environment of free trade. Canadian consumers are picking up the tab for this corporate break. Michael Wilson, then finance minister, admitted in the House of Commons during the GST debate, that the free trade agreement had given companies the right to move production to a more favourable economic climate and that the tax burdens carried by Canadian corporations had to be lowered to keep them in Canada. David Buzzelli of Dow Canada warned in 1989 that, without tax harmonization, "investment and jobs will gradually shift to the U.S." Tragically for Canada, the GST has not stemmed this exodus and has accelerated the cross-border shopping trend.

ENERGY EXPORTS As Canadian law is required to conform to the free trade agreement, our energy legislation was rewritten to remove Canadian control of energy exports. The National Energy Board was stripped of its powers and now performs only a monitoring function. The vital supply safeguard, the requirement that there always be a 25-year surplus of energy sources for Canadians, was dropped. Even a pathetic little power the government left to the Board – that exports must be deemed in Canada's net economic benefit – was scrapped under intense American pressure. Free trade would permit no recognition of a Canada-U.S. border, argued American gas companies and the U.S. government, and Canada capitulated. The sole Canadian authority left under the trade agreement, that control of healthy Canadian oil and gas companies should remain in Canadian hands, was recently relinquished by the government under pressure from the industry. The FTA put in place, forever, a deregulated, first-come, first-served energy future. In good times and in bad, transnational corporations have virtually unfettered right to export Canadian gas, oil, and hydro-electricity.

WEST COAST FISHING For eighty years, Canada supported a lively West Coast fish-processing industry by requiring that salmon and herring caught in its waters be processed in fish-packing plants in Canada. In many communities on the West Coast, it would be hard to find one family that doesn't have at least one member working in the fishery. For many years, the Americans have been seeking direct access to these fish stocks for their own processing factories, where wages and working conditions are substantially inferior to those at Canadian plants. The U.S. sought and won a GATT ruling against Canada on this requirement. Under GATT, Canada had the option of imposing an export tax which would have had the same effect of safeguarding the Canadian industry. However, such taxes are illegal under the free trade agreement, and the Canadian government gave in without a fight. In the first free trade dispute settlement, it was ruled that Canada could not even require all of its west coast fish catch be landed and inspected before it was exported unprocessed.

ONTARIO PUBLIC AUTOMOBILE INSURANCE   One of the main promises of the NDP government in Ontario was to replace private auto insurance with a publicly administered system similar to ones already in place in three other provinces. But these provinces created their systems before the implementation of the free trade agreement. Articles 2010, 2011, and 1605 of the deal require prior consultation with the U.S. government on creating public enterprises, and financial compensation to American firms, in this case, the American insurance industry. Canadian law, by the way, does not give this right to Canadian companies. When they got wind of the Ontario government's intentions, the U.S. insurance industry began to file claims under the FTA and wrote to U.S. Trade Representative Carla Hills, who publicly admonished Canadian Trade Minister Michael Wilson at the 1991 trade ministers meeting in Seattle. Hills said that the proposed legislation violated the free trade agreement and that the U.S. would exact a high price if Ontario were to proceed. The province backed down following the release of a report by Coopers & Lybrand which predicted that Ontario would have to pay private insurers as much as $2 billion in compensation for buyouts and lost business, including $689 million to be paid to U.S. companies.

AMERICANS 'BASTARDS,' SAYS REISMAN
Audrey McClellan

In 1988, Simon Reisman called people who criticized the FTA traitors. He said they were "wrong, misinformed, and sometimes even mischievous," and he compared them to Nazi propagandists. How times change. Now it's the Americans who are "bastards."

In January 1992, Reisman, who was Canada's chief negotiator for the FTA, said that the Americans are "behaving like real thugs these days in protecting their interests."

The reason for this about-face was a series of U.S. protectionist moves against Canadian imports, which Reisman says may be just cause to tear up the deal. "If the Americans say the hell with you and we'll do what we want, clearly then the free-trade deal is over."

Recent trade actions include a new 14.48 percent tariff imposed by Washington on Canadian softwood imports; a U.S. Customs Service ruling that Honda cars assembled in Canada with U.S.-made engines don't meet the 50 percent made-in-North-America standard that is needed to avoid $22 million in import duties; and a threatened, but unenacted, increase in tariffs on Canadian beer imports.

The U.S. has tried imposing protectionist tactics earlier, in spite of the FTA. Canadian hog producers faced a countervailing duty in 1990, when U.S. producers claimed Canadians were unfairly subsidized. The duty was overturned by a binational arbitration panel. A 100 percent tariff on fish imports was threatened, and a U.S. oil-import tax, designed to cut off the flow of Canadian oil, was imposed in June 1989.

SOURCES: *Globe & Mail*; Robert Mason Lee, *One Hundred Monkeys* (Toronto: Macfarlane Walter & Ross, 1989); *This Magazine*; Vancouver *Province*; Vancouver *Sun*

SALE OF INFANT FORMULA Officials from Health and Welfare Canada and Consumer and Corporate Affairs recently advised the Infant Feeding Action Coalition that the Canadian government cannot bring in legislation to comply with the World Health Organization's code protecting breast milk and breast feeding from the aggressive corporate advertising in infant formula because the WHO code is "superseded by the free trade agreement." The code is perceived to be a restriction of private rights under the FTA.

These are specific examples of the direct loss of Canadian sovereignty resulting from the FTA. As our economy is destroyed, we are losing the fiscal capacity to provide a public infrastructure and we are eliminating our system of public service. Free trade will ensure that this is permanent. Under the agreement, it is almost impossible to reregulate a service that has been deregulated or to renationalize an enterprise that has been privatized. Our future under free trade is clear. Inexorably, we will lose all institutions that have served us as Canadians, as economic decision making is transferred to Washington. (This is unlike what is happening in Europe, where sovereignty ceded by a country is turned over to a new political body, the European Community, in which each country has a voice.) The longer Canada stays in this agreement, the more compelling the business community's argument that there must be one single, level, playing field between Canada and the United States (and soon, Mexico) – one with the lowest common standards.

> 'Support for the Canada-U.S. Free Trade Agreement has never been lower. Canadians today absolutely loathe the idea of trilateral free trade.'
>
> DONNA DASKO, VICE-PRESIDENT OF ENVIRONICS RESEARCH GROUP LTD.

The FTA cedes so much power to the private sector and the U.S. that no future Canadian government, no matter what its intentions or political stripe, will be able to do more than soften the hardships it causes. Pat Carney knew this in 1986 when she told the Canadian Petroleum Association that her government had deregulated the energy industry and would now bring in a free trade agreement so that no future government would be able to dismantle this new system. To undo free trade's damage requires its abrogation. No other option lies before us.

Legally, this is a straightforward matter. There is a provision in the agreement (article 2106) which allows us or the United States to terminate the agreement simply by giving the other party six months' notice. Once we invoke the six-month solution, we would revert to conducting our trading relationship with the United States through the GATT. Cancelling the deal will immediately give us back the power to regulate foreign investment in the public interest, manage our resource base for sustainable development, meet national food needs through our agriculture supply management system, negotiate "auto pacts" in other sectors, and increase Canadian ownership in key sectors, such as culture, energy, and high-technology industries.

SOMETHING FISHY
B.C. fish workers have been on the frontline of the fight against free trade. These workers are participating in a walk-out to protest the export of unprocessed fish to the United States.

Politically, it is much more difficult. We need a clear strategy for abrogation. It has three components:

SEEK A CLEAR MANDATE FOR ABROGATION The debate about free trade that took place before the last federal election was passionate and consuming, but was built, on both sides, on predictions of the future. By the next election, Canadians will have lived with this deal for close to five years and will be more than able to have a full and honest debate about its actual effects. It is vital that termination of the deal is an issue upon which people are voting so that no democratic government could then challenge it. The debate should be a full one, concerned with what kind of country we want.

It is imperative that the abrogation side not fall into the same trap that the Tories did in 1988. Instead of a full debate on the pros and cons of free trade, one in which the people could have made an informed choice, the government wildly exaggerated the expected benefits of the deal while dismissing the concerns of its opponents. We must not do the same. Whether Canada stays in the FTA or not, our immediate future is pretty bleak. The difference is one of control. If we extricate ourselves from the deal, we will at least be responsible for our own destiny. But the road will be long and painful and we should be willing to say so.

The U.S. will be angry and American producers will likely actively harass Canadian exporters in certain sectors. Some transnational capital will flee Canada, and the large corporations will no doubt wage a massive campaign against any government prepared to undertake this move. They will fight reconstruction policies, tax reform, and legislation aimed at stemming the flow of plant closings. There is likely to be short-term price and exchange-rate instability because international financial markets are unregulated and foreigners hold such a high proportion of Canada's short-term debt. The Business Council on National Issues is likely to wage a powerful media war, similar to the business assault on the NDP government in Ontario, to discredit any government intent on abrogation.

All of these concerns can be met with clear argument. American producers are thoroughly aggressive now, even with our "favoured nation" status. They have not abided by the spirit of the free trade deal and, in fact, they have used the free trade agreement as another tool against Canadian exporters. Capital will flee, yes, but it is fleeing now, leaving a hemorrhaging industrial sector, taking high-technology jobs

ALTERNATIVE PROPOSALS FOR DEVELOPMENT AND TRADE

Tony Clarke

An alternative strategy calls for a continental development pact designed to improve the economic, social, and environmental conditions of people in all three countries. The goal here is not trade per se but *development* – a just and sustainable form of development for all three countries.

Investment. Instead of granting transnational corporations the freedom to operate as they please, a continental development pact would include provisions to ensure that corporate behaviour is responsible and accountable to local communities as well as the host nation.

Manufacturing. Instead of allowing manufacturing corporations to simply shut down plants and relocate their operations to another country to take advantage of cheap labour conditions, a continental development pact would encourage governments in all three countries to implement domestic content rules. Under these regulations, any corporation wishing to sell its products in a particular market (be it Canadian, Mexican, or American) must make a commitment to a certain share of jobs and investment in that country.

Agriculture. A continental development pact would attempt to move toward a more sustainable food production system. Every nation has the inherent right to produce the food it needs to feed its own people.

Energy. Instead of a continental energy policy that guarantees the United States direct access to non-renewable oil and gas reserves in both Canada and Mexico, a continental development pact would emphasize energy conservation and sustainable development.

Services. Each nation would have the sovereign right to exclude foreign investors from strategic service sectors such as media, culture, and finance. Foreign service firms could also be required to employ local people or transfer technology to local firms.

Intellectual Property. Instead of treating patents and copyrights as the absolute right of private companies, a continental development pact would recognize the rights of governments to grant compulsory licences, ensuring that patent holders allow others to use their patented inventions.

Financing. A continental development pact would include measures to reduce Mexico's debt and provide compensatory financing. To assist communities in all three

with it. In fact, it is easily argued that the free trade agreement has encouraged businesses to make production decisions in favour of the United States and that once we retilt the balance back to Canada's favour, companies will be more likely to choose to manufacture at least some of their total production in Canada.

So great has the damage from free trade been for Canada, that any retaliation, even strong retaliation, is likely to be less harmful to Canada than continuing under the FTA. And upon cancellation of the deal, our trade with the U.S. would once again be covered by GATT, which gives Canada substantially better access to American markets than the FTA does, while affording Canada more protection.

> **Even strong retaliation is likely to be less harmful to Canada than continuing under the FTA**

The greater concern is the severe damage that has been done to the Canadian economy by the government's economic policies and the recession, and the danger that Canadians might believe that by cancelling the FTA, things are going to turn around overnight. The honest political message that must be put forward is that there is ahead of us a time of real financial pain and that there are no quick fixes.

---

countries with redevelopment assistance and jobs skills retraining, a North American Development Bank would also be established and financed in part by a set of luxury taxes.

Environment. A continental development pact would make environmentally sustainable development in all three countries a fundamental goal. Countries violating environmental protection standards could be subject to retaliatory trade sanctions and countervail actions.

Social Security. A continental development pact would encourage all three countries to develop social security systems to meet the needs of their own peoples. Transnational corporations that violate basic health and safety standards could be subject to heavy fines and/or retaliatory trade measures.

Labour. Instead of encouraging corporations to exploit cheap labour conditions and lower labour standards, a continental development pact would seek to work towards ensuring equal pay for equal work throughout North America. Guarantees for the right to organize, collective bargaining, and the right to strike would also be fully recognized in a continental development agreement.

Migration. All peoples have the right to seek a better life for themselves and their families. This includes the freedom to migrate from one country to another in search for more just and healthy conditions of employment.

Culture. A continental development pact would encourage Mexico, Canada, and the U.S. to foster cultural goals and cultural programs to meet the development needs of their own peoples.

Human Rights. A continental development pact would ensure that basic democratic rights be recognized and respected.

Democratic Controls. Instead of giving corporations and governments free rein in determining economic and social priorities, a continental development pact would include measures to increase democratic control and public accountability. Each participating country would be required to establish democratic processes for public participation in monitoring economic and social development strategies in accordance with the objectives of the agreement. Countries which systematically violate the democratic rights of their citizens would be subject to possible trade sanctions or countervail actions.

SOURCE: Adapted from Action Canada Dossier No. 34

The road ahead is a hard one. It will take courage to do what has to be done to forge a new Canada, but in the process we will create a society that reflects the best in us and is ours to govern.

SAY NO TO RENEGOTIATION OR DELAY A tempting political alternative to abrogation, one favoured by the federal Liberals, is to attack the free trade agreement, but promise only to renegotiate it with the U.S., in order to change the "bad parts" and keep the "good parts." This is a flawed and essentially dishonest strategy. It ignores the unequivocal position the Americans have taken that any reopening of the FTA will only be done to strengthen its provisions in the U.S. favour. It fails to recognize that the FTA cedes very substantial power to the U.S. and that in bilateral negotiations, U.S. power greatly exceeds Canada's.

Says Mel Clark, Canada's former senior GATT negotiator, "Attempts to renegotiate the 'bad parts' would place Canada in a position similar to that of a country compelled to negotiate a peace treaty after losing a war, with a victor occupying all strategic ground on the frontier and directing harassing fire at the vanquished. Canada would be the supplicant trapped in a process controlled by the U.S. which would permit the U.S. either to demand and obtain additional onerous concessions or retain the status quo."

To pursue a strategy of renegotiation, the government would have to draw up a list of the parts it wanted to discuss. If that list included all the major powers ceded under the FTA, the list would be a long one. If it included only some powers, the exercise would be a sham. In any case, renegotiated parts of the deal would require that amendments be made to it. This would mean seeking U.S. Congressional approval. In effect, the U.S. Congress would control all aspects of the renegotiation process and would be in a position to stretch out the negotiations over the span of several years until its terms were met. It would also have the right, under the FTA, to demand compensation for any changes benefitting Canada. Given the fact that the U.S. market is ten times the size of Canada's, the U.S. could take the position that reciprocity would not be achieved by following the symmetrical pattern of exchange relating to normal trade barriers, and could therefore demand additional concessions. The process would

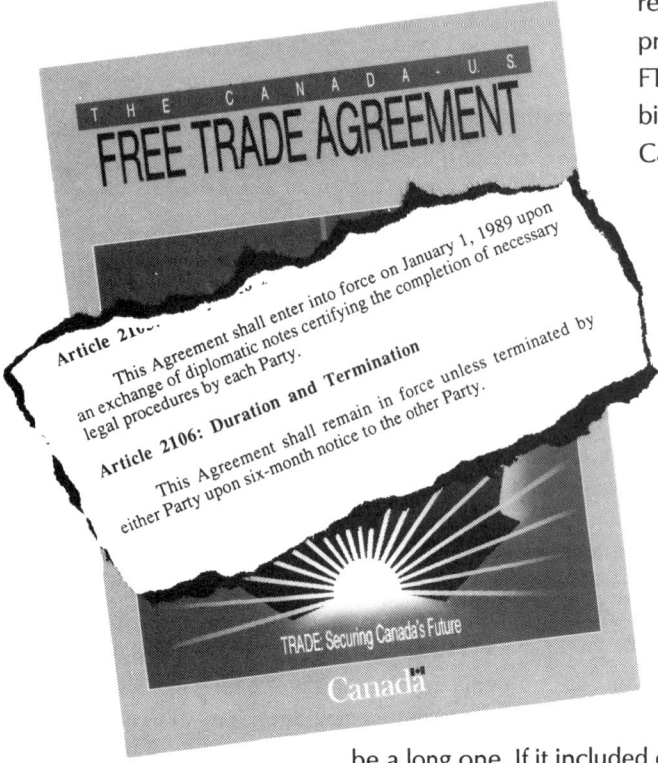

JUST SAY NO
Tearing up the deal is straightforward... on paper. Will a new government have the political will to do it?

take years, and by that time, Canadians would have long forgotten the origins of their economic surrender and the issue would be dead.

Another political alternative to immediate abrogation, one finding favour in some NDP circles, is to take power, forge ahead with government programs and policies, and when it becomes apparent that these policies cannot be implemented because of the FTA, seek the support of Canadians to abrogate it. While this strategy is preferable to renegotiation, it is also flawed. It would take any new government a year or two to start to implement the kinds of programs that would run afoul of the deal. The longer Canada is entangled in it, the harder it will be to get out, and this delay would not be helpful. Further, the U.S., well aware of this kind of government's hostility to the FTA, would be careful to keep any pressure quiet, behind-the-scenes, and out of the public eye. This is exactly how the American government succeeded in bringing the National Energy Board to its knees, and just the tactic the U.S. insurance industry used to fight the Ontario government's public auto insurance scheme.

This strategy would also circumvent the debate, so needed in the next election, on free trade and abrogation as Canadians try to come to terms with the meaning of

CREATING ALTERNATIVES

Sandra Sorensen

Our opposition though is no longer good enough. We have to be able to say more than "we told you so." We have to give leadership on what the alternatives are. In order to do this, we must build a new style of democracy based on new relationships and trust and understandings among ourselves – and with other groups around the world through new partnerships and people's movements ... It's important that we are not just fighting *against* their agenda. We are fighting *for* our vision.

Alternative economic policies will be based on starting with ... basic needs. All needs imply work (jobs) which provides the money which comes back into the economy in countless ways (buying, taxes, etc.). A more equal distribution of wealth is not only just, it builds the basis of a healthy economy.

So, when we talk about the economy let's talk in terms of people. "The economy" isn't just some abstract concept that exists on its own. A simple way to describe a healthy economy is that in a healthy economy, the people are healthy. They have food to eat, clothes to wear, a place to live, their environment isn't toxic, they are physically safe, they get adequate health care and education. On top of that I would add mental health, leisure time to enjoy family, their friends, their culture, the natural environment. They feel like they are making a meaningful contribution to society.

I'm not talking about everybody being rich – but that everyone should be able to live with dignity.

In order to achieve this I'm promoting a model of self-reliance which wisely develops our resources in the ground and in our peoples. And I am promoting economic self-defence to protect our interests of social justice.

There are lots of tools at our disposal – including expanding our trading relationship beyond the narrow bloc formations. We are open to the world, not turning our backs in a hostile, competitive stance.

We are building the relationships necessary to transform the realities. We have the experience and skills and training to develop and deliver new and better models. And we have the courage, the confidence and the vision to make it happen.

SOURCE: *Briarpatch*, October 1991

> 'If the world of free markets and competitiveness, which so dominated economic and political thinking in the 1980s, cannot deal with our needs, then maybe it is time for some broader debate, bolder "new thinking," and more dramatic initiatives.'
> BOB WHITE, PRESIDENT, CAW

the nation state, the role of government, and the question of what kind of country we want to have. Hesitation would only make worse the inevitable climate of political and economic uncertainty. Cancelling the free trade agreement in a forthright manner will signal our determination to reassert Canadian sovereignty in accordance with international law. What a gift to ourselves!

DEVELOP THE ALTERNATIVE Canadians are hungry for clear policy and action alternatives to the corporate agenda of the Mulroney Tories. Our program cannot just be based on what we don't want, but on a sense of who we are as a people, where we are going and how we want to get there. It is clear that we must create a new, equitable tax system, deal with the whole issue of trade in North America in a fundamentally different way, establish an economic reconstruction program, and restore the financial integrity of government.

These are not easy goals to reach. But any strategy must outline the options Canadians have before us, and invite us to become a part of the rebirth of our nation. Then Canada can take its place as a thoughtful, middle-sized country, devoted to the democratic process at home and internationally. The single most important question for the 1990s and beyond is the role of the nation state versus the power of transnational corporations, and the place of democratically elected governments. Canadians can succumb to the siren call of international competitiveness, relinquishing all that has made us unique, or we can reassert our historical commitment to a different order and help the world in its search for justice, equality, and environmental sanity. The choice is ours.

Maude Barlow is the National Chairperson of the Council of Canadians, the author of *Parcel of Rogues, How Free Trade is Failing Canada* and, with Bruce Campbell, *Take Back the Nation*.